'So raw, so honest, so intense. I didn't want this book to end.'
Sigri Sandberg

'A beautifully written, emotionally intense memoir.' *Sunday Express*

'The island is a metaphor for anyone who has ever been alone . . . It is about what happens when everything you are used to falls away, which is something we are all experiencing at the moment.' *Daily Mail*

'An utterly engrossing read.' Saga

'Tamsin Calidas's tale of moving to a remote Scottish croft has become a lockdown must-read . . . a glittering account.' *Metro*

'The trials and triumphs of isolated living are laid bare in this often shatteringly honest read.' *Reader's Digest*

'This is an extremely honest account of human survival in the face of unimaginable pain and loss. So poignant and stark . . . Never as relevant as it is now, Calidas' battle with isolation and loneliness is both moving and inspiring. The desire for human contact and interaction is soothed by a deep kinship with nature, which remains steadfast no matter what.' *Scottish Field*

'A wonderful memoir.' *The Malestrom*

'Powerfully observed.' BBC *Countryfile* Magazine

'An extraordinary book, a wild and redemptive account of reaching rock bottom and swimming back into the light. I'm awed by Tamsin's courage, her resilience and huge heart. Her island will stay with me for a very long time.' Olivia Laing

'The memoir of the year . . . ground-breaking.' *Vogue*

'Gripping . . . Tough yet compulsive reading, carried by crisp, vivid prose.' Amy Liptrot

'A meditative breath of fresh air. This book will fill your lungs, sting your eyes and catch in your throat. Soaring prose like birdsong over the harsh lands that compelled Tamsin Calidas to breathe deep.' Ruth Fitzmaurice

'An extraordinary book of limitless resilience, Calidas' leaping prose is a love song to the natural world. What she achieves with an open heart and a will of iron is nothing short of remarkable.' Sarah Langford

'Combining intensely beautiful nature writing with the excavation of deep emotion, this brave, startling book examines what it really means to lose yourself in nature, and in doing so find a completely new version of yourself, too. A powerful, unsettling but ultimately redemptive account of one woman's deep communion with the natural world.' Clover Stroud

'Astonishing, raw and clear-eyed. Tamsin charts how she comes to terms with loss, loneliness, hardship and prejudice through immersing herself fully in her island habitat. *I am an island* is a powerful, affecting book; glittering and visceral.' Nicola Chester

'A brave, beautiful and unforgettable book. Tamsin writes exquisitely about life, love, pain, death and rebirth and the healing power of nature. A sea of hands will reach for *I am an island*, carrying it like a great flock of birds, across the world. I cannot recommend it highly enough.' Elena Bonham Carter

I am an island

Tamsin Calidas

BLACK SWAN

TRANSWORLD PUBLISHERS

Penguin Random House, One Embassy Gardens, 8 Viaduct Gardens, London SW11 7BW

www.penguin.co.uk

Transworld is part of the Penguin Random House group of companies
whose addresses can be found at global.penguinrandomhouse.com

First published in Great Britain in 2020 by Doubleday
an imprint of Transworld Publishers
Black Swan edition published 2021

Map drawn by Neil Gower
Photographs by the author

A CIP catalogue record for this book
is available from the British Library.

ISBN 9781784164782

Typeset in 11.5/16.5pt ITC Berkeley Oldstyle Pro
by Integra Software Services Pvt. Ltd, Pondicherry.

Printed and bound in Great Britain by Clays Ltd, Elcograf S.p.A.

The authorized representative in the EEA is Penguin Random House Ireland,
Morrison Chambers, 32 Nassau Street, Dublin D02 YH68.

To Cristall, all the wings, wilds and bright waters

Nor fire shall burn me
ni teintera teine mi

Nor sun shall burn me
no mo ghrian a losgadh mi

Nor moon shall blanch me
Cha leg a 'ghealch mo planadh

Nor water shall drown me
Cha teid usage a bhathadh dhomh

'The Descent of Brighid'
Carmina Gadelica

Contents

Map xiv

ACT I 1

1 Gulls 3
2 Atlantic 13
3 Island 20
4 Croft 37
5 Graft 59
6 Winter 73
7 The Unborn 83
8 Brakes 96

ACT II 113

1 Hands 115
2 Foraging 126
3 Auction Mart 146
4 Dead Grass 158
5 Swallow 167
6 Tup 182
7 Wild Cry 193
8 Raw Element 202

ACT III   213

1 Water   215
2 Fire   227
3 Kin   241
4 Earth   251
5 Air   259
6 Stars   269
7 Sun and Moon   277
8 Wild   283

Acknowledgements   290
Reading group questions   293

Tamsin Calidas is a writer and photographer living in the wilds of the Scottish Hebrides.

She worked in various roles in advertising, publishing and the BBC before giving it all up in 2004 to move to a tiny, remote island in Scotland to run a derelict croft with sheep and horses.

to the World

Sunrise

N.G.

Rocky Ridge

Croft Grazing

Sheep Hill

Cliffs

Croft Grazing

Barn Cottage

My Tree

Shelter

Lambing Park

feeders

The Woods

Hills

Bonfire Hill

cobnuts

Hawthorn

LOCH SHORE

Fields

Scrub

buzzard fledgling

Rocks

ACT I

1

Gulls

Arriving into Oban, the first thing you notice is the grey sea and a close, huddled bay that shelters inside the protective arm of its sunken harbour. From a distance the tide is strangely thick, an amorphous mass of slow-moving, restless water. Step a little closer to the fishing boats and great hulking vessels and you will smell the rippling, dark metallic sheen, the striated channels where the diesel runs off as each hull is safely berthed, winched close or tied fast to the metal-ringed quays.

The sound of the waves is not so different from the traffic of the city. But as soon as you lift your face and taste the fresh tang of salt on the air, you will mark how this sky is as different, fickle and changeable as all you have left behind. Then, if you listen, you will hear the laughing gulls. And beyond that, heading off in a low V-shape, the haunting call of the geese.

It is an extraordinary moment when you recalibrate and find your compass. I had been dreaming of staring out at a raw, open horizon for years – ever since I found an old map of Scotland and pinned it up in the hallway in my flat. It was positioned across the full length of a narrow wall where I always saw it as I was passing, at an angle where your eyes fell into that empty space between giant masses of land. It is always during that notion of transit, of passing from one space to another, that your heart opens and all of your dreaming begins. I would press my nose to that thick paper, inhaling its musty scent, as my finger traced the ragged coastline of the fractured islets and islands of the Western Isles, straining against the bracing tides of the Atlantic, across the Minch, the North Sea and the Little Minch, to the tortuous fjordic coastline of the Norwegian Sea. In those moments, as my eyes closed, the traffic, shouts from the street, neighbours slamming doors would evaporate into the hurl of fresh spindrift, the thick, curling crests of the breakers drenching the salt-stung air, the gulls tearing the skies apart with an aching, screaming call.

I would imagine how those great birds were somehow daring me, if not to follow, then at least to dream of living a wilder life. I don't know what it is about gulls but they have a way of inviting your eyes to lift above the skyline, to seek some further-flung sky beyond the immediate vicinity or low horizon. Yet, always, as I sense their keening cry, my heart catches and something else dares to drift. It is as if something inside untethers, unsnarls itself from all the finer ties and close meshes that snare you within a life you know is too compressed for you. It can be startling when you open your eyes, and see that creased paper close up, pressed hard against your skin. Then I would walk quickly to the door, throw it open and stand with my eyes raised, shoulders braced, looking above the cars and buses at a thin, pale-blue sky. I would hear the gulls and see them, floating far away, white spattering drifts of light, circling far above the city. Held within a blue orbit that stretches around all continents and spaces, my compass was pulling me, leading unbroken from central London to Oban and those same wave-flung islands, washed by their restless sea.

On Oban's rain-drenched promenade, the needle of the compass is wavering.

'So, what do you think?'

'Hmm?' I ask, pulling the high neck of my jumper up to meet my ears.

'Here.'

I look up as my husband Rab thrusts a rain-spattered newspaper at me. We are huddled together, honeymoon-close, in a narrow doorway, only it is the kind of clinch spurred by necessity rather than desire, fighting to catch our breath and to dodge the wind and rain. We are both shivering, skin drenched, in unsuitably thin jackets, the cold masonry providing scant shelter from one of those torrential downpours that will become familiar as a regular feature of Oban's climate. It is a rain that comes out of nowhere, as if all the open waters of the skies are descending, a furious sheeting-down. All along the grey promenade, water is shearing off the glistening pavements, bouncing back and ricocheting into whatever surface it can find. It is an impressive soaking. I can feel my toes wrinkling, whitening, cold-drenched inside my shoes.

As the wind nearly rips the paper out of his hands, we run, laughing, jeans completely sodden, across the street into a smoky, peat-steeped inn. As the door opens, it is like stepping into another time, another world. It is all wood inside, toasty and warm, lit by small kerosene lamps. When I look through the window at the boats, I am struck by the thought that I have no family, kin, friends or emotional ties here. It is an unfamiliar yet strangely liberating feeling. Already the sky is darkening, a deeper blueing at its edges, so your eyes cling to the light, and blink, stupefied, as it dawns on you that you are a long way from home. And even after the long weary drive, I am excited because suddenly I realise that Scotland is a different, vibrant country, a whole world away from the constraints of our London life. Sometimes, a life can feel tight, like a jumper you have long outgrown, that restricts your movement, so you feel an urge to stretch and be rid of it. For years I had secretly been longing to wrench that last thread free. And now, still tingling from the chill wind wrapping around me, I feel unexpectedly alert and exhilarated. Change is fresh, sharp and invigorating. It makes you shiver with excitement and cold.

'So what do you think?' Rab asks again, half an hour later, two drams poured out on the bar glowing amber in the soft light. He wraps his fingers around the water-stained glass.

'I think I could get used to this,' I say, eyes shining. I take a nervous gulp of the whisky and feel its warmth flood through me. Suddenly our daring to imagine the prospect of embarking on a different way of life feels both dreamlike and also scarily real. I am still shivering, my jeans clinging to my legs, my hair soaking, dripping water into my eyes.

'Here, take a look.' Rab hands me the sheet. It is so fragile and wet it is tearing at the edges. I lay it flat and smooth it out carefully. Some of the ink has bled with the rain. And then I see it.

The advert is small, with a tiny stamp-sized photograph of a derelict, run-down island croft. For years I have been dreaming of the waves and a ragged skyline, and here it is.

All the detail was blurred, yet I knew it was one of those chance moments that can change your life for ever. That open sky with its cottage, outbuildings and weary fields was speaking to me. Perhaps it was its aura of quiet abandonment that drew me instantly to it. I put down my glass and felt something inside me lift.

Don't say anything, I thought, willing Rab to keep silent. I held my breath and balled my fingers into fists. In my heart, I had no doubts. In my head, I knew it was perfect, apart from one thing. It was on an island. And living on an island was the one thing we'd said we'd never do.

'So, it's got everything, right?' Rab's voice rises with a questioning upward inflection. We look at each other. And then we look away. We both know what it is that we don't say. So I say it aloud before he does, this promise we have made.

'Not on an island,' I grimace. 'It's too remote. Too impractical, difficult to do anything, impossible to find work. And it will be hard to settle in. Can you imagine island life?' I flick my eyes off into the distance, shaking my head. 'No, I don't think so. Way too insular.'

'OK, next.' Rab shrugs, flicking over the page. But there is nothing else, nothing next that catches our eye.

We linger at the inn, wrapped in close conversation, hatching ideas. As I look out of the window I see the clouds clearing. Out there, floating in that sea, are all the islands. And one, lying just apart from the others, has a tiny derelict croft standing empty, just waiting for someone to love it, to come and find it, to make it a home at last. I try not to think about it, but it keeps drifting through my thoughts, coming to find me. As I look out at the dark sea, I know that some new direction is waiting for us. And, even though it makes no sense, it feels as if we, like the geese, are following a wilder sight or some call of the heart, each somehow coming home.

I had loved my early years in London. I lived in Notting Hill in a garden flat with a little iron gate leading out on to the communal gardens. It was a quiet sanctuary in the heart of west London, with a buzzing, cosmopolitan local community on tap. I was there years before the film came out, when you still bought your vegetables in a brown paper bag with cash, knew all the street vendors, and got your cigarettes from the cashier at the toy shop on the corner of Kensington Park Road. Life was a mandala necklace, a glittering brittle string of parties and un-relenting, rapid-fire movement. It was a time of hope and dreaming of your beautiful life, and Brit Pop singing the world real again.

I could never understand why no one else used the gardens. They were quiet and beautiful, so I used to lie out there at night, wrapped in blankets, listening to the waves of traffic rising and falling into the darkness, and looking up at a pale handful of stars. We were all watch-ing the skyline in our different ways with some anxious feeling that it was now or never. Everyone was trying to make it, to find their own slipstream. In reality, most days, just like everyone else I knew, I got by holding on tight.

Those early months, I lived off udon noodles, miso soup, rice cakes, eye-watering sour-sweet lime-soaked caipirinhas and brown rolls of 35mm film. Photography shoots led to the BBC and then to publishing and eventually to advertising. Brand names rolled off each day of the week. Time passed. My career began moving fast, as I started directing new business pitches and flying regularly to the US on shoot location work. As work hours increased, even crossing the Atlantic above the cloud line there was no let-up in sight. Just a browning urban haze clinging to the city's skyline, like some overspill of anxiety.

And then one day, life slowed to a sudden, jarring stop. I was in an accident. A black cab ran headlong into the taxi I was sitting in, jump-ing a red light at speed. The ambulance arrived, lights flashing, whisk-ing me to the hospital and placing me into a long metal tube for an emergency MRI. The pain was unbearable. I was barely able to walk, sleep or lie down in bed, let alone stand, sit or move my neck without screaming in agony. In the end, they administered morphine. It was a relief to have a brief interlude in that searing pain. I had a smashed sacrum, whiplash of the neck and thoracic spine, an anteriorly tilted pelvis from the impact, a fractured and dislocated coccyx spun completely around at 90 degrees and a severely prolapsed lumbar spine. It is amazing what the body can withstand and endure. During the intensive rehabilitation, I drew a line under and through my life. Overnight, my daily existence was shuttered with a different light and dark lens. Suddenly I was aware of my own mortality. It felt like the whole of London was walking a tightrope between life and death.

After I recovered, I realised I was looking for something different. And then I met someone. It was the catalyst to moving from my home in Notting Hill into a bigger space just a short mile north up the road. I fell in love with Rab. There was something about him that was quirky and original. An irresistible, carefree charm emanated from him and we connected straight away. Our new home was close to a reservoir so I could always hear the sound of the gulls, a wilder cry that I loved. Our small community, with its outwardly bright face and tiny streets, was local, family-orientated, and different from the one we had known. One day, I won a bag of goldfish at a local fair that we visited with friends and afterwards we tipped them into a homemade pond in our back garden. I started to dream of one day having a family of my own, and hoped that I might still be able to have children, even after so much structural trauma to my body. And then one summer everything changed.

In London, neighbourhoods are transient and can shift as quickly as the low skies gusting overhead. There was a disconcerting invisibility to the formerly gregarious community, and a disheartening, unsettling and desolate feeling that permeated the neighbourhood. It seemed that we were not the only ones to sense it. On the streets, people started walking more quickly, heads bowed, barely meeting your eyes as you walked by. Humanity is a vulnerable, vigilant thing. Overnight our building was spray-painted with graffiti, windows were broken and the police were called. But after a while even they stopped talking to us, because there was nothing anyone could do. We hoped to sit it out. One day, arriving home, I screamed as I walked through to the back garden. The plants were torn apart, some that were flowering had been uprooted. I held my hand to my mouth, fighting tears as I looked into the pond. Cans of paint had been poured over the wall and the containers left floating in the water. Amongst them, hidden in the reeds, were the faded, bloated corpses of our beautiful bright little fish. Something died in me as well that day.

A neighbour was mugged, then another knocked to the ground. I stopped walking around the neighbourhood. Those weeks were a tense, nail-biting time when everything became dark and feral. Stress is invisible; subtle and insidious, it builds up over time. Anxiety is like a smouldering fire. All it takes is a scream, a moment of fear, to whip those flickering embers into burning flames.

Worn down by months of this, I start waking in the night, feeling breathless, my heart thudding. And then one day I witness a man throw a woman out of his car and try to kick her while she lies on the ground. She is a beautiful woman, with fine features, and smartly dressed. I look on in stunned silence, frozen until I hear my own voice screaming. Sometimes it takes you a moment to act when you see violence right in front of your eyes. It shocks me. I feel I am being drawn back into a past I don't want to remember, a silent slow-motion movie in which a young child is being thrown down, wrestled to the ground. It is my scream that wakes me from paralysis. It is disturbing to hear my voice. It sounds different: wild and furious, unleashed from a place inside me I didn't know existed.

'Get off her!' I yell, dragging the woman by the arm towards the house. The man is tugging at her jacket. He is tall, with broad shoulders and a thick, angry voice. I am scared that he will lunge for me, because he keeps on at me, 'Shut the fuck up, you stupid fucking bitch.'

So I carry on screaming and hold on to the woman in a crazy tug-of-war. There is no one on the street, but I am sure people are watching from their windows. I am desperate, but no one comes to help; the cars just keep driving by. And then I announce: 'I'm going to take a photo of you,' and make as if to pull out my phone, which I know I left inside the house. At last he leaps into the car, shouting, 'YOU FUCK-ING BITCH! I'm coming back for you!' Then he floors it, leaving dark tyre marks on the road.

I watch him go, and now I am crying and shaking. It is a strange sensation, being so angry and so frightened, as if you are being pulled in two directions. I feel frozen inside, and yet my body is pumped up, so full of adrenaline that my voice is too loud. I hear it crack through my angry sobs. The woman stops crying, looks at me as if for the first time and says, 'Thank you.' And then, 'Can I come inside for a minute? I think I am going to faint.'

When I get her into the house, I rush away quickly to make her something hot. Shock is like that. You need something hot and sweet inside you. I leave her sitting alone on the sofa in my front room. When she leaves an hour later, I give her my number. 'Call me when you get home,' I ask her, 'so I know that you're safe.' Only she doesn't.

Later, I ask Rab, 'Hey, have you seen my keys? I can't find them anywhere.' And I am surprised when the taxi company rings me. 'She gave us your number. She said you were going to pay her bill.'

'Why did she do that?' I ask Rab.

He looks at me, and then says, 'Because she could.'

That night, I wake again with my heart thudding. As I open my eyes, I know instantly something isn't right. I hold my breath, and there it is – a noise on the landing. A second later, a stranger comes into the room and stands over me as I lie there, immobilised by fear. A tall, dark shape with broad shoulders. It is only later that I think, I have seen you before. At first I open my mouth, and I think I am screaming. But no sound comes out. It is like being underwater and pulling so hard through that darkness that you can see the surface just above you, but you know your lungs are going to run out of air before you get there. And then, suddenly, I am screaming for real. So I feel I am slowly coming to and waking from a dream. But this nightmare is still happening: the man leans in and comes closer. Rab wakes up.

'What the fuck!' he roars, jumping up. He stands shouting and furiously waving his arms and then I watch him sprint naked after the intruder, feet thundering on the stairs and away down the street. I wrap myself up and run after him, shaking, some minutes behind. I do not want Rab to meet that man alone. I do not feel safe in my home, or anywhere that I know.

We stare at each other. My hand covers my mouth, and I start to shake again.

'It's OK,' he says, 'I'll change the locks.'

I think of those bright little fish.

'I can't do this any more,' I say.

We got married. We spent our weekends by the reservoir, gulls crying, glittering clinks of metal and sails flapping in the wind. We started planning our move to a new place, where our life and work might be more in balance, and home a safe, quieter haven. I set my dreams on a space to raise a family. Already there had been losses and disappointments, and I was touching thirty-four years old.

2

Atlantic

As you drive north of the London Westway, you soon hit a sprawling urban wasteland of smoking industrial sites and desolate concrete forecourts, all framed by a neon luminescence that glows so aggressively it is hard to see the first flickering light of the natural dawn sky. Above, black-backed gulls fly mostly silent, landlocked, occasionally keening. It is a bleak, forlorn cry. I imagine they are bereft.

Travelling this route in darkness into work each day, I am aware of an unsettling, restless feeling. Slogging away day after day can make you ask all kinds of open-ended questions. Sometimes you get to a point when you look to the sky for answers, your shoulders bracing, always loaded with fresh angst.

And then one day we make the decision to take a few weeks to go on a prospecting road trip up north to Scotland, looking at places we might like to live. We leave in darkness so that we will miss the traffic and arrive around lunchtime, and won't waste our first day on the road. With your destination determined, you know not to stop when you reach the start of the soft greening. You fix your eyes on the road, your foot on the pedal and keep on flooring it, heading north. And the wild beauty is shocking – if you keep driving out of the darkness and into its sunrise, straight as the crow flies, slowly the sky opens, lifts, and the light becomes porous. Here there are only the mountains, heather and fresh rain-spattering drifts of air. For a few hours, the horizon is sheared steep, precipitous, punctuated by the slick swish of wipers and steady fall of rain, so you have to tilt your head back to view its summit. The long drive is exhausting, but we are fired up.

As I get out of the car and stretch, I hold my breath. Over the bay, the geese are flying straight as an arrow into the heart of that fragile light, a smirr of squalling slate wash just where the horizon falls into the sea. As soon as I hear the geese calling, their voices breaking those skies, that's when I know to start to breathe again. The air in Scotland is different from the stale air in London. I inhale great lungfuls of that clean, sweet, fresh wet breeze.

'This is wonderful,' I say, turning to Rab. Only he does not hear me, because the wind tears the words from my mouth, and cuts my voice away. It is a relief not to say anything. There is no point fighting the elements. I turn my face into the wind and I just breathe.

A few days later, Oban is empty in the rain. Only the estate agent remains to give us directions. 'You won't get your car on the ferry at such short notice, so be ready to go on foot,' she informs us.

'So if we get off the ferry, and then walk three miles, someone will meet us there?'

She shrugs. 'But if they're not there, it won't matter. The door will be open. Don't expect much. No one has lived there for five years.'

As I am leaving, she stares at me, a cool detached once-over. 'You're not from these parts. Sure you don't want to think about it before going all the way over? Best not to get your hopes up. It's a different world out there, just sheep and farmers, one small store and nothing but sea all about.'

'It's OK,' I say. 'We'll go.'

'Island life, it's different. It's not for everyone.' She flings these words after me as the door slammed shut behind us.

Maybe not, but maybe it would be our slice of heaven. A tiny rock of an island, cut adrift from the rest of the world. Just a long horizon, empty skies, and a beautiful blue sea. In my heart, I hoped it would be for me.

It was a bleak March day, leaden overcast skies, and the wind was up. The crossing over had been difficult, and the skipper warned us that the return ferry might not run. The forecast was wind over tide and some fierce squalls. In the end, we had decided to risk it. If we had to, we reasoned, we could try to stay at a bed and breakfast. We did not know that there was only one and that it was closed in March.

As predicted, the vehicle deck was already fully loaded, a large agricultural lorry stacked high with hay taking up three spaces of the available four still remaining. Two cars queuing on standby were left behind as the ramp was raised up off the slip.

The island was barely fifteen miles long, its narrow girth tightening to just half a mile, with close to 120 residents, another ten or so renting temporarily. The skipper assured us that if we walked the three miles from the ferry, up an empty single-track road with deep potholes, we could be there and back in just a few hours. He cautioned us not to miss the last boat. It felt momentous watching that bright ferry bounce away over the waves, across that fast channel and back to the mainland, as we set off along the track.

'I guess this is the main road,' Rab mused, looking back over his shoulder. 'More like a backwater than the main drag.'

'I wonder how they cope in the rush hour.' I smiled, thinking of London. There is nowhere to pass or turn. 'Still, far better to walk.'

Every now and again we would quickly step on to the mud-spattered verges as a battered car or rusted, vintage tractor rattled past. The road was so narrow you couldn't fail to catch a glimpse of the occupants. The vehicle would slow down, faces inside closely scrutinising us through steamed-up windows before slowly driving on. Sometimes we came across passing cars that had just stopped dead in the road. Windows rolled down, cigarettes lit, the news of the day shared as the cars' engines ticked over. On one halt, a bottle is passed between cars. Lilting, cadenced voices talking the day through. All eyes stare at us curiously as we walk past. And on one occasion, someone says, 'Incomers.' I listen to its sound, like a piece of litter thrown on to the road. Yes, I think, but hopefully not for long. I pick that word up and feel its tone and resonance. One day I hope that it will sound different, as we become familiar and known.

The wind cut bitterly through our coats; even through gloves and fleece-lined hats. Gulls huddled by waterlogged sheep-feeders, the ground covered in rushes and old windblown hay. On the high *beinns* and hills, snow still lay thick, the steep corries glistening, waterfalls roaring off the high tops from the first snowmelt.

We found the small cottage set back a few minutes' walk down a rough track that ran from a slope and curved behind an ancient stone barn, still showing its original thatching posts. There was no door on the barn. Underfoot were smooth cobbles and flagstones, the only contents decades of muck, straw and empty swallows' nests. The uninhabited stone cottage was rundown, grey-walled, damp and desolate-looking. There was no lock on the front door, and it opened on the first try. We hesitantly knocked and walked in. There was nobody here. The interior seemed even smaller: just four bare rooms with three-foot-thick stone walls made of rocks dug up from the ground. There was no sound of traffic, or neighbours. Our eyes darted searchingly.

It was the fall of silence that struck me. It had a porous feel to it, as if the whole sky had been spilled into it until there was room for little else. No raised voices, no bricks through the window. No rattling of sticks on a metal grille, or buses thundering past. Inside, there was a stillness like cool, clear water. And I knew that it was this quiet I had been seeking for so long. It did not matter that the cottage had no water, electricity, outside drains or paint on its walls. It did not matter that there was no heating or insulation. Nor that it was as freezing cold inside as it was outside, with just a single stone grate in one end wall. It did not matter that it was unloved and had not been lived in for over five years, nor that there were signs of mice, birds' nests and rats in the roof.

There was an antique leaking caravan outside that would do to sleep in, for however many months it would take to make the place habitable. And a freshwater loch at the bottom of the croft, from which pails of water could be brought up to wash. Outside, an unheated cor-rugated-iron lean-to was propped up against the north gable, where the lambing help had once bedded down. The dirt floor was comple-mented by walls carefully papered with sheets of 1950s *Oban Times*. I was struck by the care that had been taken to do this. I picked up a tiny housekeeper's book sitting on a wooden kist, with shillings and pence noted in the margin. Beside the thin, damp mattress was a King James Bible with minuscule print and a small Tilley lamp with a lint wick. When I stood outside, all I could see were hills and mountains.

'What do you think?' Rab asks me as we walk back to the ferry.

I do not hesitate. I just look at him, and smile.

As soon as I get two bars of reception on my phone, I make an offer. Six weeks later, the island croft is our home.

The day we moved to the island, the most terrifying challenge was finding myself standing on the deck alone as the ferry pulled away. There had been a problem. The tailgate of our lorry was too low to board the antiquated boat, despite assurances from the booking team when we'd purchased the tickets six weeks earlier. On the quayside, Rab lifted up his arms in resigned surrender to the unexpected turn of events of the last hour.

'Don't worry, I'll come find you,' he shouted. 'I'll get a boat and get over some other way.'

'How?' I yelled back. 'There are no other boats. This is the last sailing today.'

'I don't know,' he shrugged. 'But I'll find a way.'

As the skies cleared, I sat on the deck and watched Rab and the mainland disappear into the distance and my previous life drift away from me. I had no food in the car. The only possessions I carried were the clothes I stood in. And my elderly cat, in her basket, staring wide-eyed as the ferry juddered into the channel, the waves building into a stronger swell.

Driving off the ramp and up the island was a strange, unsettling feeling. We had planned this day meticulously together and now I was arriving alone. I found the croft again, and the cottage, sitting in its own beautiful wilderness. The yard was conspicuously more overgrown with brambles, and any semblance of a path to the house was covered in an abundance of wild flowers – bright aconites, foxgloves, marsh marigolds, flag iris and wild orchids growing with abandon.

As I pushed open the door, I sighed with relief. It was just as I remembered. With no water or electricity in the house, nothing was plumbed, and the floor and walls were filthy, covered in dust and what looked like a nest of birds or mice. But it didn't matter. It was home. And before I started sweeping away the debris of generations of wild creatures living inside its fabric, I placed my hands flat on the thick, bare stone walls and whispered, 'I am here now. I don't know who you are and I know you don't know me. But I know we're going to get on together. I'm here to stay. You are my home.'

Afterwards, I lit a few twigs and burned the sweepings and the rubbish on a small grate out the back. I listened to the crackling flames licking the dust and dirt of those small offerings alight. I turned my face to the wind and the now deepening blue sky, and watched the Evening Star brighten as the skies turned from dusk to the island gloaming time, and on into a hazy, luminous night sky. I listened to the silence and felt the breath of solitude wrap about me. And for a few hours, the silence transformed into unfamiliar wild sounds – of owls, bats, buzzards and geese calling out of that darkening sky. Those moments were so precious. They felt saturated with a limitless potential.

I will never forget that day I travelled to start my life on the island. Arriving alone, as a stranger, was one of those unnerving twists of fate that only holds a deeper resonance in later years. I like to think it was my first test of facing my fears and putting my trust in the unknown.

Looking back, I had no idea that those early years would only be the start of a fiercer, wilder, intensely difficult period that would tax my courage, resilience and endurance to breaking point and beyond. Growth is not always easy, and sometimes a new seed has to be encouraged, even forced, to grow.

3

Island

E VEN BEFORE I open my eyes, I know it is too early. A fragile lunar
light streams through the cracked caravan windows, some of
which are stuck half open, and condensation shines clear on the glass.
Limp tea towels, strung over a nylon fishing wire fixed to the thin
walls, gently flutter in the breeze. Drowsily, I blink at the tiny croft
house crouched low in open fields, the mountains deep in shadow
behind. I watch the wild grasses flowing. And suddenly, I remember
where I am.

'There you are,' I whisper. I trace the cottage with my eyes. Its low
outline glows ghostly pale, like a will-o'-the-wisp flickering in the
gloaming. I love to see it there waking with me, waiting for the sun to
rise. I am counting down the days until we can finally move inside. It
is a longing, a deep ache that I have never felt for any other place
before. When we first saw the cottage, it felt so abandoned and

unloved. It matters fiercely to me that it is loved and lived in, after so many years left untended, unkempt and alone. I am longing to make it a home, and for those solid walls to hold me. And one day, I hope to fill it with small running feet and laughter.

Above, scattered across a liminal emptiness, the Milky Way is a glittering, exploding phosphorescence. Fiery pinpricks of brilliance cluster, illuminating an iridescence of a myriad gleaming white lights. I have heard of these star-flecked, eerie lemon skies in the Highlands, but nothing prepares me for their startling luminescence. I have never witnessed such beauty before.

'Are you awake?' I whisper, as Rab stirs next to me.

There is a long pause. So I try to lie still, watching his body breathing, willing him to open his eyes.

I am amazed at the difference a few short weeks can make, free from the stresses of London. I can feel subtle changes in my body as my tight skin relaxes and starts to stretch, responding to the salt breeze and sunshine. My salt-tangled hair is tousled to a dark russet gold. We are getting fitter and leaner. I have not worn make-up in weeks. A small pocket mirror, stuffed hastily into the depths of my bag, has long since vanished. In the end I stop looking for it, and it is strangely liberating to feel unmoored from our old ways.

The rough stone walls have white-flecked my hands with cuts and tiny pink hicks. When I turn them over, my knuckles are raw and reddened from scrubbing the dry, flaking render. When we have finished scrubbing, we splash brilliant-white masonry paint on to the weather-stained walls, and I paint the cracked door and windows a clear-sky blue. At sunrise, the glass panes refract a shimmering lazu-line haze, until the light sinks below the horizon and the sky drifts into its gloaming again. At sunset, the bronze-fired skies burn themselves to oblivion from within. And that is another day passed. We are slowly making progress but already it is close to midsummer. There is no sign yet that the heatwave will break.

'Never thought we'd do this, but here we are,' Rab often muses. And I smile shyly as he gently twists my hand, because I am still pinching myself to see that ring on my finger. Its thin band is like a ray of hope. We are married just six months; already six short weeks, 600 miles and a stretch of water from our old London lives. It is striking how full our new life feels, stripped so far back to its essence. We are living with nothing apart from two bags crammed full of our small belongings, an old Vespa scooter, a barbecue rack and a tiny gas camping stove. Sometimes I laugh at how little we need. And at other times it feels precarious. I wonder if the land can really provide us with our basic wants. I hope we can sustain this raw simplicity, our self-belief and determination. I know our life will not always be this smooth and uncomplicated, for all our free thinking and lack of clutter. I am conscious that we may not be sufficiently prepared for when the summer ends. And yet I am glad we have not held back out of an excess of caution. I tell myself it's up to us to make this work. It feels like a gift, as if we have nothing at all to lose.

Each morning, we are still holding hands under the covers. An unfamiliar landscape allows you to feel things differently so your eyes look out, clear and open. It instils calmness. Yet some days it stops me in my tracks. It is strange how a presence so quiet can draw you to it. Even with the taller grasses growing, sometimes that long horizon can feel disconcertingly bare. It is a space utterly devoid of the usual distractions. There are no shops on the island, except for a small post office that sells a few well-stocked groceries, or social hubs such as restaurants, hotels, cafés, pubs or places to meet. Services are limited. There is a small primary school, but no GP or police officer, only a part-time nurse and a fire brigade of volunteers but no other emergency services. The church provides occasional recreational activities for the small congregation, with cups of tea supplied by the Women's Guild, yet with such an ageing population, most Sundays only a few hard pews are filled with the devout. A single-track road stretches north to south, with occasional splinters that all run aground on to shingle and rocks. Its land mass is small and restrictive, held by a fiercely tidal sea that washes off the wilder Atlantic. It is impossible to forget that you are surrounded by water. Wherever you stand, the salt-stung cold tides and clamouring of the gulls are felt. Sometimes, gazing out across the waving grasses to the restless sea, the view can feel strangely overwhelming.

Some days it can feel so empty, I ask, 'Where is everyone?' It is hard to grasp the reality that little more than a handful of other folk live here. The road has scarce traffic, just the odd tractor or dilapidated car clattering past. As days pass into weeks, it feels natural to look for others to share that sky with and to seek a closer company. Belonging requires a community and people. I do not say it out loud, but it also necessitates an acceptance. We are well travelled, but this island feels more remote in its landscape than any other place we have travelled to. Exploring the hills, I feel an unfamiliar freedom coursing through me. There is a raw, energising presence inherent to the landscape itself. When you have no other distractions, you start to quieten into nature.

Lying close, in a battered caravan, watching someone you love softly breathing, a pale dawn light streaming through the windows, framed by the shadows of the mountains behind, fulfils all my bucket-list wishes. It is wild and liberating. Seeing Rab happy makes me move quietly. It is a relief to see our life on track again. Only, this morning something is different. As I sit up, tilting my head to listen intently, the caravan starts to rock gently. I can hear its dry, rusting panels shard, peeling away in rough splinters.

As Rab stirs, rolling over with an arm across his face to block out the light, I slip my feet to the floor. I wrap a soft woollen blanket about me and push open the door of the caravan to investigate. As I step out, seed heads brush against my bare legs and the grass glitters, shimmering quietly, across the empty fields. The fresh air and starlight fall cool on to my skin.

Out of the shadows, a gentle blowing snort accompanies a sudden startle of limbs. A swishing sound meets my own gasp of surprise. Our cows with calves at foot have wandered freely over the fields up from the croft. A moment later, Rab is at my side.

'What the hell?'

We look at each other. And then we laugh. It is so wonderful and ridiculous.

'We'll have to drive in some posts and fence them in,' Rab sighs, tiredly running his hand over the sheared panels of the caravan. 'And fill up these holes.'

'Ssh,' I say. 'Not now.'

Neither of us says what the other is thinking, of how, come the autumn, the wind will blow through.

'Look, they are just being inquisitive.' I stretch out my fingers to lightly touch their sleek summer coats. It is our first real encounter with the cows since we bought them at the market on the mainland. It was nerve-wracking watching Rab placing our bids in the frenetically paced auction ring with a raised hand or a quick nod of the head. All of us pressed too close, sweating bodies pushing hard against the bars of the low bidding pit, the bright lights, wet sawdust, the stench of dung and urine, the slamming gates, the deafening bellowing of cows as they were driven into the ring. It was hard to think with the relentless, ear-splitting voice shouting over the tannoy, driving the pace of the sale. I noticed how there were no other women in the crush surrounding the auction ring, just small groups clustered together high up in the hard wooden stalls. I wondered if I should be sitting there with them.

It has taken the cows a full ten days to settle here on the croft. Their breath is warm and sweet, fermented from the herb-rich summer grass and tiny wild flowers. I take care not to move too quickly as their wet noses blow softly, cautiously scenting us, their tongues slowly rasping out as they taste the air, their flanks quivering, nervous, full of a dense, contained energy. One that is a darker tan reaches forward, nudges me gently and then, startled, backs quickly away. 'They are not yet used to us,' I say. 'But soon they will be.' And I think of the sheep we are still to buy which, similarly, we have no experience of handling or breeding. I tell myself, it is like anything in life. There is always a first time.

'How did we get such a large family?' I wonder, as Rab turns to pull me close.

I yearn to be heavy like a moon suspended, waiting as the seasons pass. I close my eyes and make a wish. It is simply for a child to hold in my arms.

Sometimes I long to hold the day in suspension. For this idyll never to break. Time glides slow as the brown trout sifting soundlessly under the loch's still surface. A lone heron flaps out of the reeds, its great body working. The dry heat is stultifying. And all the while, the summer flits as effortlessly as the swallows skimming for insects, dipping their bills before whirling back into the sky.

Every morning, we pull on our overalls, naked underneath. I fill buckets from the burn, soaking the walls, rubbing away years of debris, dirt and thick soot. It is an unsettling feeling, knowing we are about to live in a place devastated by unforeseen hardship, and that its owner was unable or unwilling to remain on the croft where he or she was born. With our arrival, this life is dead and gone, another heir opting for pragmatism over legacy and selling this home to us. As I scrub, I can hear Rab outside, crawling over the low roof, fixing old slates, and fastening the thin metal ridging to the roof. The roof is full of holes and gaps, its cracked and weathered tiling soft with moss. I try to imagine the unknown winter, when the seas will start lifting and the winds will come funnelling through. I am glad that our cottage is hunkered down, with an unassuming face, and keeps itself close to the ground. I remember the proverb about bright poppies growing too tall being ruthlessly cut down.

Claiming the land around the house, we discover places of beauty and desolation. The grass is studded with wild orchids, dog violet, flag iris, celandines, bright-blue speedwell and the first pale harebells. But dig a little deeper, and beneath its thin skin are its broken graveyards and shallow landfills. A pile of rocks covers twisted horns, a fractured bovine skull, broken bottles and a pile of thin, whitened bones. And it makes me wonder what else lies just out of sight.

One day, we decide it's time for a long-overdue day off. And because the rugby is on and we don't have a TV, Rab goes across on the boat to Oban in search of a pint and a few hours away on his own. We have been together without a break for weeks. We both need a little space. But I do not want to go to Oban, so I stay on the croft alone. The grass is so long, when I lie down in the sunshine I think I am completely hidden – so I lie back, take off my T-shirt and jeans. The grass tickles my skin. It smells delicious, all the seed heads bursting. And then I think, if not here, under empty sky and rolling grassland, where else can I be free? I strip off completely. The sunshine is hot on my face. I doze, listening to the birds and the sound of the breeze.

Some time later, I wake abruptly, aware of a subtle change. The birds suddenly burst out of the tree above me. Something that tells me

I am not alone. Instinctively I reach for my clothes, and then I freeze. Two men are striding towards me across the fields, at a fast pace somewhere between a jog and a run. I know they have seen me. I think, how embarrassing, but at least now they will give me some privacy and head off another way. But they do not. They neither deviate nor slow down. They are coming straight towards me. Suddenly, I am dragging on my clothes as fast as I can. It is a struggle to get dressed without standing up and exposing myself still further. When they are almost on top of me I roll away from them, with my back towards them, furiously fastening my jeans. The next minute, they are standing right over me as I lie flat on my back, their shadows falling across my body. I put my arm over my face, squinting into the sunlight. But all I can see are two shadows; the sun is blazing behind them, its flare full in my eyes.

'Didn't mean to surprise you,' one of them says, apologetically.

The other laughs, leaning forwards, and offers me a hand. 'Well, look what we have here.'

I do not take his hand. I roll over on to my side and get quickly to my feet. I am flustered. I scrunch my hair tight into a knot and take a step backwards, clumsily brushing off seeds and grassheads. I glance from one to another. Then I look down at my bare toes.

I feel hugely at a disadvantage. And yet I am standing, fair and square, with two feet planted on my own croft. I wonder if it is commonplace to find others walking across fields that don't belong to them, or are things seen differently here?

I don't know why, but I find myself apologising. And that both confuses and annoys me even more, because I feel all the more off-guard, out of my comfort zone.

'I'm sorry, but I didn't see you,' I say awkwardly.

The second man laughs. 'Aye, but we saw you.'

Flushing, I flash him a look and he winks at me. My cheeks are burning so I quickly look away.

'Oh, don't mind him, lass.' The first man shoves him mockingly. He has clear hazel eyes, piercing, shrewd. I feel them looking right through me.

I lean forward and pick up my things: a book, a pair of trainers. The men do not move.

'But what are you doing?' I ask clumsily, 'I mean, why are you here?'

'Good question. What were we doing?' He turns to his friend. 'Think I must've been looking for you.' He winks. 'But that's not right, either,' he chuckles, shaking his head. 'Sun's gone to my head.' He stares at me, unabashed. 'Stock's gone walkabout. We came looking for a ewe.'

I fold my arms. I am not sure I believe him. It feels a flimsy, powerless gesture, and it is perhaps because of this that my words blurt uncharacteristically out of my mouth. 'That's funny, because these fields are empty,' I say. 'There are no sheep, just cows grazing here.'

And it is true. There is not a sheep in sight. The auction where we plan to buy a flock is still a few weeks away.

'Ah, that may be true, but it wasn't a minute ago.' He grins. 'Strange what you can find tucked away in hidden places.'

I look at him, speechless. It is at moments like this that I long for a quick, fiery wit. I am starting to learn you need a keen edge to your tongue for all the sparring and staking of territory and boundaries that takes place here. I hunt in vain for an apt response. The right words will only come to me, uselessly, hours later at home.

'I'm sorry, I don't want to be rude,' I say, 'but there are no sheep here. And this is my croft.'

At which the first man fixes his eyes on me and slowly folds his arms. 'Ah, but that's where you're wrong,' he says quietly.

I look at him, confused.

'Aye, lass, always mind you're staying at *Hector's* croft.'

I shake my head. 'No, this is our croft, mine and Rab's. We just bought it.' But as soon as the words are out of my mouth, I want to pull them back.

'Aye, so you did. Well, you can call it what you like,' he counters. 'But this croft has always been *Hector's* croft.'

And suddenly there is a prickling tension between us. It is as if we have each taken a step further back from one another. I can feel a wind blowing between us, as if the day has suddenly turned cold.

'Bought this wee place as well, did you? Put your wee flag into it, too, no doubt. Conquered with the chequebook where you failed with the sword.'

He stares at me. His gleaming eyes run up me and back down. I am being sized up. It is discomfiting and intrusive. I feel vertiginous, unsure of my ground. There is a long silence.

And then he laughs, shrugs. 'Well now, let's call it quits. Nothing more than a daft wee storm in your precious china teacup. Maybe next time you'll invite us in to share some proper Highland hospitality with your good self.'

Only the way he says this, it is provocative. I look down at my feet. I feel I have been churlish, but also humiliated. Above all, I feel confused.

'I'm sorry,' I say. I do not know why I am apologising again, except that I sense I have only just avoided making a serious faux pas. So I tell myself it is worth it for this reason.

'Next time,' I say carefully, 'you are welcome to a dram with me and Rab up at the house.' I hold out my hand. The gesture seems overly formal but it is the only way that suggests itself to close or seal this exchange.

When he takes my hand, he squeezes it so hard I wince. I meet his gaze, and still he doesn't let it go. And then, without warning, he drops my hand contemptuously.

'Never forget,' he says pointedly, 'in Scotland, every man has the right to roam. So be careful where you go putting on and off your clothes.'

When I look up, I feel dazed. I have wronged them. And yet I too have been wronged. I rub my hand and watch them leave at last, confused and disorientated. They are laughing together as they walk away. And the man who gripped my hand slaps the other hard on the back. All the warmth of the sun seems to evaporate. And I feel weary, the sunshine of the day tainted.

'You stupid, stupid idiot,' I scold myself fiercely. Only exactly what I have done, I am not sure. It is no clearer when I play it back in my head. When I tell Rab, he laughs. 'They're just chancers. Of course they came over. You were lying there half asleep without a stitch on.' I look at him and wonder, is it my fault, then? And I think, would you have done the same? It bothers me for days, like sunburn that prickles its heat beneath the skin. I feel that I have stepped too close to an invisible boundary. I am alone on one side and, inexplicably, for the first time, Rab is standing facing me from across the line.

I am missing my friends, and Rab is missing his. It is tiring only talking to each other. I wonder if birds too can weary of each other's voices. Is that why they congregate in flocks – to hear a different song?

During the long weeks before our off-grid address is connected with a landline, I walk to the phone box, located outside a nearby farm, to keep in touch with friends and family. My fingers push coins rapidly into the metal slot. Each minute is precious. 'It's great to hear your voice,' I say to a friend. And to another, 'Will you write? Call it that coffee or lunch we used to have.' Only no one uses ink any more.

It makes the few letters that come all the more important. Even opening a bill feels special in the absence of other communications. Post is delivered daily. It is always a hopeful time. Every morning the post office van drives down to the shore to meet the ferry. It turns around, reverses down the slip and on to the boat. The sacks are loaded into the back and then it drives up the island to the tiny post office, where the post is sorted before being delivered direct to each mailbox or placed inside each unlocked household door. Later, the outgoing mail will be stamped, bagged, put on to the ferry and taken to the mainland central depot in Oban. Each day is marked by this routine. It demands accurate timing. The ferry waits for no one, not even the post. Only the weather or a mechanical fault will stop its clockwork precision.

We long to know other islanders; to hear of the gatherings that take place behind closed doors. The key, it turns out, is on the road. One day the cheery red post van comes to the house as I am working in the yard and the post lady toots the horn and rolls down the window. 'Doing anything tonight?' she asks, and laughs as I shrug and shake my head. Truth is, I cannot remember the last time I had a night out. 'Well, it's my birthday – I'm making a girls' outing. I'll come by to pick you up close to the back of six.'

'Don't be late and don't get drunk,' Rab jokes as we hear the blast of a horn outside and he pushes me out of the door. 'You're on your own now.' I have clean jeans and make-up on. I have washed my hair and left my work boots at the door. For a minute, I do not recognise myself.

'Jump in!' a voice shouts, but when I try the handle, I realise that others are already squeezed into all the available seats. 'Full house up front!' the voice shouts again, 'Let yourself into the back.'

I heave the back door open and say hello in surprise. The back is already nearly full as well. I can see at least five women squashed in there. No one says anything but legs and bodies move over. There is a squeal and then someone laughs. 'Mind, you clump – you're sitting on my foot.' It is an ice-breaker. A hand reaches out, hauls me in and the door is slammed shut from the outside. Inside it is completely dark until a torch flicks on. There are giggles, and then a bottle is passed around. It feels wonderful to be included in this celebration, whirling about the island, picking up still more revellers along the way and, later, to sit crammed with them around a small table at the ferry bar across the water. After the last tenner is slammed down hard on the table, and glasses are downed, there is a dash for the boat, and the ferry sings its way home.

Although I cannot remember everyone's name, I now know a handful of others who live here. It occurs to me that perhaps I have always taken friendships for granted and brings home the enormity of the step we have taken. With hindsight our old life seems incredibly simple, trustworthy and dependable. Everyone needs to feel the presence of other lives close by. Strangely, it makes you less discerning of the company you have found, so grateful are you to have found it at all.

It is an old island custom to look for lights in the darkness. A light in a window, I learn, is an open invitation to knock on the door of the house for company, and others expect hospitality on seeing a similar light in your own home. Our first visitors are an elderly couple. They arrive on the doorstep and pass the time of day. They will not come in or sit with us, but their warmth is welcome, as is their kindness and genuine curiosity. They bring a tin of shortbread and homemade tablet, a delicious sweet made from sugar, condensed milk and butter – it is so hard it is safer to break it with your fingers than risk your teeth – and then they walk away up the road. Visiting from door to door, unannounced, is an altogether different and unexpected way of socialising.

'Why don't we practise?' I suggest.

I hastily wrap some bread and biscuits I have made using our basic cooking equipment. I am excited yet it feels daunting to go knocking on strangers' doors. In the end, the outcome is as we might have anticipated. Some doors open with warmth, curiosity and a cheery welcome, whilst others pull back warily. And at a couple we experience open hostility.

'Well, it was never going to be easy,' Rab reasons. And then we look at each other. It is unsettling to arrive in a place and to be so swiftly unsure of your welcome.

Conversations run in a linear way, following well-rehearsed, formulaic patterns, leaning into each season or what is happening in people's lives. Exchanges are economical; words are chiselled. Though little is said, much is implied in subtle nuances – the flick of an eye, a quick-witted aside or a curt rebuff. I am missing deeper interactions. There is a reserve and innate guardedness hiding behind a casual, well-oiled warmth that gives nothing intimate away. It is a shield that is difficult to penetrate. Instead you have to wait for it to lift. It takes time to inhabit a landscape and to familiarise yourself with its traditions. Simultaneously, I am occasionally unsettled by the lack of privacy or anonymity. I wonder what is said of us behind closed doors.

Small gestures of help and kindnesses burst into each week like bright blinks of sunshine. They counter any early off-kilter impressions and are all the more generous for being random and unexpected. A lift from the ferry on a rainy day. A friendly wave as we walk past an open window, a sudden shouted invitation to come inside. Headlights that appear on the driveway, long after dark, as hearty 'bumper' drams are splashed out from a bottle carried in the deep pocket of a sheepskin coat to wish us well in our new home, or simply to find out, through more uninhibited talk, exactly who we are. Sometimes it is startling and bewildering to receive such a full-spirited yet testing welcome from folk we have barely seen in passing a handful of times, and others we have not yet seen at all.

One morning a van disappears at speed out of the yard. An old wooden chest of drawers has been left there with an unsigned note stuck on to it, the words 'We hope you can find a use for this' written in a beautiful script. I am moved by this thoughtfulness and generosity. In all our years in London, I cannot remember such care being taken over welcoming new neighbours. Later, once the chest has been sanded and oiled, tiny mother-of-pearl flowers are visible, like all the flowers of the croft, etched into the fine detailing of each drawer. I hope we will have the chance to return these favours, with our time or in kind, so that this goodwill does not run dry, or change course suddenly like the wind.

There are always those who abruptly turn away, or who won't meet our smiles. But, as time passes, we learn which doors will open with a warm greeting. And how, as an incomer to the island, hospitality, and belonging to the community, mean opening your own door to all, regardless of the reception you are given in return.

The day the summer breaks, we are still in the caravan. The rain is hammering down. It drums hard on to the leaking roof and soaks the bedsheets, seeping in through those windows still stuck half open. We drag the mattress clear and place buckets on the torn lino floor beneath the windows. Outside the water starts to collect in deep puddles around the house. Even the cows look subdued.

'Ready or not, it's time to move,' Rab says.

We struggle to combat the chill inside the cottage. The thick, un-insulated walls are barely warmed by our logs hissing on the hearth. Our skin shrinks from washing in unheated water. Cold is tiring. But afterwards, you feel a glow.

As the rain persists, the dry, browning grass gradually turns green again. The day I notice this, the electrician arrives from the mainland. We have been waiting for weeks for him to connect us to power, lay pipes across the bog and link our empty water tanks to the spring. There is a shout as Rab waves jubilantly out of a window. Fresh water is at last bubbling through the limescale-crusted taps. We suck hard on a hosepipe and draw the airlocks out. And although the bathroom is chilly, it is a small miracle not to have to lug buckets, and to feel hot water running out of the taps. The tank is so small it barely fills the deep cast-iron bath. But even a few inches of warmth on the skin is luxurious. Stepping over the high sides of the bath, I sigh as that welcome heat soaks into my bones.

I listen to the wind and the rain blowing outside. It is a wonderful feeling to be living inside our home at last. And although the summer and those first short, idyllic weeks are over, I am grateful for this roof over our heads. It teaches us that comfort and discomfort are only a drop of water apart. It makes me conscious of how strangely feral that seems, because even animals have the dignity of being able to groom and wash themselves. It is shocking how quickly we struggle to navigate around each other with ease when basic comforts are denied over an extended period. I hope I will always feel that startling shock of gratitude when water runs out of the taps, or my bare skin steps steaming out of a bath. It is a relief, too, that our conversations flow more easily again.

Yet as doors start to open with our neighbours, I notice how, for all its banter, our dialogue is loaded with everything that remains unsaid. The question asked on each new encounter – 'Who do you know?' – is different from the obligatory 'What do you do?' to which we were accustomed in our old lives. We are strangers. We do not know anyone. We have no kin on the island. Always I am aware of the implicit, unasked follow-up question: 'Then why are you here?'

At the end of the summer, we are connected to the internet. The signal is slow – with the mast offshore, it is received first by Oban and then beamed across miles of fierce sea to the dish at the fire station. All the same, it is a relief to be reconnected to the wider world. I have given up asking my friends to write letters. 'Just send an email, it's quicker,' they say. It is hard to explain how much more personal a letter feels. There is a beautiful fall of silence that drifts between handwritten words.

I watch the gulls screaming in off the water, tilting their wings, angling precipitously into the wind. They make it look so easy. It takes time for your impressions of the world to be subtly broken, realigned and reconstructed. Rab and I act differently as soon as our feet touch mainland soil. On the island there is little interest in the lives we have left behind. It is as if that part of us has been wilfully disconnected. Sometimes I am uncertain if this part of ourselves will forever stay invisible. We are caught between our desire for acceptance that we belong and a fear that, if we stay, we might end up different from the people we know ourselves to be.

4

Croft

THE GRASSES ARE running free in flowing waves over the hillsides. The wind breathes on them, billowing a great rippling fullness and swell. Everywhere, seed heads are ripening, flaxen husks swollen taut, straining to shear and scatter next year's crop along invisible opening seams. As I walk across the hills, the air is heady with a rich abundance. It is a herbaceous, aromatic scent, warmed and seasoned by a strange sirocco that blows in gusts off the sea. It is wearying, at the end of the summer, waiting for that harvest. Some days I wonder if it will ever come.

Once the birch bark splits and clouds of thistledown drift, the fields are shorn and another cusp is passed. Hare streak from the hollow, quivering rushes and sea eaglets stretch adolescent wings over the bare hills. I watch those cruel talons soaring seaward on to the freshening salt uplift, suspended, scarcely moving. Below, tufts of fleece snag across the rough grazing, fluttering like torn prayer flags. It is then that a slow aching hunger is felt keening in the wind.

I walk everywhere. I explore every pocket, parcel, hectare and furlong of land. The granite faces of the mountains come alive in the pale, fallow sunrise. With every flux and fluctuation of light, the landscape becomes chiselled, stark-lit and strangely potent. It throws up its gifts, its bright stories like hard, ringing stones.

Each hill, brae, glen or valley holds a secret. I hear those forgotten lives breathing, their voices echoing on the wind. The old villages sit empty, thick nettles showing where once the midden would have lain. Mice nest in the broken cornerstones and tiny ferns cling to the walls. I follow the overgrown main street winding down through each small settlement. Sometimes, as the wind shifts direction, I can hear the echoes of children running through the grass.

Soon I have a favourite place to go – a rocky headland that sits alone, riven off from the hills by steep gullies and precipitous cliffs. It is in the northwest of the island, hidden and not easy to reach. To see it, you have to commit to seeking out its hidden paths. It is approached by sea, or on foot through ancient, twisted, stunted woodland of birch, oak, alder and ash. There is no track or clear marking on the map. I find it only by noticing a lean scatter of grazing on its far shore. These secret, winding paths are long-forgotten songlines marked only by deer and sheep, narrow cleats pitted into the soft, peaty soil. The dense thickets are impassable, ripping my clothing and snagging my hair with briars, until I fold forwards. I learn to make myself still smaller. It is calm and restful out of sight.

Southwesterly gales have shaped this remote headland differently. Here is the massive contoured profile of an uplifted face, eyes staring blind into the sky. Its blunted chest, fierce head and fine aquiline nose are carved of igneous and basalt rock. It is here that the legends are rich: this is the ancient resting place of Ossian, the keeper of the soil. Man is an anachronism; the land does not belong to him. Its strata of rock, from a darker time of myth and instinct, is primal; a creative and destructive force of the earth itself.

Stones are hewn, duns are raised and razed, brochs and forts laid, and then laid over. Sheep come, the people go. Times change. All about, the tides ebb and flow and the waves keep breaking. Later, the people return. And still this island rock remains. Regardless of how it is divided up into small strips of grazing: the stringently demarcated, shifting territories that are called crofts.

Our croft is called Rocky Ridge, or the Rough Farm. Our house is built from island stones. Its memories are woven into the landscape, knitted together of ancient Gaelic and Norse names. My mouth wraps about their unfamiliar shapes. The Norse is angular, hard like the fjordic mountains, but the Gaelic is soft, like the fields. Rocks and memories are the island's geological and cultural backbone. Stories are shared over cups of tea, drams and buttered scones, and are passed on by the bearers of the same names as those carved into upright stones by the church mason over generations. Acquiring the right to belong is as arduous as prising those hard-won rocks from the island's soil. It is gifted joyfully to each island child, and to those bonded by marriage to its tight-knit cluster of families. It can be earned only by bleeding your own life, joys and sorrows into its dark, shallow earth.

Each pocket of soil is as jealously guarded as any close kinship. Kinship and soil are fiercely defended territories. To name it you have to claim it. Yet, for all your effort, you never deserve it. Belonging is at the behest and tolerance of others jealously guarding their own right to the soil. The history of this croft matters. Its loss is a palpable grief to some and a source of enmity to others. Disused tools, ploughs and anvils which lay forgotten before our arrival gain a sudden provenance.

It is strange to see and feel the missing of these items where they used to lie. It is hard to understand how it might be when strangers come and disrupt the croft's old ways. I wonder if we will ever be forgiven for taking a piece of the island's soil.

We work our own croft. We drive hard stobs, or wooden posts, into the soil, anchored by corner strainer posts buried three feet deep; we secure tension Rylock fencing wire with gleaming, sharp, double-pointed nails. We fix our march lines, our boundaries, and finally the croft is stockproof. In autumn, at the Oban livestock auction, we buy our first sheep, a mixture of Cheviots and cross mules from the older Black Face sired by Blue Leicester, for its strong bones and fine wool. Our first lambing is scarily, viscerally real, no longer just the topic of pastoral talk, as a three-season tup immediately sets to work.

'Well, that's it,' Rab says proudly, leaning over a metal gate. 'Nothing wrong with that boy.'

And I think how nothing will stop those lambs from coming. And how easy nature makes that gift of new life seem.

Our first lambing is bleak, beautiful, challenging and uplifting. It is too easy to miss the early signs unless you know what to look for. It takes skill to detect the 'show', the creamy, mucous plug released from the cervix, and a keen eye to pick up on a weary dropping of the sacrum as a tailbone dips, concealing a ripe swelling of udder and teats. I learn to look for a thin water bag hanging or bursting a steaming spray on to the ground. Once those waters break, a period of restless agitation follows. An anxious circling, pawing of the ground and inability to settle can take minutes or presage complications if it lasts longer than a few hours.

It is a relief when the ewe lies down. I watch her eyes glaze as she lifts her head and starts straining. The real lambing begins with her stuttering, harsh cries. Sometimes the lamb comes just as it should.

Tiny wet hooves peek out at the vaginal opening, wrapped in mucus and birthing fluid. Shortly after a slippery crown appears, I look for dark-blue, unseeing eyes. Once the shoulders are through, the effort is over. The body slides out quickly in a warm, streaming gush of life and afterbirth. Our hands swiftly remove the suffocating caul from the mouth and airways. With every birth my heart leaps at that first fragile, high cry.

'If only it was always this simple,' Rab observes as he deftly turns the ewe over, releasing the first creamy spurt of colostrum from a gently worked teat. I am elated when the lamb staggers up and sucks.

But lambing is not always simple. Sometimes the head emerges first, ahead of the legs, and then it needs pushing back inside the ewe or no amount of straining will release it. The strength of a ewe's contractions against your hand, working gently inside her, is a brutal, crushing force. Sometimes the neck flicks back, or the shoulders get stuck, or an elbow is caught in the birth canal, or the lamb is twisted with a sibling still in utero. It is difficult delivering a breached lamb without severing the umbilicus or damaging its soft internal organs. Rab's hands carefully help to guide these unborn lives. There is so much at stake. I do not hesitate to administer mouth-to-mouth resuscitation, my lips pressed hard to the lamb's airways, fingers gently working a tiny stuttering heart. A life is only a life once there is air in the lungs. It is a desperate sight when a perfectly formed lamb lies cold on the ground. With no knowledge or experience, we take each moment as it comes.

One morning I find a tiny lamb stretched out in the darkness, born just before dawn and abandoned by her mother. Her stiff body is freezing, her tongue swollen and already turning blue. I wrap her in my scarf and come running indoors. I rub her with towels, and place her carefully in a box filled with straw. Only time will tell, I think, as I switch the heat lamp on. Tears spring to my eyes as she opens her mouth and cries. Humanity is extraordinary like that. You appreciate life so much more after each brush with death.

Painstakingly we slide a thin tube from her mouth to her stomach, and as powdered colostrum in sterilised warm water slowly resuscitates her, I know she has a fighting chance. Later, though, her mother rejects her. She brutally lowers her head and charges her again and again. The hard, bony forehead hammers into the lamb. We make a crate and tie the ewe with a soft halter so that the lamb is protected. But she is too bruised and dazed from the birth, her tongue is still swollen and she is unable to feed from the teat. There is no option. Until she can, she has to be bottle-fed. 'Still have to twin her on,' a farmer tells us. Another shrugs: 'Why bother? Simpler to just knock her on the head.'

'I can't do that, not whilst she is trying to live,' I say.

After each feed, we put her back into the pen. We hold the ewe so that the lamb can learn to teat-feed, but her healthy sibling is stronger and pushes her roughly out of the way. Each time, the mother lunges for her. She will not settle with her in the pen. When I lift the lamb, she leans into me, trembling.

'I can't bear it,' I say, as she is knocked down again and again. It is agonising to watch. Soon she hides from her mother. After three days, I cannot stand it any more. I remove her from the ewe and raise her as a pet. I name her Tilda. She sleeps in the barn, surrounded by the sights and sounds of the lambing, but in the daytime she follows me everywhere. As soon as I wake, I warm a milk bottle, fix a sterilised teat and run to the barn. I can hear Tilda making the very special call that a lamb bleats to its own mother. It is an intimate sound of recognition, joy and hunger. For three weeks, Tilda needs help to feed. But slowly the trauma of her difficult birth heals. She has a beautiful face with a strong conformation. 'I think you're going to have beautiful lambs of your own one day,' I tell her. When I lift her up to feed her, she eagerly nibbles my nose. She falls asleep in my lap. She is fascinated by the cat and has a passion for fresh-shooting raspberry leaves.

'She can't stay in the house,' Rab tells me. I am using an old biscuit tin as a makeshift litter tray. This arrangement will only be viable whilst she is very young, and I know she will soon need to live outside. 'She needs a friend to keep her company,' I say. When a tiny triplet arrives, unable to keep up with its siblings in the daily struggle to feed, she joins Tilda. I call her Milly. She is so small that on colder days she sits inside a straw-filled terracotta flowerpot to keep herself out of the wind. Her miniature nose and bright eyes follow Tilda everywhere. At night, they play inside the cottage on the bare floorboards, sucking greedily from warmed milk bottles before bedding down in a straw crate.

When lambing is over we bury others that did not make it. Lambing brings you close to the miracle of life and to the shattering pain of its losses. It inures you to the exhaustion of the spring grind.

The sheep know where every herb and fresh blade lies. It takes hours to herd them in from the open grazing. Once they find the trees, no amount of persuasion will draw them out of the narrow tracks that zigzag sheer above the cliffs. 'I can't do this,' I yell to Rab, in position above me ready to direct the flock as I attempt to steer them out from a treacherous ledge. It is nerve-wracking trying to find a foothold and branches to hold on to. One part of my head is screaming, 'It's too dangerous!' while the other part insists, 'Hold on, just don't look down.' We are both exhausted by the time we push the sheep back to safety. 'This is crazy,' I say. 'We need a dog.' The sheep are running rings around us. They have a canny intelligence, none more so than the matriarch ewe who leads the flock to where they are most inaccessible to us.

One day I arrive home from a local farm with a scrap of a pup in the truck. She is long-haired, downy, like a soft, dark fox. She has tiny white paws and a white tip to her tail. As I hold her, my fingers sink deep into her silky fur. 'Hello, Maude,' I say. She stares up at me with bright amber eyes. I fall in love that day. She is more than a working dog to me. She fills the vacuum I am feeling as I wait for motherhood.

'She can't stay outside,' I say.

I want to bring her into the house. She is so tiny, I don't want her to be alone in the cold stone barn. But Rab is firm. 'She's not a baby. She's a working dog.' And one of the farmers, who is in the kitchen, nods in agreement, pours another dram. 'Only way for a working dog.'

'She'll be too soft. And she'll learn bad habits.'

'You'll be a laughing stock, ruining her for work.'

She is my dog. But the croft is man's work. So we end up putting her in the barn.

That first night she cries and cries. I cannot bear that such a small life can feel so alone. So I go and sit with her in the straw. I have wrapped a hot-water bottle in a soft blanket and brought a ticking clock to echo the sound of her mother's heartbeat. In bed in the cottage, I lie awake. I wonder why it is OK to keep a dog alone, away from a pack or company, for long hours of the day, and not a child.

She grows fast. 'You love that dog more than you love me,' Rab says. And I laugh. Because although that is inconceivable, I suppose in one sense it is true. Maude and I seek in each other a mutual trust and unconditional love that is unfailing. Our bond is as deep as the sky. We do not tire of each other. Some things are hard to put into words.

Every day Maude and I walk the length and rounds of the croft, familiarising ourselves with its sudden dips, hidden corners, cliffs and trees. It is a difficult terrain. With only a single enclosure, the ground is wild, open. I do not want to tie a rope about her, or let her drag a weight, as I have been instructed. I want her to be free. So I put words, signs and sounds to her movements and teach them to her.

I spend hours working and playing with her, introducing prompts of voice, whistle, arm and hand signs. Quickly we progress to working the sheep together. We are inseparable.

Later in the autumn, the months of hard work pay off. Hail is flying like bullets and the skies darkening as I track back, head down, barrelling into the freezing fields. We are gathering in the sheep from the high, exposed land of the north-facing croft into the southerly, more sheltered fields. The sheep have broken their cover, and a flighty gimmer, barely two years old, has recklessly split away from the flock. It is an anxious moment. The flock starts shredding. It is like a weak seam that is suddenly torn, so that the fabric on either side shears as its edges fray.

As Maude bounds away, the wind changes direction. 'Come-bye,' I yell, but she does not hear me. She is still a young dog. My lips are blue from whistling. I want to cry with the cold. I watch as she scales a cliff and then veers off to the left, looping back on herself. My heart freezes as the sheep scatter, heading towards the rough side of the cliff and a forty-foot sheer precipice below. It does not bear thinking about how wrong this may go.

'Maude, look up. Please look up.' Only she doesn't. So I am running, hard into that wind, willing her to turn around. Suddenly I stop. I do not shout. I give up my calls, cries and whistles. I try to speak to her. Not with my voice, but with my heart. Whatever it is that reaches her, sheer determination or sheer desperation, it seems to have its own voice. As she looks up, I can feel something connect. It is like a key finding its lock. Gently I guide her in, semaphoring her whirling body like someone guiding a plane coming in to land. I can feel her effort, that intense, conscious intelligence, flickering like a live wire through the circuit board of her brain; a rippling intuitive response to my silent call.

As the sheep come skittering past, I run after them. I pull the gate bolt shut and lean on it, panting, rubbing the wind and hair out of my eyes. I crouch down and hold Maude. Looking at those sheep, safe out of the wind, I feel like my heart will burst.

It is a joy to be in the cottage. For weeks after we move in it is bare. We live with a couple of chairs, an old cooker and a thin mattress on the floor. One day I salvage a small traditional table from the barn. It is covered in cobwebs, dust and fusty old haylage. As I strip it back, tiny silverfish wriggle out of its hinges and joints. I imagine its life before, the conversations and secrets it has heard. It makes me wonder if our hopes and struggles are the same as those of our predecessors. I find an old torn photograph in the wooden kist left in the cottage and pin it up on the wall. It is a portrait of a man and a woman. They have strong faces and watchful, reproachful eyes. 'They must be family to this place,' I say. Only Rab takes it down. 'There are enough eyes watching already,' he says. I think I know what he means.

I notice him, some days, staring out at the sky. He is drinking and smoking more than he used to.

One day I stiffen when he remarks: 'Sometimes I wake thinking, is this it? This and only this?'

I glance at him to try to read his expression. I am so tired of moving. I remember how Rab was before those London streets got too close. I thought we had left that all behind. Restlessness leads to a disruptive unhappiness. I try not to dwell on that. It made our city life feel cramped and small. The skies here feel immense to me. It worries me when I catch that look on his face.

I smooth a dark oil over the table. When it is dry, I bring it inside. I lay a cloth and put plates on it. We have not sat at a table for months. I pick a tiny posy of wild flowers, harebell and wild thyme, gathered on the hill. We have caught two brown trout in the loch. That evening, we wash, dress and sit down to eat. It feels like a date. We look at each other and laugh. 'So stupid, but I feel shy,' I say.

The next minute, Rab jumps up. There is the unmistakable noise of a tractor approaching. 'Holy shit, it's going to crash into the barn!' It doesn't, instead braking hard to miss the tight corner. But it comes so close it clips the water butt. Then, abruptly, it stops.

'This could be interesting,' he says. 'Some island action at last.'

I have just put the beautiful, steaming pink trout on the table. 'So much for supper, then,' I say, suddenly annoyed. Rab is already out of the door.

In the yard, two men are lying sprawled in the dust. I can see they have been working at sheep. Their checked shirts are covered in fleece, and muck spatters their jeans. An empty bottle lies on the ground. Slowly, the younger of the two hauls himself up, leaning heavily on the other. His face is thickset and reddened, but the rest of him is slim and pale.

'Sorry.' He shakes his head, slurring, 'Think I must've tripped up there.' He leans over, pulls his companion to his feet. 'Tricky turn. Stopped a bit smart. Came to see our new neighbours.' He sways over to Rab, slapping him hard on the shoulder. 'Now you think you're staying at Hector's croft.'

I walk over and stand next to Rab. He steps forward to offer a hand to the older man, who suddenly sinks against the tractor wheel. I turn to face our upright visitor and realise I have seen his face before.

'Ah, a bonny lass for all that,' he reasons, roughly jostling my arm. It is not quite a handshake. His fingers wrap about my wrist so it is hard to disengage. I try to step away but he doesn't let go.

I glance around quickly, looking for Rab, but he is still assisting the other man and his back is turned to me.

'Not at all,' I say, taking another step back. 'If you don't mind . . . you're hurting my arm.'

'Ach, like that, is it?' His face flickers, switching from a smile to something harder. One minute he is holding my wrist, and then his fingers slide down the back of my arm. It happens so quickly, I am not prepared. His hand catches my armpit, fingers resting close to the straps of my dress. It lingers there, for a probing second, against the soft skin hidden just under the posterior curve of my breasts. My skin burns at that unwanted touch.

He laughs as I flinch and wrench my arm away. Rab turns around, oblivious to what has just transpired. It doesn't feel safe to explain. I look at my wrist. I can still feel the impression of the man's fingers, see the white marks they have left on my skin. I look at him, confused, lightheaded and on edge.

'So now we've made our introductions,' the man banters testily, 'are you not going to let us in?'

He stares at Rab, eyes darkening. 'Don't want us to think you're not . . .' I watch his lips, as each syllable is enunciated deliberately, '. . . not very hos-pit-able.'

'Of course, you're welcome,' Rab says carefully. 'And now you've met my wife,' he flashes me a look, 'you're welcome to a dram.' He frowns at me, not understanding, as I shake my head. My eyes are fierce. They tell him no.

There is an awkward silence.

'I don't think that's a good idea,' I say, to fill it. 'I'll go and get some tea.'

Rab scans my face, bemused, uncomprehending. Then he shrugs and walks ahead to the door.

'You do not confront this,' he tells me silently in that look. 'Or over-react. Not here, not now, not with this level of alcohol.' I know to him it is important to emerge none the worse for this exchange. But from what I can see, both of our visitors have had more than a skinful. Any more drams and both will be out cold on the floor. Suddenly I am furious. I wonder, if not here, and if not now, when? I am not sure which side is right or wrong, not sure what to do, aware only that our home is not our own. And that somehow Rab has distanced himself from me. I do not like how that feels.

We file silently into the room. The fish look up at me with cold, flat eyes. I switch the oven off and put them back in to keep warm. Rab goes to a cardboard box and takes out two more glasses. I watch him pour out hefty drams. He makes an effort to keep things light, but the atmosphere is strained. After about an hour, both men pass out.

'What do we do?' I ask anxiously. 'They'll be here all night.' I feel so upset and angry. 'Rab, for God's sake. This is our home.'

We stare at each other, unseeing. I hate it when we react so differently. And then Rab kicks a chair. 'Don't be so uptight.' And that is worse than anything I have felt before.

As he shakes the men awake, he is rough and casual. He is still processing my hasty explanation of what happened out in the yard. It irks me that to him this is merely a move in some kind of game.

'Well, thanks for coming over. Time you were on your way.'

In the yard, the atmosphere changes right in front of my eyes. It is excruciating. One minute they are going. Then, in a flash, something sparks. The younger man shoves Rab from behind. He stands shoulders squared, legs braced, fists balled at his sides. I feel my own hands clenching, my nails biting deep into my skin. As I watch his fleshy lips working, I feel my own mouth go dry. I freeze as he thrusts his reddened face up against Rab's. Then he turns to me and leers, 'So, you're here, all nice and cosy. Think it's going to be easy, do you? Well, if there's one thing I hate more than fucking incomers, it's a shower of bastards coming up to where you don't belong.'

I blink as I feel my limbs move slowly in that slick way they do when you are pumped full of adrenaline. Rab puts a hand on the man's shoulder and I gasp as, roughly, he shakes it off. He must sense my fear and incredulous anger because his face is so close I can feel his breath hot on my cheek. I fix my eyes on his, and for a moment I stare back hard. Then I drop them quickly. I want to hurt him but there is real hatred in his look. I stare at the spittle on his chin, his too-soft lips, his tongue slurring his words, and feel the space around me shrinking. 'Nice tits, breeding hips,' he leers. 'A sweet young heifer for bulling is what this croft needs.'

After they are gone, we don't eat the fish. They are dried and burned. We sit in silence.

'Fancy a dram?' Rab asks eventually.

'Make it a double,' I nod. And then I pick up the bottle myself. My hand is shaking as I fill up my glass.

By the autumn I have a beautiful Highland mare. She is a cream dun, as bright as pale winter sunshine. I call her Fola. She is a brood mare, as wild as the hills. But after a long summer running with a stallion, she is still barren. 'Time you got rid of her,' a neighbour tells me. 'No use for a freeloader on the croft.' And I am sad. Because I know they are right. Yet there is something gentle in Fola's eyes that stops me. 'Let's give it a bit longer,' I argue with Rab. 'Maybe we can think of another use for her.' Rab is unconvinced.

On rainy days, her hoof marks fill with water. 'It's poaching the soil and wrecking the croft,' he says.

'But what about the cows?' I ask. 'There are so many of them. Their hooves make far more mess.'

'They pay their way with calves,' he says. And then he folds his arms and looks at me challengingly.

I cannot argue with this. 'Let's keep her till the spring,' I suggest. 'I'll try to find a way to make it work.'

I am determined. We have discovered that our croft used to be the home of the blacksmith. Below the broken thatch posts, in the derelict barn, cobbles and stalls remain where gentle working horses used to stand. I love that, with Fola, horses are returning to the croft and I wonder if she might one day work the land.

In the increasingly mechanised world of farming, I can understand the resistance to a working horse. Yet I begin to notice how, when other farmers stop by, my ideas or contributions are ignored, regarded with cool amusement or swiftly talked down. Sometimes I wonder if, to them, there is no legitimate place for a woman in the fields either.

I catch Fola and rub my hands, featherlight gentle, over every inch of her body. 'It's OK,' I tell her. 'You can stay here, with or without a foal.' And then I whisper, 'But you have to help me.' And I am excited, because I think I have, if not a solution, then at least a working plan.

'Takes a long time to break a horse's spirit,' a farmer tells me.

'I'm going to do this gently,' I reply firmly.

When we are alone, I make a promise to Fola. 'I will never chain you to the back of a lorry and drag you,' I tell her. Her sensitive eyes are watching me. I know she is listening. It takes time for a horse to trust you. I talk to her, smoothing every inch of her coat with a cloth. When a fly lands lightly on her back, I see the skin instantly ripple. It makes me think of how responsive that acute sensitivity can be. That day, I dream of us running across those hills together. The sun on our faces, the wind on our backs and all the sea for a view.

'Are you sure you should be doing that?' Rab asks when I sit bare-back on her. I am elated and terrified as she steps nervously, in unsteady circles, on the grass. The next day I fall off. I learn to make my body soft just as I am slipping away from her. I practise this. I lie in the grass, quietly, and allow her to come and find me. Backing takes a long time. It takes longer than it might, because we are both learning. And then, one day, as I sit on her, and feel her body breathing, pressing into my thighs, I pat her soft neck. 'Come on Fola, it's now or never.' Her pricked ears quiver, listening.

I lean forwards, my head close to her mane, her eyes shining as she starts to gallop. And suddenly, the wind is blowing against us, the hills falling away and I am flying with Fola. We are flying together. The sky is above us and the solid earth is drumming below in a steady beat of hooves. I have found a part of myself that is fresh and new to me. I am wild and free.

In the autumn, the deer swim over from the barren hills. The island sees them coming. It watches with a harder face. But the deer keep coming. Desperate with hunger, they risk the fierce crossing as tides set the island adrift. Survival depends on risking all for that sweet bite. Inland, rich furrows of pasture and common grazing running longi-tudinally up the island's narrow spine hide this feral struggle. Yet at dawn, occasionally I spy the deer daring to follow those ragged rock seams in the hope of a smooth, shallow skein of grass. By breaching territory, they risk their safety. They remind me to watch where I tread.

There are some who wish us well. And others who, even before they meet us, appear to want us to fail. Sometimes it makes me sweat.

'We were going to buy this croft.'

There is an edge, a hostility and the suggestion of an illegitimacy to our ownership that makes me catch my breath.

'I'm sorry,' Rab says, rubbing his neck uncomfortably. 'That's too bad. I'm sorry it didn't work out for you. But on the other hand,' he adds, 'I'm glad we are here.'

Later, when the subject is not dropped, and glasses are filled and emptied, he asks straight out, 'But did you put an offer in?'

And it transpires that, whilst it was a close-held intention, no action was taken either to offer or to take steps to buy.

'Just let it go,' I say. 'It doesn't matter. We are here now. These feelings, they will disappear in time.'

Only it does. And they don't. Years later, those resentments are still there. We hear whispers of a handwritten scrap of paper and a hushed-up inheritance dispute. Sometimes it is easier to bury a half or a whole truth. Or to turn your back on those unsettling gusts. All whispers, just like the stinging salt wind, eventually lull, tire of themselves or simply drift away.

'But it makes no sense,' I say, the day after another bruising exchange. 'If families so want to stay together, if communities only want their own to stay, why blame us and not take the quarrel to the vendor? Surely it is the family or individual selling that sets and accepts the price. Why not take less, and have more, in that case?' Their argument seems unjust, a hypocrisy that rankles for its slight and sleight of hand. And it worries me. Sometimes it feels strange that where we live, we will always be invisible. No matter what we do, how long we live or stay, this will always be 'Hector's croft'.

As the wind freshens with the hard edge of the season, the waves fall ever harder, dashing on to the rocks. We keep quiet and keep on working. We tidy up the rough ground. I am aware how infinitely more difficult this would be without Rab at my side. Crofting is about teamwork, and pulling together, each with a role and a willingness to work. About the effort of creating a system that is streamlined, in tune with the seasons and the cycles of the sun and the moon. As autumn tips into the early winter, some days the winds are up, the seas are too fierce and then the boats do not run. We pore over the forecasts and tide tables, planning for those times when we are likely to be unable to get to the mainland to stock up on groceries and animal feed supplies.

We do not know anyone in Oban, so we rarely go out socialising there. Sometimes I browse in the local bookstore and charity shops, catching the last ferry home, picking at an eye-wateringly hot, vinegar-soaked wrap of chips, or I treat myself to a freshly dressed crab from its shell at one of the pier shacks. So although trips to the mainland for anything other than supplies are not frequent, with rough weather it somehow makes life feel tougher knowing that you cannot get away, even if, some days, just for a few hours, you might like to.

It is a big moment when one afternoon the mainland haulage lorry makes it across to the island with a long-awaited delivery. 'Please be careful,' I blurt out, as old ropes are used to hoist it on to the dirt yard. I try to help as it is unloaded with difficulty and manhandled into the small kitchen and sitting room. I have bought the piano for a few pounds from an advert at the back of the *Oban Times*. When I run my hands over its keys I am astonished. It is undamaged, and has a beautiful action and tone.

It takes time to customise your mental checklist to every eventuality. Inevitably, there are times we are caught out. There is no petrol or diesel pump on the island, and our low usage does not warrant installing an agricultural bunded tank. It is raining the day the Vespa's petrol tank suddenly runs out, and too windy to cycle, so I wrap up in waterproofs and get soaked walking to where I need to be. The next day I take a jerry can in a black plastic bin liner across to the mainland but I have not filled out the necessary forms, or notified the crew, and on the return trip the full can is discovered and confiscated. In the end we piggyback on to a shared use of a boat and, on a calm day, we crouch on the wet boards and make our own fuel run, the motor chugging as the salt wash sprays across the wake and the cormorant huddle together on the seaweed-strewn, craggy skerries.

Those early months on the island, time spins on a different arc. I sense how the landscape watches our own small lives struggling to fathom its rhythms. We start moving to a different pace, more closely attuned to the waxing and waning of the seasons, the birthing of calves and lambs, cutting of silage, fishing of mackerel and gathering in of the hay. Mechanisation has changed lives here, but not so greatly as on the mainland. Clearing the old stone barn, I find scores of cracked lanterns and tapering wicks. I learn that gas lighting replaced Tilley lamps and paraffin lints only in the late 1950s. Electricity did not light up the island until the mid-1970s. The carts pulled by great cob and Shire horses were replaced by tractors and, much later, by heavy haulage fuelled by red diesel that began to leave run-off slicks over dark puddles and potholes in which rainwater had once pooled fresh and clear. But the skies remain still and dark. Times have not changed that much.

One morning, the sky darkens and the air subsides into a hushed silence. Lying in bed, I can feel the ridging on the roof shivering. I draw the blankets closer as the panes rattle and bitter draughts shudder through invisible gaps. Downstairs, the cold grate moans and hums. I light dried kindling and kneel in close, gently coaxing each guttering flame to ignite. When I switch on the radio, the forecast is for 150mph winds. All day I listen to the news and watch the barometer. The island is buzzing with the shipping forecast, which informs us in a flat monotone that strong winds will keep rising. Rab is on the mainland today. When he rings I learn that he is stuck there for the night, with winds and waves now battering our shores.

'Tie everything down,' he tells me, with an edge in his voice. 'And for God's sake, make sure the barn roof is tied on tight and secured.' I grip the phone and nod, my heart beating fast in my chest.

As I step outside, the wind is whirling with a low, gleeful sound, the branches thrashing about. When I look up I see that all the trees are bare. Where does a bird go when its home is destroyed? I wonder. And how do feathers stay dry or withstand this wind? I hurry off in search of ropes but find nothing that is not too short, or too thin. In the end I uncoil an enormous length of agricultural hosepipe and, climbing on to a ladder, I attempt to manhandle it over the roof of the barn. It is unwieldy and difficult to manoeuvre singlehandedly. At last, I manage to tip it over the ridging and feed it down the leeward side.

I scour the yard frantically, searching for a suitable heavy object to tie it to and weigh it down. This presents its own challenge: the heavier the weight, the harder it is to lift. In the end I drag the Vespa scooter, Rab's prized possession, from its shelter. I do not have the key and it is cumbersome to move. I am sweating with the effort, but fear and adrenaline combine to give me a strength I never realised I owned. I manage to wrestle it into position but I cannot hold its weight steady as I try to lower it down. I wince as it tips over with a crash on to the ground. There is no time to wonder if it is damaged. Battling with the wind, I struggle to secure another length of hose across the rear gable, heaving masonry blocks to secure it on one side and tying the other end to an old, rusting tiller that would once have been harnessed to a plough team. I pray that all this will hold.

At midnight, the cottage starts humming with a menacing, low-voltage buzz. It is hard to place that sound. I cannot take my eyes off the flickering lights as they dim to a stale, sullen brown. I have no idea if the power is protected or if a surge could blow the fuse box off the wall. I realise I do not know how to put out an electrical fire, and that I should know this. It is disempowering staring at something you don't understand. And frightening waiting to face the worst alone. Outside the trees are roaring, the storm is wailing and the windows are being buffeted with an incredible force. I feel a skin-prickling sensation an instant before the blinding flash comes, and then a deadening thud. The power cracks out. The darkness left in its wake is effervescent, alive and impenetrable. My eyes still branded by that searingly bright flash, I cannot see my hand in front of my face. But I can feel my heart beating in my chest. My breath in my throat. When my elderly cat cries and jumps up on to the bed, I hold her. It is comforting to feel her soft warmth.

A few hours later, I am suddenly alert. The wind is still screaming; the cat is nowhere to be seen. I listen, my ears straining, fingers reaching blindly ahead of me as I move to the window. My breath quickens with a glistening fear. A shimmering white light is flooding the yard. A mains power line is down and the live cable is coiling, firing sparks, like a furious electric eel. Its glittering beauty is mesmerising. And then there is a crash and a slow shrieking of shearing wood. The cherry tree is coming down.

Dawn comes slowly. For hours I sit on the wooden stair, shivering under thick blankets, my arms wrapped about me and my eyes fixed on that blinding darkness thrashing itself with its own whipping coil. It is a relief to see the skies lightening, wan and streaked pale. The power mast is split in half, but the white sparks, still strung high on the wind, are wrung out by daylight. I blow out my candle and go to the window to meet the dawn. I am glad my worst fears have not been realised, and the live electricity has not burned its way up the cable to reach the house. Later, it comes to me that, as I sat through those dim, glittering hours keeping watch on it in the dark, I was experiencing something significant. Fear is like that. It is incandescent.

It reminds me how sometimes facing the thing you fear the most can be empowering and incredibly beautiful.

When I go to open the door, the fallen tree is obstructing it, so I climb out of the window. Branches, leaves and debris are everywhere. I gaze around the croft. The exquisite quiet is shattering. As the cows walk up for their morning bucket of feed, I go to meet them. And, strange though it may sound, I am glad of their company. I wonder if, after such a night, they are glad of mine. I feel a new respect for the creative and destructive forces of this landscape and that, in getting through the night alone, I have passed some test or initiation. I pull the blanket closer. It is a relief to watch the sun as it starts to rise.

5

Graft

WE NEED WORK. We are draining our savings. There is an old saying in the islands that there is no contrivance against necessity. Regardless of our dreams of living simply, it is not possible to live solely off the land while we are still setting up and trying to finish the house. It worries me. I can feel hands reaching into pockets, drawing out bills faster than I can accommodate them. Piles of receipts stuffed into an envelope each week are building at an alarming rate. Existing close to nature is not for the faint-hearted: the reality is that sustainability comes at an eye-watering cost. Setting up from scratch is an expensive business, with precious little return on our outlays. It makes scant difference whether we labour ourselves or pay for the help that is required. Time has its own value and waiting is not always efficient when a job needs undertaking, especially when its purpose has a knock-on effect. You have to cover each element, seeing each task through from start to finish, or it is left half completed or botched. There are days when the croft looks at us reproachfully.

Nature is forgiving but our own expectations are uncompromising. Each day consists of its own weights and balances. When you start reckoning the cost of living, you wonder where it all goes, and why it takes so much just to keep breathing. Some days it feels as if even the sky needs to be paid for. It is an irony that, day after day, I struggle to make sense of. The land throws up its gifts but it costs the earth to sustain.

At the outset of each year we plan for every outcome, making forecasts and imaginative projections for every likely scenario we can envisage. We calculate our outgoings cautiously, writing down and crossing out each item. We budget meticulously for every penny and pound. But as the year runs on, we grow too blasé. We take risks. We make mistakes, waiting too long to acquire equipment that would make our lives easier, or splashing out on other kit that we could do without. It is a strange barter. You give yourself freely, but nothing else comes for nothing.

I want to measure that exchange by some different gauge; to value farm machinery, or equipment such as gates, hurdles or cattle crushes, not by its retail price but by the minutes and hours of my own life. When you think like that, it makes you re-evaluate value. I am finding it helpful to slow time down into minutes. It makes sense of all the hours, days and years used to pay for our material possessions. I am calculating worth in terms of a truer currency. It is not just years of work we are spending. It is years of life.

Looking at value this way brings a spiritual dimension to commercial dealings. Some days I wish we had thought of it earlier. Often, I think back to those first eight carefree weeks after we first landed on the island. The sky and sunshine were enough. Rab counters, 'That was before we started living.' But for me, we were living much more genuinely then. Money can be deceptive like that. You think it will always be there, only one day you look up and it is gone for ever. You think that running river will always carry you with it – until the day it runs dry.

We are not yet at the brink, but I have a feeling it is not too far off. That nagging worry is always there, like a tender place you keep pressing gently, sounding it out with your fingers in the hope that you will find the soreness easing. But it does not go away. The few short visits from friends falter. We live less comfortably than others are used to. I am elated when my brother arrives briefly from Hong Kong with his young family. But, even though he says, 'That was the best holiday!', they struggle with the rough conditions and do not visit again.

Rab is frustrated because we don't have all the kit that other farms have. He is entitled to feel weary; it is hard work digging for days, or working by hand at what might only take a few hours to achieve with the right equipment or heavy machinery. We trade help for use of haulage when it is needed, but it is one aspect of self-sufficiency for which we are ill-prepared.

'It's OK. I'm sure we'll get there, when we're a bit more set up.' But it is hard to pay for tractors, diggers, loaders and trailers and to convert the barn into a workshop when neither of us is earning. Rab is renovating the cottage, a job that has to be done. He is reluctant to take on other employment: he wants to live off the croft. 'I didn't come here to work,' he jokes, 'I came here to retire.' I smile, but sometimes I hear it too often. One of us has to secure a payslip. I, too, would prefer to be on the croft all the time, so I have mixed feelings when my application for the post of a childcare support assistant at the island's primary school is accepted.

My job is to look after the nursery. There are only eight children in total enrolled, and at present that age group consists of a single three-year-old. It is only a few mornings a week. Every day the child and I put on our waterproofs, gloves, scarfs and hats, regardless of the weather, and arm ourselves with bumblebee-black-and-yellow walkie-talkies on a string. We roam freely, like swifts learning to fly on the wing. I enjoy my mornings but the job falls short in other ways. Whatever its rewards, sometimes I feel empty. It can be hard to see the children's faces light up as their parents come to collect them at the end of the day. I am not blind to the unspoken understanding that the legitimacy of my being here in this role comes with the promise that one day soon, I too will help sustain the school's small register with children of my own.

There are the politics, too, that tend to go with any job. Some people are resentful that their choice of candidate, or a family member, was not given the position. Others want to sharpen their own dogma, political opinions and ideology. I learn to turn away quietly. Discussion all too quickly flares into accusations or argument if your accent is not local and, worse, from down south. It is tiring always to be watching your back. Yet as soon as you relax, you unwittingly make yourself a target. Sometimes it feels like a game. But we need the income, and I love the children, so I smile, and persevere.

It is perhaps harder than it might be for others. I know I am different. Yes, I am English, but it is not just that. I never thought of my skin colour when I first arrived. My skin is sensitive so I burn in the sun, even if I tan. My hair is naturally tousled with dark, red, auburn and sun-bronzed strands. My mother is Anglo-Irish, and her family's fabric is densely woven of Irish Celtic and Scottish threads. But my father, from the second of two generations born in South Africa, is of Asian descent. I always wondered how we have blue eyes and light skin on both sides of our family. As I delve deeper into my heritage, I find a suggestion of the clear, desert eyes of Kashmir or India's north and western plains.

Difference is scrutinised with circumspection on the island. A foreigner, approached outwardly with idle curiosity, is often mocked or pitied behind closed doors. A cold apathy or boredom meets my attempts to integrate. I am the stray dog.

While colour is not something that is spoken about publicly, I start to dread break times at the school, which is always the time when these loaded topics are casually broached. It only takes a word or two to alert me that someone has something to say. So I wait. One question is aired shortly after my parents have visited for a few days. It is never easy when they come, but I am always sad when they leave.

'Weren't you ashamed to walk in the town with your father, when he came to stay?' a woman confronts me in the kitchen.

'Why?'

'Because he is a darkie. He is a coloured man.'

I know there is more coming. So I say nothing.

'You don't see many folk like him, just walking about like that.'

I have to hand it to her. It is true. You don't. Only somehow it is shocking to hear it. It casts a shadow between us. And, looking at her face, I know that this is a struggle for us both. And I wish I could make it easier. But I do not know what else I can say to bridge that chasm in our tolerance and understanding. It makes reaching an acceptance of each other harder to attain.

Sometimes I question if it is worth it. The thin wage slip barely covers our bills. We need a way to supplement this meagre income. Rab is better equipped for work, yet he is fully committed to renovating the house. I sit down with a fresh piece of paper to draw up a list of my practical skills. I write down 'child support assistant'. It feels a grandiose claim for someone in charge of one toddler in a school of eight pupils. Whichever way I look at it, I am that list's basic flaw. I have no practical skills.

I screw up the sheet of paper, sigh and start again. 'Can you help me?' I ask Rab. But he buries his head in his hands. 'I've got enough to cope with as it is.' I look at him and wonder.

Eventually, I settle on writing a small ad on the back of an envelope. It is simple, discreet and to the point. 'Gardening. Hoeing, weeding, planting: £8/hour.' I am careful to keep it simple. I have no formal experience, just a love of the outdoors, two strong hands and a willingness to work hard. I walk a mile to pin it on to the noticeboard of the island post office and store.

A few days pass. When the phone rings, I hear a strong, clear voice. It is a woman. Although she has an educated English accent, having lived overseas for many years, she is from strong Scottish ancestry. Yet it is not this, not her voice or her family roots, but the warmth in her voice that ignites a glow of recognition inside me. It feels like a ray of sunshine and brings a smile to my face. Some voices do that: they imprint themselves on your memory by how they make you feel. I will always remember that voice because of the way she says her name. It rings like a bright, clear bell. Cristall.

'Well, let's see what you're made of,' she says. 'If we get on, we can talk about a few regular weekly hours. That's really all that matters. Wouldn't you agree?'

My heart is laughing as I put down the phone. I say her name again: Cristall. It feels like a promise.

Beyond the crossroads, where the north of the island shifts into its south, the hills steepen. The single-track road narrows until it is a thin, winding ribbon. My bicycle flies down the hills. On its inclines, I stand panting on the pedals. Highland cattle and birds are my only company. Occasionally I pass a farm where hens wander across the hills, and at one lies a dairy cow, chewing her cud contentedly in the middle of the road. When I run out of breath, I dismount and push the bike up the steeper ascents. Not for the first time, I have underestimated the ruggedness of this countryside. It is wilder, more windswept and more remote than the softer, undulating agricultural heartland of the north.

At last, I stand gasping at a summit. It takes me a moment to get my bearings. The view is so exquisite it hurts my eyes, but then I see a white house sitting quietly, surrounded by trees. Later I call it by its Gaelic name, Brea an Aluinn, meaning the Beautiful of the Beautiful. I could not know then how dearly I would come to love it. Only that I loved it at first sight.

'Don't let's come in,' a voice greets me as I knock at the door. 'It's such a day waiting to meet us outside.' I gaze at the woman as she clasps my hands. Her skin feels cool and worn rough, only thin, like fine paper. She has an open face that complements the clarity of her voice. I seek her eyes. You do this, when a stranger takes you by the hand. It is an unexpected, startling familiarity.

She contemplates me inquisitively, like a bright, beady bird. I can feel something in her eyes, reaching out to understand. It makes me feel as if the world is once again a safe and a beautiful place, and wish that every meeting could be like this, open and welcoming. As she briskly takes hold of my arm for balance while she puts her old wellingtons on, I look at her shyly and examine more closely. A tight cluster of curls is jammed under a hat, so it is hard to guess her age. But beneath the strong fingers clutching my arm I sense an unexpected fragility. They are gnarled like branches and weathered, reddened by the sun and the rain, as if they have always lived outside. 'Ugly old roots,' she quips, catching my gaze. 'But they're all I have, so they'll have to do. Here,' she adds, reaching for an elderly trug containing some gardening tools. 'Take the secateurs, the wires and the gloves, and come and see the garden. That's why you're here, after all.'

Our hands thread soft wires through the thick foliage, tying sweet peas and runner beans to upright willow canes. When our fingers brush as I wrap the ties around each shoot, I learn not to keep apologising. Somehow such intimacy feels natural when working outside. 'Thank you,' Cristall says. 'These wretched hands struggle with those fiddly fine knots.' We begin to share the work like that – me tying, and her holding – and I am glad because it clearly helps her aching, swollen joints.

Initially our arrangement is measured by the exchange of two hours of simple chores for a cup of tea and a freshly cut lettuce stuffed into a frayed string bag to take home. And then she says, 'You know, I think you and I will get along just fine.' I begin to go more frequently, and on each visit I end up staying a few minutes longer, until the minutes stretch into hours.

Slowly I learn to work more closely with the plants, rather than trying to force them into angles they do not want, and to pair leafy shoots together in a mutually beneficial alliance, to give the maximum possible strength and support against the winds. We look to the skies to predict the weather. It fills most of our conversations in unexpected and subtle ways.

'Everything needs something to hold on to,' Cristall tells me. 'Sometimes even nature needs help to keep it safe from itself.' It is tough finding shelter when a cold wind blows. We all feel the brunt of those winds in this often harsh environment. We talk, as our hands weave in and out through cold-freshening weeks and months. I love to listen to her stories. Each day I am awed by her resilience and stamina. She is out before 7am every morning, working all day in the garden, coming in only to eat, or at nightfall. She takes her energy from the seasons. She is, I learn, of strong Scottish ancestry and her roots lie deep in this land. She has lived this way on the island, with her husband Anthony, for over twenty years.

'We all need to know where we belong. Everyone needs to know they are cared for,' she explains as I learn to companion-plant for next year's growth. 'There is no point in facing those together that would rather look the other way. Plants are so much wiser than people. You will find your own people once they start looking for you.'

I think I know what she means. Everyone has to find a way to live in their own small community. Some days, as we talk, we walk out and look at the trees. It is calm and peaceful surrounded by that rustling, dense foliage. The fields around the house are planted with young oak and birch trees. I notice where beech saplings and fir have seeded in an adjacent field. One day, Cristall explains how bonds are forged in this green, leafy community. 'Even trees have friendships,' she tells me, 'some closer than others. They are no different from you and me. Some don't get along, others even have enemies. Sometimes you just have to learn to coexist. Trust me, it can be difficult for everyone. See how this tiny birch is still being nourished? It has a friend over there.' A single shoot bravely grows from a stump of close-chopped wood. 'It often happens when birch and firs live together. Yet over there,' Cristall nods sagely, pointing at a sickly oak surrounded by beech trees. 'Those, I'm afraid, do not, and will not ever get on.' And she gives a sigh. 'And there is no point trying to persuade them otherwise.'

I admire Anthony and Cristall. Their own roots are closely entwined. Their bonds run so deep, they sustain each other with a self-sufficiency so complete, the ground around them feels nourished, fertile and rich. It makes me think how like those great trees they are. Their love creates life around itself, sustenance for others. I wonder what happens, in such close relationships, if roots break, fall away or start to fracture. And how those roots are able to salvage or repair that straining or broken bond. Sometimes Anthony seems more tired than he might. I try to help as much as I am able. Working outside in the natural world teaches you that patience, strength and love are all relative terms. You place your trust in the sky over your head and the sap growing all around you. As I handle seeds, plants and saplings, I stop looking elsewhere for answers. Sometimes I am sure Cristall sees the things I don't say. I trust in that, too.

One day we are picking broad beans. The air is chilly and the wind is keen. My eyes are glistening wet. I do not wipe them. In my hand lies a smooth green pod. I take off my gloves and gently tear it open along its string thread. It is dark and quiet inside the womb of this fruit. Its small naked globes stare blindly up at me. Their skins are calm, pale, translucent. Each nestles its imprint into the soft, fibrous interior of the pod. It matters that I can feel such small lives breathing. My hope of having my own feels increasingly like an empty promise. Time rolls barren on. Infertility is a silent weight. It smothers early hopes in an all-enveloping, crippling darkness. Sometimes it is hard to know if my childlessness is early miscarriage or simply an inability to hold any precious life inside me. It feels as if your own body is gaslighting you so that you do not know what to believe or trust. Every month the darkness extinguishes the early flickers of hope. By contrast, in this tiny shell is a whole miraculous world. I flinch as my fingertip gently breaks a minute embryonic cord. We work on in silence, but I feel Cristall's eyes watching me. There is no hiding from that all-seeing gaze.

The next day I sit down and write a letter to Rab. I tell him all the ways that I love him. Writing is relaxing – it distils all that is held inside. It is only as you relax that you realise how tense you are; only when you smile that you know how sad you are. I give him that letter. There is a small drawer full of others he has not touched. But this one I give him. And I hope he will open and read it.

It is a relief to have somewhere to go. My connection with Cristall and Anthony is not just one of friendship. Trust creates its own safe haven. Sometimes it is enough that someone else is listening. Sometimes it matters to know that you are seen and heard, and that your voice is wanted and cherished. These days, these things are important to me. There are days when I feel invisible at home. I have lost my voice, and with it all the bright sounds have gone underwater. It is hard to feel that only those thick walls are listening. With Cristall and Anthony it is different. When I am with them, I can finally breathe deeply, fill my lungs with air. They are more than just friends to me, they are like family; the one you choose for yourself.

In the months that follow, I visit more frequently, and she comes to see me at the croft. Gradually, gardening becomes secondary as a deep friendship grows. We sit for hours watching the swallows. I lose myself in their effortless rising and falling motion. When I look at Cristall's eyes, I smile. 'You have eyes like a swallow's back,' I tell her. And when she laughs and says, 'Blue as the sky,' I begin to think of her when I look upward. Anthony's eyes, too, are blue, but they shine pale as moonlight. They twinkle like glittering powder snow. In his eyes I see bare branches, breath clouding with ice, dappled shadows. Laughter is a precious gift we often share. We laugh because we do not talk about what we do not talk about. We do not speak of the lack of laughter in my own marriage. And I am grateful for that.

'Will you play for me?' Cristall asks one day on a visit to the cottage when she senses I am troubled. And so I sit down at the piano and run my fingers over the keys. Music is always a source of comfort and inspiration. Ever since I was a child, I have turned to music to help me to make sense of all that is hard to articulate or seems incomprehensible or overwhelming. As I play a Bach prelude, a cool breeze blows through the open back door and windows. I smile as Cristall sways, waving her hand at our sheep all clustered together on the hill overlooking the garden, watching us.

'Look! They are listening!' she exclaims, delighted by the idea that those clear, beautiful notes could summon sheep. At the sound of

Cristall's laugh, I feel suddenly transported, light. Music connects me to a bigger world, even when the space I inhabit feels lonely or small. After that, we often sing together on walks, or take my old portable vintage gramophone, bought years ago from Portobello Market in London, out from the cottage and on to the hills. It sounds strange, but hearing music outside in the wilds makes you feel that even the mountains are listening.

As autumn advances we stack logs. When they are dried, we bring them inside. Each kind of wood has its own scent, and its flame burns differently. I love to watch the fire wrap our lives closely together. Cards are shuffled, chess pieces moved, poetry read, confidences and laughter shared. Our lives gently take root, our fibres nourished by small, mundane, repetitive tasks enfolded by our voices. It is a bond that makes my heart beat true. In those moments my heart floods with something as vital as oxygen. Each day I look forward to these times we share together. It is hard to imagine life on the island any other way.

By the arrival of autumn Rab and I have sold the cows. I am sad to see them go, but the prospect of winter feeding costs when we are not making our own hay are exorbitant. Although twenty-two acres sounds like a lot of land, with our flock count increasing, our livestock is running at full capacity. While the cows know us and are generally peaceable, once they calve they can become aggressive and unpredictable. Rab is lucky to have avoided serious injury when a protective mother charged him, pinning him to the ground, as he was tagging her calf. It feels like a warning of sorts. The sheep are gentle and easy to work by comparison, and more resourceful.

One day I drive up to Cristall's house and return to the croft with her to pick the season's last windswept flowers. When it starts raining, we bring the wet, broken stems into the cottage to fill vases and bottles, and to have tea. Already there is an atmosphere. The rugby is on the radio. Rab insists he is allowed to listen to it in silence. I try to talk quietly, but when Cristall laughs at something, I am embarrassed that Rab makes a cutting remark. I know what is coming. I can feel that dark cloud approaching. I get up quickly. I can hear that my voice is too bright as I say, 'Let's take our things with us. I have something to show you outside.' I know how stupid that sounds, and that there is no hiding from it, because it is still raining.

As we leave, he kicks the door hard behind us. I can hear him shouting. My hands are trembling. I am upset and embarrassed – it is hard to be exposed like this. But more than that, I am so weary, the rain is tipping down and I cannot see for tears. 'Let's wait a moment in here.' In the barn I hunt about in the straw and pick up a fresh, warm egg for Cristall from where a hen is nesting. As I drive her home, I feel her bright eyes watching me closely. 'I am so glad we have each other,' she says gently. And then she reaches out and squeezes my hand. 'Island life is tough at the best of times. But trouble at home makes it even harder. You know you can come here any time.' One day, I hope I can keep her heart as safe as she does mine. I look back at her steadily, without blinking. I know she knows, without any words shared between us, that I understand she has troubles of her own.

Kinship is invisible. I am struck how it can be conveyed in a fleeting glance. I wonder, too, how, with so little movement, laughter and sorrow etch themselves so deeply into our faces. All those tiny fine lines are the Braille of our lives. All that we experience, intensely, but don't speak of aloud. Sometimes we can read what is left unsaid in each other's eyes or faces. I know to hide my cares from others. Some things that matter are safer held inside your own walls. Over time, I learn to read Cristall's face as well as she reads mine. I start to see a worry that sharpens her beautiful blue eyes to a freezing sapphire.

I notice how Anthony's cheeks are chiselled like bare branches, how his own eyes gleam pale as a winter sky.

I promise her, 'You know I am here. You can talk to me if ever you need to.' Only some things are so hard to talk about. I know that. She knows that. Driving that beautiful, winding road together feels like a promise and a hope. I do not know where it is heading. But I can't help but feel I have travelled it before.

6

Winter

WINTER ARRIVES SHARPLY, like a breath of ice. Its bitter northeasterly wind ravages the exposed cliffs and headland. Wet, blackened stumps of heather are barely distinguishable from the glistening grey rocks. The livestock rounds become a daily sliding battle after the grasses and rushes die back. Forty hungry mouths wait desperately by empty troughs, foraging lean pickings. Each ewe weighs sixty kilos. Each step is a hard, staggering push against the tightly pressing flock. As the mountains darken to sullen crimson, the bright cottage lights beckon. I turn swiftly, scattering hay bales with raw fingers, my snow-wet cheeks smarting from that cruel, stinging wind.

Ice barricades the island for days as fierce blizzards shatter the skies. White-capped waves batter the windswept rocks. The low horizon gleams sulphurous, but it is a momentary lull. Shortly afterwards, the ferries flick their amber warnings to red: storm-force alert. The boats are winched in tight on metal chains, hauled close against fenders and protected by high harbour walls. The island is lost from low to high water, cut off by raging winds over tide. The winter seas are dragging broken shingle and snowmelt off the fore-shores. The great ruckling stones lift in a churning suction of hissing foam, bladderwrack and plastic-littered surf. As the grey waves thicken, I watch mesmerised by the dense rising weight and force that curls not from their crests, but drives irresistibly forwards from each rippling truncated core. It is a muscularity that rips my breath away.

It is shocking to witness the destructive power of the waves and weather. Offshore, a lighthouse funnels a beam across the dark water, spindrift flecking the howling darkness with a bright salt spray. Inside every household, lives move quietly as the mercury plummets in the barometer glass. The shipping forecast stutters its clipped updates whilst the open seas rock, oblivious to its news. Carefully, I tune the radio across crackling surges of interference. I learn how, out in the channel, an adolescent seal is struggling against the current and high water. It has been washed offshore from its safe anchorage between the smaller rocky islets. Exhausted, it strives to beat against the tide. As volunteers arrive to help, snow is still falling. The seal is nowhere to be seen. And still the waves pound on.

At the slip, engines are left running, exhausts juddering, as a collection of vehicles assembles on the shingle-strewn tarmac. Wipers glide, slicking slow as blank faces peer silently out to sea. It is one of the season's strange contradictions. Winter is a time of solitude and isolation yet also one of gathering together, a winding-in of the skein of the year. Each day we watch the falling snow whirling and the sea wrack building, our eyes fixed stoically on the horizon. Christmas is only days away, and no one can move.

I rest my forehead against the window, eyes narrowed at the dark, whirling treetops. As my breath freezes against the glass, the bright lights across the water suddenly feel a world away. I hold on to every last chink of light. I worry that Christmas with our families will be cancelled again this year. Our excitement builds as the holiday draws closer, yet inevitably the weather takes a turn for the worse. I wish we could leave early to reduce the risk of disappointment, but the school term finishes so close to Christmas that it is often too late to seize any brief lull in the conditions. I feel guilt at the thought of once again losing this time with my family. We so rarely get together and we all live so far away from each other. The hope of seeing old friends, too, is as precious as a wrapped gift under a tree. Rab's frustration is palpable.

I am already seizing my coat as the ferryman's voice crackles over the phone, 'If you don't move now, you might not get over till after New Year.'

Sheep on the road cluster together for warmth. The slippery surface glints treacherous as the Land Rover heads up the track, screaming in second gear in order to keep a tight grip. As we approach the slip, it is heartbreaking to see the ferry pulling away across the water. 'Stop!' I shout, but already the boat is turning towards the spit. Rab keeps driving furiously, flashing his headlights and hammering the horn. As the boat ploughs about, rocking from side to side, I cannot believe my eyes: it is turning back. 'To hell with this!' Rab yells. Slamming the wheel into lock, he runs us on to the high shingle at the top of the beach. 'I'm not missing this for anyone!' We hit the ground running, our arms laden with bags.

'Think you must be two bright chancers, finding that gap,' the skipper nods as the tiny boat lurches bravely across the choppy water. It is a relief when the ropes are tied up on the other side and Rab's face lifts. He slaps the ferryman on the back. I sense that we have pulled out of a tight corner. And suddenly I feel lightheaded and ready to dance.

Six hours later we are driving back up the island. Snow clouds have thickened over the mountains. There is fresh falling snow and a whiteout in Glasgow. The trains are cancelled. The planes are grounded. As the traffic begins to back up, the gritters have started closing the roads. We stock up on provisions in Oban and head for home. I do not trust myself to speak. After such a window of opportunity, these hasty supplies feel lacklustre and meaningless. For hours, Rab has been smoking furiously in silence. As he switches on the ignition, his face turns pale with fury. He slams his fist hard against the dashboard. 'For fuck's sake. Well, that's another year on this fucking island. And that's Christmas off.'

And then I know to hold tight to my seat, because he rams his foot hard on the accelerator, crunching gears as the exhaust burns dark fumes. I grip on to the dashboard and feel my body start to brace itself. 'Please, Rab, enough,' I protest, through clenched teeth. 'Calm down. No one's going to have Christmas if we crash.' Only he doesn't. After a minute, I compress my lips and stay silent. I hate it when he shouts or gets so angry. But it scares me more than anything when we drive this fast. My body remembers a shattering windscreen, splintering metal and screams. I shut my eyes and try not to think of how it feels to crash. But it is something forever stuck inside me. There is no point in talking to Rab when that dark cloud finds him. When I get out, I am shaking. That day, I lose him for more hours than I can count. And the dark cloud takes longer than usual to evaporate.

I long for Christmas Eve to be crisp and starlit, and when it comes, it is. The skies are clear and alive at midnight as our footsteps scrunch through the snow. We are talking and laughing again as we walk up the little track to the ancient stone church. The door creaks on its hinges when I lean my shoulder into it. Inside everyone is huddled close in coats and scarves, knees pressed tight together, backs hard against the wooden pews. There is a simplicity to the gathering that is deeply moving. I seek out familiar faces as jam jars are handed out and candles lit, and there is a peal of laughter as someone's coat nearly catches fire. Faces glow soft in candlelight, rapt with a childlike excitement. My breath steams blue frosted wings. Sitting close, drawn together by our humanity and small company, it feels good to share others' warmth. I close my eyes and feel my heartbeat slow. And although my family is hundreds of miles away, I would not have missed this for the world. A few minutes before midnight, the huge bell is rung. Its voice sounds ancient, strange, hollow from inside the bell tower. And then we stand and sing carols. Our voices illuminate the dark as thick snowflakes start falling.

On Christmas Day there is a power cut, but eventually we call our friends and family. We cut up our plucked bird and cook it slowly on the open grate. Later, we split chestnut shells with the coal shovel. When I take Maude outside, our shadows are blue in the fresh powder snow. The silvering birch trees, lifting up their bare arms to winter, glow pale in the darkness. I wonder at their fortitude and resilience. They ask for nothing, scarcely drawing life from the cold air and hard, frozen soil.

On Boxing Day we go visiting. The skies are crystalline, a pale turquoise that makes you feel exhilarated, like the snow glittering on the trees. We walk the few miles of the island, carrying small gifts as thanks for small favours over the months. I know Rab feels as upbeat and energised as I do. We talk of our plans for the coming months. And I feel close to him, like we did when we first arrived. But as soon as we knock on the last door and step inside, I immediately sense an atmosphere. My breath quickens and my eyes become alert. 'Are you sure?' I ask Rab. He just frowns and says, 'We've been invited.' And I am torn, because instinctively I want to say, 'Let's go home.'

When it comes I am not surprised. A voice greets us: 'What the fuck are you doing here?' There is a hostility underlying the jovial tone. So even after the speaker is told to hold their tongue, and we are offered a glass by our host, I am tense and on edge and keep my eye on the door. I do not feel right. I will ask Rab to finish his drink quickly so that we can get away. But he gives me a steely look and pours another dram. When talk turns to land, and some grazing that is up for rent, it all kicks off. 'Think you can just walk in, like that, and snatch it away from under our nose?' This single ill-thought comment provokes an argument that flares up in front of us. I say to Rab, 'Come on, it's time to go.'

'Yes, you go home, why don't you? Just fuck off back south where you came from.'

We leave quickly, because I am weary. And weary of hearing those words.

Later I am still trying to make sense of it. All it took was a second for that tinder box to ignite. And for a minute I think back to those London streets we have left behind. I tell myself not to overreact. But I know that that is only half the story. We understand that it takes time for an outsider to feel safe in a mixed gathering, and for one group to feel comfortable to invite another to sit by its fire. Proximity is both a challenge and a bond. The arcane law of kinship draws us closer even as it keeps us apart.

I want to find the key to the secret passage that will bring us in from the cold. I long to slip that bright key into its lock. Every day I seek to fathom that impenetrable mechanism. But the harder I try, the more those subtle cogs keep shifting, as fast and fickle as the salt winds gusting in off the sea. Some days it wears you down, that sting-ing wind, playing you like a piece of flotsam. It hurts to feel perpet-ually buffeted by its force. I hope that one day it will change direction. That it will quieten, rather than always be exerting its bitter blast. Fuelled by alcohol, it is a different experience. Its strength is unstop-pable, immense, of a scale and dimension that is altogether frighten-ing.

After the winds die down, the quietness is shattering. On the loch shore, the fragile reeds and bulrushes sparkle with hoar frost. Their long, graceful necks dip to the crystalline sunshine, like pale, frozen swans. The water is petrified. It breathes in sharp cracking gasps beneath the ice. Deep below the choked, disused mill, fresh springs are bubbling. They keep on flowing, rushing their run-off in clear, singing pools down to the sea. Salt light thaws the ice. It draws my eyes to the low horizon, revealing the brilliant-white shell sands of the islets dotted with young and adolescent seals. They lie basking, dark-mottled and snow-brindled, fat pelts gleaming. Onyx eyes watch for sleeker shadows, diving smooth, fast as bullets, through the black waters. Whiskered mouths glean kelp from the rich subterranean matriarchal feeding grounds before the return. I love to listen to the seals singing, luxuriating in frozen warmth on the rocks as the sun lowers into the viscous, frozen tide. There is a strange beauty, and also a loneliness, in that sound.

As the ice cracks and creaks on the loch, shallow waters are frosted, marbled with whorls and pockets of air. If you stare through, you can see tiny worlds held frozen inside. Tentatively, I glide my feet over the glistening, slippery surface. I watch the ice fracture, imploding in white clouds, crushing itself to powder under its hard skin. The tem-peratures have dipped so low there is no chance of these shallows thawing. A hard permafrost has gripped the island and there is no talk of a reprieve for the foreseeable future. Once a week the fire engine fills up its water tanks from the loch and crawls to the cottages and farms. Domestic tanks are redundant; frozen outside pipes that would normally replenish direct from ground springs all unworkable. Our galvanised outdoor tank is filled, but we have to carry buckets to and from the sink. The pump is insulated with Kingspan, hot-water bottles and warm blankets. The pipes from the spring to the pump house across the bog are lagged, but sit shallow. We try different tools to thaw the ice – a hairdryer and, in sections, a blowtorch. But nothing will shift it. I put my head against the pipes and listen, straining to hear sounds of melting. But it is dead, silent. We are locked in a frozen world for another six weeks.

That year of the freeze, I could see how the quiet was starting to get to Rab. I saw it on his face. I felt it in his thinning body. In years to come, I saw it deepen until it became etched into his features and skin. December and the long cold months in London are a whirl of parties, events and late-night lock-ins. Sometimes I think of our old lives, sitting around a full table, surrounded by friends. Those years, those memories, are full of bright lights, glasses chinking, eyes illuminated by laughter, reaching across an intimate space and a shared outlook on life. When I look at Rab now, I sigh. I do not know how I can help him. I do not know how I can help us.

Celtic knots are frozen on the twisting fence barbs. The crisp, dry air burns away the stench of dead crows strung on gibbets. Desiccated feathers blow ragged along the sprawling boundary lines of the small crofts and farms. It is a bleak warning to wildlife, and a summons to spring. The piercing call of the buzzard echoes the thin cries of lambs already born on the frozen hills. Visitors turn in horror from those dark, dead flapping shapes, skewered cruelly on to metal barbs. Yet they are blind to bleeding eyes and pink tongues ravaged by talon and beak. Winter is brutal, but early spring is rapacious in its savagery.

There is an old saying in the islands that winter is the dead month. Walking across the fields, I remember that we are one head fewer on the croft. It is the time of year when male wether lambs are slaughtered. When I get to the twisted elder tree, I stop, take a deep breath then walk hesitantly towards the open barn. A dead two-year-old is hanging, skinned, suspended from a meat hook to cure in the salt wind. Its back and rear haunches are striped with pink and white darkening streaks. The bare muscle and fascia are already hardening, as their moisture is sucked dry by the freezing temperatures. Its abdominal cavity is hollow and empty, the glistening white coil of intestines having been scooped soft and steaming into a bucket.

It is a necessary procedure, one that takes out weaker animals and provides food for the coming year. There are no euphemisms for the stark realities of eating meat. There is no turning aside from the harsh verities of taking life. Death is death. Yet I always pray that it comes quietly and with dignity. After the stun bolt is drawn back and pressed close against the temple, it is fired at high velocity, instantly traumatising and deadening the brain. A razor-sharp knife is pressed into the aorta and a swift, clean incision is made. It is then that I would like to be present. For my own hands to hold that life gently, talking to it softly, for all the time it takes for the river of blood to stream away. But I cannot. It is a step too far.

'Killing's no place for a woman.' The farmer shakes his head firmly. 'Can't have fuss and hysterics when a beast's getting killed.'

I am frustrated because I believe I should be there. Brutalising though it may be, it is a matter of taking a final responsibility for the meat that is placed on the table and the life we have chosen to lead. But I am also quietly grateful.

'I will help butcher,' I tell Rab. It is strange to see that solid carcass, once a living, breathing body, being pared away for meat. It is a relentless, forensic process. I try to do the same with my emotions. Butchering a carcass from start to finish strips you back and leaves you exposed, compelling you to examine your own life, the interconnective tissue of your own relationship, dispassionately – in its entirety as well as its minutiae – and not to turn away your eyes.

7

The Unborn

IT IS A beautiful day. I am sitting next to Rab. Across the desk, a clear light is spilling through the window. The gynaecologist is encouraging us to visualise their tiny faces. I try to imagine the nails on their fingers as little hands reach out to mine. You do that when you are given permission. Hope is like that. It feels reckless, like taking a beautiful drug.

I trust my gynaecologist. It makes the four-and-a-half-hour journey to Glasgow worthwhile. She has been here before. She knows how arduous it is to travel down from the islands. I am a statistic. I know this. But I am grateful that she tries not to make me feel like one. 'These are real babies,' she tells me. 'Real, living, beating, breathing. You have to believe in them. Trust me. It works so much better this way.' So I do what she says. I put all those hopes, expressed and unexpressed, into an oak box. It is my birth box. Every part of me goes into creating beautiful thoughts and dreams. Each morning, I pick flowers, paint small sketches. I collect feathers and write poetry. I offer my hopes to the moon.

When you have had years of disappointments, you tell yourself you will never go through it again. But you do, and every time, you cling more tightly to those hopes.

Later, the gynaecologist's advice is reiterated by my consultant. 'It's important you see them, really feel them,' he tells me as we wait for fertilisation to take place in a Petri dish. His voice is earnest. 'Blastocyst cells are microscopic. But you have to trust that these are your own little ones.'

I try to imagine this. It is easier when I picture us walking together. I imagine their tiny faces looking up at me, and a great blue sky above us.

There is so much at stake. After years of failed treatments, I am only now receiving the specialist IVF procedure that can at last offer us fresh hope. We have lost nine years trying to conceive naturally, exploring other options and jumping through all the hoops that each medical stage has demanded to reach this point. It has been painful, invasive, uplifting and agonisingly destructive in that uniquely intimate way that only trying desperately to conceive a child can be. Every month you carefully build an increasingly fragile, medicalised structure of hopes, only to find it torn to shreds again a few weeks later. I am sickened by the debris of that silent war zone. Whilst Rab can walk away, I live amid its dust and rubble. I am weary of inhabiting my failing reproductive body. Sometimes I think of giving up but I am not yet ready to walk away. Sometimes you have to trust in your own future, so that when you reach it, you can say, 'I did everything possible. I tried.'

Stress takes its toll on both of us. Some days are better than others. In an ailing relationship you hold on to the bright times all the harder, so that the darker moments feel less dark. As our relationship slowly deteriorates, I have questioned whether I should keep going. But I long for a child. I hope that child will touch Rab, motivate him to commit to testing himself in ways he is reluctant to test himself now. Sometimes it feels as if he has a switch I just can't reach. I think, if only I can get to it, some inner light will come on. At other times, I reason, if, God forbid, it comes to it, I will raise this child alone. When you have got so far, investing so many years, including your childbearing years, it becomes harder, almost unimaginable, to let go. IVF binds you to its looping circuit and it becomes increasingly hard to step off its track. There are days when it doesn't feel right to continue, yet, for right or for wrong, it also feels too late to stop. I hope our relationship will improve, and with it our chances of success. Outside the treatment, I do my best to keep our lives simple.

Initially the treatment was scheduled for Edinburgh. With timing critical now on every front, I had rented basic accommodation so that I could more easily make the tight windows for scans, blood tests, hormone injections and monitoring. It seemed a small concession to make. Rents in the capital are expensive, so I found a tiny cottage in the Borders. 'You'll have to take Maude,' Rab told me. 'She won't cope with you away.' And I was glad at the thought of her company, because Rab would have to stay on the croft. 'You'll be fine,' he smiled. 'It's only a few months. We can talk on the phone. It will be too hard for me to visit. And who else will look after the croft?' I felt uneasy but there was no other way. I wondered how other couples cope when one has to stay behind.

I had packed my bags and readied myself, when, at the very last minute, the hospital rang. 'We're switching you to Glasgow.' I was confused and inexplicably tired at the thought of this unforeseeable change of plan. It felt more than I could cope with. It was too late to cancel the accommodation without losing the first month's rent and deposit. It meant more travelling and a dog-sitter to look after Maude. Suddenly it seemed a step too far. 'I feel overwhelmed,' I confessed to Rab. 'I don't think I should go.' He looked me in the eye. 'I think you should. If you don't, you will never forgive yourself.' I hugged him, with tears in my eyes. Sometimes all you need is that extra push to set you back on track. I told myself, 'Life can turn itself round in an instant. All it takes is a little luck.' Every bright spark can give you hope – and hope can change everything.

And then one day, everything does change. Finally, I am given a little-known blood test. It detects that I am lacking sufficient levels of an overlooked but vital hormone. Without this, it is near impossible to produce any mature eggs. It is the one hormone that cannot be replaced synthetically, but I can be better supported. 'You have a chance,' my consultant smiles. As each procedure is more rigorously monitored, I am given ever higher dosages of drugs to inject into my abdomen every day. It is painful, but when you are given fresh hope, that discomfort feels pleasurable.

After five arduous weeks, I have produced only two eggs. I listen quietly to the consultant. I know to stay positive and relaxed, but my heart is stretched as taut as a tripwire. You want to believe it is going to happen, but you have to be realistic. There is every chance it might fail. Two eggs mean I have only two chances of fertilisation. I try to keep my spirits up. I tell myself, 'One is better than nothing, and two is double that hope.'

Later, when the phone call comes, my eyes are shining. The fertilisation was successful.

'Oh my God!' Rab jumps up, elated. 'Twins!'

He clings to me, tears in his eyes.

And then we hold each other, unable to speak.

Our twins are only a cluster of cells. But every family starts this way. I know it is too early. But I need to mark the start of their life. 'What shall we call them?' I ask Rab.

His eyes light up. 'You name one,' he says, 'and I'll name the other.' We do not talk about what sex we think they might be. Yet, when it comes to their naming, I write down Maggie and he writes down Eve. There is no discussion, but there it is. Two girls' names. We hug and, for an instant, our fatigue is swept away. Because we are having twins. And these are their names. And suddenly our life is beautiful again. These are the names of our children. It matters that we name them. Even if we never get to see them born.

And then we put those scraps of paper into the oak box, with tiny flowers and shells from the fields and beaches. I add a blank card on which I have written down all my dreams. I have read it's important to write them down as if they are real and concrete. They are quite simple. I dream of my children. I dream of being a mother. I hold that box every day.

It is the day for those wishes to come true. It is an incredible feeling. When I wake up in an hour, two new lives will be breathing inside me. I imagine minuscule hearts beating and the soft tissue of lungs opening and closing, a fluttering of breath, like beautiful shells underwater.

'Are you ready?' the anaesthetist asks me. He smiles, squeezes my hand. I lie on the trolley bed, a thin white gown over me, wearing a wristband with my name on it and a hospital blanket. It is bright yellow, like a ray of sunshine. I watch him slowly load up the syringe. I nod. I am elated, barely breathing. Full of hope, wonder and fear.

'Don't worry,' he says. 'There's nothing to worry about. Just close your eyes and go to sleep. When you wake up, just think, it won't only be you lying there.'

'I know,' I say, and I am moved by his words. I look at his name tag. He is the senior anaesthetist. 'Thank you, Will.'

'Just a small scratch.' I wince as the sharp point of the needle pierces my skin. It takes a while for him to find the vein. It hurts, but not as much as daily self-injecting. My skin is covered in bruises. Blue, purple and brown marks mottle my belly, my arms, my buttocks and thighs. I clench my teeth and lift my jaw, and I stare hard into his eyes. He has kind, serious eyes.

'That's it,' he nods, as the vein stands up. 'Not long now, and then your baby will be safe inside.'

My eyes widen as my heart contracts. I feel something twist within me and try to pull my arm away. Suddenly I want my husband here beside me. He is in the hospital – I am so glad that he has finally taken two days away from the croft to be with me – but at this precise moment he is nowhere in sight.

'Not one,' I say urgently. 'I am having two.'

He looks away. And because he doesn't say anything, I panic.

'Not one,' I insist. 'I have two babies. Will, I am having twins.'

There is a long silence. My heart fills with fear. And then the thin curtain rustles, and the nurse breezes in.

'No,' she tells me. She pats me on the shoulder. 'Just one today.'

'But I have two babies. They are together in the Petri dish.'

I look at the nurse and back at Will. He fiddles awkwardly with a fresh syringe, and moves it closer towards my arm. And suddenly I am trying to get up off the bed. 'Where are my babies?' I demand.

'Lie down,' the nurse says, 'or you will rip this drip out of your arm.'

As I lie back down, Will tells me not to worry. I feel the cold solution flood my vein.

'But where is the other one?' I ask faintly.

He looks me straight in the eye. 'The other one died. I'm sorry. But look, you've got one. It's going to be OK.'

'Don't worry, hen.' The nurse leans over and pats me on the arm. 'Trust me, one is more than enough.' And suddenly their faces blur and I feel myself drifting away.

As I lose consciousness, I whisper, 'I am going to be a mother.' I try to go to sleep focused on manifesting and welcoming new life into my body. But those words stick in my throat. I am overcome by a great wave of grief. As the anaesthetic kicks in, I feel I am drowning. It is like diving into cold water: the world disappears, and all that should be warm inside is suddenly cold as ice. All I can think about is that I have already failed. I feel the loss of that little one so sharply.

I wake in the middle of the procedure. The pain is excruciating. It feels like being hooked on to a piercing barb. I only realise I am awake when I see the anaesthetist chatting to the surgeon. My mouth is open and I am crying out, calling as hard as I can, but no one can hear me. And then they notice as the low murmur becomes a high, strangled cry.

'Oh Jesus, she's awake!' I can hear their panic. The clatter and glint of bright metal instruments. There is a flurry of activity. Bodies move quickly. I am in that room but watching from somewhere more distant, above the operating table. Something inside me struggles to reach them. All I can hear is a constricted, high-pitched wailing. It is not my voice. It comes from some place deeper inside me. And then a rush of sleep overtakes me. It comes like a train and all goes dark again.

When I wake I am unable to walk. I cannot stay in the hospital overnight because there is no room. So they wheel me out to the car and lay me down on the back seat. My husband is pale. He does not look at me. It feels strange to see him here. Sometimes I feel like laughing, and other days I feel like crying. I wonder if it is like this for everyone. I feel as if I am having an immaculate conception. We are making IVF babies but we haven't been near each other in weeks.

It takes three things to make a baby. Sperm, ovum and a lot of luck. I have two out of the three. I think our luck died when I was told that fragile life had perished in the Petri dish, for a few weeks later, its twin – the embryo they put inside me – dies too.

Yet some part of you still carries on believing. Some days drift by more easily than others. It is so hard to let go.

Sometimes I wonder which of my children was lost first. I think it was Maggie. In the end it is of no consequence. Because after I knew Maggie was dead, I knew Eve, too, would be grieving, in that dark place beyond gravity. Sometimes I blame myself. I wonder if my crippling sadness that day stole the breath of my other unborn child. Whoever it was that was left was dead in a matter of weeks.

It does something to your head when a child dies inside you so early on. My body is tied to the earth and the seasons, even as it resists its natural cycle; my instinct harnessed to an imprinted map designed to pass on our genes. In the island community, my voice is one of a few concealed under a crippling weight of silence. It is hard to know how to break or heal the silence of buried motherhood.

With each failed attempt, the doctors advise just to keep going. So I persevere. I try to do everything right. I am a baby-making machine. I eat right, sleep well, go for walks with my dog. I visualise that I am a mother. I imagine a tiny glimmer of light like a falling star.

Eventually, I have my last chance. So when, after weeks of injecting myself with drugs, I have produced only one egg, the disappointment is crushing. That egg looks so lonely on the scan in the darkness of my womb. It feels as if my body has given up after losing the twins. It is impossible not to place all my hopes in one Petri dish, because I have no other option. No further treatment will be offered. This time I go through the procedure alone. Rab does not leave the island. Every night I ring him. 'Will you come and visit me?' I say.

But he just sighs and asks, 'And who will look after the croft?'

'It is a strong embryo,' the consultant smiles at me. It will have to be, I think. Creating a flicker of life is harder than I ever imagined. I wonder how this can be, when it should be so effortless, so natural.

Once the embryo has been put inside me I wrap my hands about my tummy. I go to sleep with a smile on my face. 'Stay with me,' I whisper to my baby. And this time I am convinced it has worked. I feel different. I am sure I am having a boy.

When there is no sign of my period, I take a home pregnancy test. It shows positive. I am elated. So it does not matter when the hospital is unable to confirm the pregnancy. 'You'll have to wait another week to ten days,' the receptionist tells me. 'The systems are down.' Only it takes longer.

I keep my secret to myself. I do not want to jinx it until I am certain. With every crushing disappointment you tell yourself it is not your fault, but you don't believe it, and the weight of expectation gets harder to bear. But each day that passes brings me another day closer. I cannot wait to tell Rab. I am so happy, even when I make a last trip alone to the hospital. I still have not had a period. My baby has been growing inside me ever since it was implanted six weeks ago. I sit and wait after they take my bloods. I am smiling when the nurse comes in with the results. At first she looks at me without recognising me. And then she smiles uncertainly. 'You shouldn't be here,' she says. 'Your test was negative.'

I stare at her, my smile draining away. 'Are you sure?' I say.

'You should have received a letter.' She frowns. 'I'm sorry it was a wasted trip for you to come all this way.'

And then she moves on to the next patient in the queue. My legs are shaking. There is no one with whom to share this news or hold my hand, so I put one hand in the other and sit like that on my own, squeezing my own hand.

When I get home, I have to face telling Rab. He is in the barn, and doesn't stop working.

'I don't know what to say,' he says. It is a relief that we don't have to speak about it. I put on a jumper and start making the rounds.

That day he gives me a sickly newborn lamb to look after. I love it. I nurture it. I spend every waking hour keeping it alive. Then one morning it is not breathing right. It dies in my arms. And that is when something breaks inside me. I cannot stop crying. I try to stop but the tears keep on flowing. It is exhausting but strangely comforting to hold the warm, dead body. I am still holding it when it turns cold and stiff. I keep it in a box whilst I say goodbye to it. After a week Rab incinerates it.

It takes me a long time to get over losing that lamb. It takes me even longer to talk of my own lost little ones. I cannot bring myself to throw away the box containing the names of our babies. I put it under the bed.

A few months later, I am in the shop. One of the old ladies from the island 'granny bus', a local service that offers free vehicle transport to the elderly, approaches me. 'What, no babies yet?' she says, tutting and shaking her head. And suddenly it seems everyone is listening and has an opinion to give.

A farmer jokes, as he brushes past me, 'Should put a notice up. Looks like you're needing a new bull.'

I am too broken to say anything. It hurts that I am unable to be a mother, to fulfil the basic task of creating life and giving birth. I want to ask, 'What if the problem is me?' But I don't. I know what happens to cows and sheep and bitches that are unable to have offspring. They are discarded as 'yeld', meaning barren. Even in the market they are worthless. No one wants a cast ewe.

I am disorientated. I don't know what to trust or believe or feel any more. When your body fails you and you stop trusting yourself and your instinct, it alters your bearings.

I try to keep myself busy. I go out walking. When I am tired of walking, I just lie down. I am so exhausted that sometimes it feels as if it is the only thing I can do. Lie down in the grass, on a hill, and feel gravity holding me even as my eyes fall into the sky. Sometimes I just close my eyes and sleep. Often when I wake, it is nearly dark. As I feel the evening dew on my face, it is as though some inner hurt is soothed. I do not sing or whisper their names any more. I just stand and watch the sun set. I write my own name in the wind. Then I walk slowly home. I start to wonder if I should carry on with my job. I am not coping. I am finding it increasingly difficult to look after the under-fives in the school. Sometimes I have to make excuses to leave the room.

It is hard working in a world made up of tightly knit families when I cannot turn to my own. My brother is overseas, my sister is estranged and my parents have not been to stay since a disastrous visit the previous year, during which my father anaesthetised his usual anxiety by getting drunk and abusive. It is horrible to find your own father stealing whisky from the house like a teenager and your parents screaming at each other in front of you. I am tired of having to lift him up off the floor. In the end I had to ask him to leave, and he looked me in the eye and said, 'I wish I had never come.'

I know, deep down, he didn't mean it. As upset as I was, I remain protective of him. I know it is his way of coping. He is as worried about my mother as the rest of us. They stayed in a one-bedroom rental cottage down the road, because ours was a tip amid fresh renovations. For all her pretence, it didn't escape me that she could not find the bathroom or the bedroom, or simple things like the fridge in the kitchen. Everyone has secrets and problems. Knowing I cannot share them for fear of adding to the chaos makes it harder. Our roles are disrupted, my parents behaving like children.

Sometimes it makes me question if I am crazy to long to be a parent myself. Yet it does nothing to lessen my desperation for children of my own. It hurts even to see friends who have young children, creating another distance that means their sporadic visits become even rarer.

I am a season out of kilter. My heart is still frozen from such a long winter. Infertility is like a great fault line running not just through my body, but through my life. It is strange to think that when I die there will be no part of me that continues. It used not to matter, but now it sometimes stops me in my tracks.

When I am feeling brighter, I know in my heart this is not true. When I die, I will be in all and everything. I will breathe a lungful of sun and a heartbeat of moon. And even though I am childless, my spirit will beat with the fullness of love. I will be out in the wild places, free on the winds. In the high clouds and the early dew. In some part of the soil, or salt, or the lift of a wave. I will be in a songbird's throat and on the spit of spray of a gull's wing. I may not be seen, but I hope that in my death, as in my life, I will be felt. That my life will help to nourish other lives. And that one day, in my own small way, I will be mother to all.

Most days I go to the shore. I watch the sea furling and unfurling as I stand with Maude, listening to the waves. In the half-light, the geese are calling. A graze of sound on the horizon, tearing a low glimmer of sky. Out there, in the further darkness, a stirring wind is up.

Whitecaps crest an incoming tide. Above, gulls are circling, thin cries skirling, white feathers fraying against the sharp edge of the northerly wind. Sounds blur, carry, lift or are lost. Every few minutes, a gust of spray hurls itself fierce against the sharp limestone rocks. My cheeks are wet with spray. I listen to its steady-building crescendo, a lull, and then its inevitable fall. A low rushing sound follows, like a slow, heavy release of brakes.

I whisper softly to the waves, 'If it's meant to be, one day a child will find me.'

I gaze at the horizon. Its fragile light has never looked quite so far away, so untouchable. But as I breathe, I feel those waves quietly gathering and spilling a deeper strength inside me.

8

Brakes

IT IS EARLY spring. Around the croft, the neighbouring fields are burning with acrid, dark fires. Ashen, dense plumes of smoke drift slowly upwards, curling like wraiths into the air, and catch the back of my throat. Fiercely, I blink back hot tears. It hurts me to look at these charred, shriven fields. It is the traditional culling of the season, a vital paring back of dead growth. Some farms set small areas aside where wildlife can find safety, but others just laugh at the desperate, shrill cries. 'Nothing but vermin. No good for new growth.' Once the grasses are lit, and the wind catches and lifts, nothing will stop the fierce flames. Afterwards, it is hard to imagine life returning from those charcoal-blackened stumps.

I am beyond fatigue, yet still I do not move. My heart feels leaden. Inside, I am consumed by a deep sadness and a slow, smouldering anger. Rab has been playing away. Every day I try to smother those close-licking flames but it is like trying to put out a fire with your bare hands. Yet I cannot leave it alone. Betrayal hurts like a burn. It ravages my heart and keeps my skin alive at night. I long for the cool, billowing grasses that once ran over these hills.

My lips are too cold to whistle, so I start calling for Maude. I call for her again and again. When she does not come, the pain and fear well up. I am so tired. I am scared not just for her, amidst those burning fields. I am scared for me, too. And suddenly, I am crying uncontrollably, sobbing at the sky, 'Please, help me . . . someone . . . I don't know . . . what to do.'

It hurts to know you are vulnerable. Infidelity comes in many guises, but it shows itself long before and long after each event. It is a subtle language built of whispers. But on an island whispers are like the wind that flicks the low, smouldering flames. It hurts to discover an abuse of trust. I am sick of sadness, retching ill with it when I think back to all my hopes for the New Year: injecting myself daily, and then the miracle of twin embryos waiting to grow inside me, the light of their life shining like bright stars. All of this joy was shattered on the night of the Hogmanay dance at the community hall when, inexplicably, Rab didn't come home.

On New Year's morning, I woke leaning into a cold space in the bed. When I went downstairs to let out Maude, I did not understand why the door was locked from the outside. Rab appeared at lunchtime. He refused to talk or look at me. 'I got drunk. I should have come home. I stayed over with friends down the road. Big deal.' I stared at him, furious and hurt. 'But we are in the middle of treatment. Why did you even go back after dropping me off?' His face turned dark when I asked him why the door was locked and he pushed past me, saying, 'For fuck's sake, just let a man sleep.' That New Year was quiet. He slept like the dead. So I went out visiting friends, wishing them a Happy New Year, on my own.

Everyone on the island knows Rab's secret. Everyone knows her name. Their silence is deep and impenetrable. They are all waiting, holding their breath. Wondering who will do it. Who will tell me what everyone else already knows. Humiliation is a glinting, sharp blade. It draws others to it, irresistibly, in a dark fascination.

It comes as I am watching the children at school. A string of words, trailing smoke, so you know its embers were lit long before. I listen, my gut wrenching. It hurts to finally hear the truth. And to realise that you are the very last to know.

The bright lipstick on the mouth shaping the words somehow defines them more precisely. With the rain hammering so hard outside, and all the schoolchildren playing noisily in the small, narrow hall, it is difficult to hear myself think. I stand motionless, trying to concentrate on the message they are conveying.

'Cheer up,' one of the women shrugs. 'It's not like it happened yesterday.'

'So you knew?' my voice stumbles. I try to hold her eyes, only she laughs, awkwardly, and then she looks away.

It is hard to read her intention, but I want to trust.

'I don't know what you're upset about,' she tells me sagely. 'We all got over it months ago.'

I accepted that my husband was not present during my treatment. But I did not know what everyone else knew – that it was because he was with someone else down the road. I thought we were trying for a family of our own together. Afterwards, that knowledge makes it all the harder to face those days when she helps out with a school run and comes into the playroom to collect or drop off children. I tell myself to be professional. I smile. My voice is level but strained. You do what you have to do.

'You did not say thank you,' one of the children wonders loudly. 'You always say thank you.'

I look at him and sigh. It is hard to explain to a three-year-old that thank you is something you don't always have to say.

There is only so long you can keep pain buried. It is like a seed that embeds itself deep into your tissue and starts to germinate. Its bitter harvest is reaped a few months later – a year to the day the seed was planted. It is Hogmanay. 'I'm not going to the party,' I insist. Cristall, my closest friend in all the world, tells me, 'You can't hide away for ever. I think you should go.'

She is right. She is always right. So I go.

At the bar, which is nothing more than a shelf with a few bottles, I hand over my contribution. With the raffle over and the tea, scones and sandwiches cleared away, the hard drinking is starting. The room is packed. Later, I am back at the bar, filling up my glass amid a crush of people, when I realise she is standing next to me. I do not know what to say. So I don't say anything. And then I swallow. I am drunk. She is drunk. It's now or never, I think.

'Why did you do it?' I ask.

'Do what?'

'Fuck my husband,' I say.

She smiles, catlike. 'Lies. Just lies.'

'That's not what he says.'

And then we talk. We were friends, of a kind, before this.

'I thought you were my friend,' I say. 'I invited you to my birthday.'

'Yes,' she says. 'And you know what? I didn't go.'

'We were trying for a family.'

She just smiles. 'Bad luck,' she says, and then she walks away.

Sometimes I wish we had never spoken. And other days I am glad we did.

It cleared the air. It helped me to feel stronger. But later things took a darker turn. Her friends dragged me outside. They were drunk, totally mortal, and the tension was palpable. Voices were raised and someone swung a punch. I saw it out of the corner of my eye, coming at me in slow motion. There was no time to think. With my reflexes already alert to the inherent risk of this situation, my body instinctively glided out of harm's way. The punch missed me by a hair's breadth and connected heavily with the face of one of their own. All it took was a glancing blink of comprehension and suddenly a full-scale brawl was underway.

Only I was not in it. I didn't think about it, I just followed my legs and slipped away. Pure instinct was telling me to quit those bright lights and blend into the soft darkness, to leave that world behind me and to seek the peace of invisibility.

As I left, I heard a voice screaming behind me: 'I'll fuck whoever I fucking want to.'

If it wasn't so pitiful, it would have been funny.

I am in excruciating pain physically as well as emotionally. I am not usually accident-prone but I have been unlucky. That spring I have two terrible accidents. My left hand is badly broken in a fall on the croft. And a few weeks later, my right hand is also severely injured in an incident that is still hard to talk about.

It is extraordinary to me how such an unremarkable fall could result in such a horrific shattering of bone. One minute I was upright, walking on the croft. The next I had tripped and landed awkwardly. A grassy bank shelved up to meet me, my head hit a rock and my left hand met a steep incline. It was that simple. Grass has an unseen violence when you slam on to it, head down, with your full body weight. I did not feel my hand snap. All I felt was an odd emptiness in it, a sudden giving way. I had a sense that breathing was vital, but all I could do was gasp and hold myself tight inside.

Strange, the clarity that comes when you lie stunned and immobile. I had a sudden awareness that I had been holding my breath for a very long time. That the earth is solid, stable, comforting; the dew cold, fresh and sweet like the rain. As I lay crumpled, face down and inhaling the silence, something inside me shifted. Drifting in and out of consciousness, I felt it go. It is exhausting experiencing a relationship imploding around you. You don't hear it break until the last supporting structures shear apart.

When Maude started shoving me, over and over, I dragged myself wearily back to the empty house and crept under a blanket, my cold cheek against her wet nose, her bright amber eyes holding fast to mine.

Inside I am falling, too. Our house is empty of kindness and laughter. Outwardly, I put on a brave face, but underneath I am frightened because I do not know how to catch us. I do not know how to catch myself.

My injury makes Rab angry. He finds it hard to cope when I am ill or in pain. Sometimes our best is not good enough. And our worst has an awful inevitability that is predictable, shocking in its familiarity. It is only later that I wonder how vulnerability can fuel such deep frustration and rage in another person. Sometimes it triggers a sullen silence and at others an anger that is hard to comprehend. I am tired of hearing 'You are making it up, there is nothing wrong with you.' I turn away, hurt, with tears in my eyes.

Each morning, I wake afraid. I jolt out of sleep with my heart pounding in my chest. I am having a recurring dream that takes me into cold, dark water. I know I am deep below the surface but I keep struggling to reach it. I have to get there or I will run out of breath. I wake just as my breath runs out. Other times I find myself shouting with all my might but making no sound at all, my legs working, as if trying to hit invisible brakes, my right foot kicking out desperately. It is as if I am trapped in a runaway vehicle. As I come to, even though I can see my room, the light coming through the window, the sensation continues: the car is still speeding, out of control, with me in it. I cannot stop because there are never any brakes in this dream. Always, I wake properly at the same point – just before the moment of impact – with an abrupt gasp and a high, stifled cry. I sit bolt upright, trembling, hyperventilating. Then comes a dull ache as I become aware of the empty space next to me. Yet it has been this way for months.

Our life, my life with Rab, is unravelling. It is like watching a spool of thread unwinding at breakneck speed. I am sick at heart because, deep down, I know where we are headed. There is only one way this road goes.

And then one day I am sitting in the passenger seat of the Land Rover, hammering up the single-track road. I am huddled forwards, lurching from side to side. All I want to do is shut my eyes, I am so frightened, but I force myself to keep them open, wide, alert, focused on the road. I am not dreaming now. It is daytime, I am awake and my nightmare is really happening.

I am slamming my foot down hard where I want there to be brakes, but Rab fails to notice. And suddenly my voice is screaming at him, 'Please slow down! You are scaring me!' But he keeps driving and I keep screaming. I know we are going to crash. Abruptly, I fall silent. Screaming, or even talking, is a total waste of breath. And I need every ounce of my energy to try to stop this car.

But Rab is driving so fast and is so angry that I cannot grab the wheel or reach the brakes. I crouch in a ball sideways against the seat, doing my best to keep my hands in my lap to protect the one that is freshly set in plaster.

As we climb a hill, I can see a car approaching in the distance on the single-track lane. At the top, I know there is a blind corner and a steep bank that sits high above a ditch. And then I am screaming at him again at the top of my voice, to stop, to please just stop and let me out. It is as if he is hell-bent on driving the car, our relationship and our lives to destruction. And then, because I have nothing to hold on to, cannot hold on, I fold my body forwards in a brace position.

'Fucking stop, Rab, for fuck's sake, just stop!' I am yelling. 'Please stop, I want to get out. I just want to get out.' And then the car cresting the blind brow of the hill is coming right at us.

I do not think. My body reacts. My fingers are on the door handle, my shoulder is leaning hard on the door and I tuck my arms into my body, make myself soft and tumble on to the road, just as Rab rams the car on to the soft verge, the heavy diesel engine spewing out burning fumes.

At times of crisis your body knows exactly what to do. All that practice slipping off Fola's back pays off. You learn to make yourself small and invisible, wait for the ground to come rushing up to meet you and trust that the earth will be kind. Instinct is more than the fight-or-flight mechanism. It also tells you when to freeze.

I lie there, sobbing and swearing, on the road. I am shocked but unhurt. Everyone is shouting. Rab slams his fist against the dash and yells, 'You fucking cunt!' I think, at least it's not just me. In a way I am relieved to hear him screaming at the other driver, because that is the moment I know for sure that he is not well, not himself. The last year, and longer, suddenly makes blinding sense. I also know that I cannot help him, for all my wanting, hoping and trying, because he will not take my help, or any that is offered. We are beyond help now.

When he yells, 'Get in, you fucking bitch!' I refuse. I am so tired of being scared. I do not want to get back into that car ever again. I turn and I start to walk the long road home. Only when I get there, I do not feel safe. I know that when he returns he will be silent, his rage simmering. And that feels even worse than when he shouts. I call for Maude, and immediately she comes running. When the door closes behind us, we go straight out on to the hill. I do not look back. I keep on walking. I am bruised and shaken, but I keep my eyes fixed on the sky.

Sometimes that is all you can do.

I do not understand how we have reached this point. As I walked home, I asked myself over and over if I am to blame. But in my heart I know I am not. We all make our choices and Rab has made his. His anger is self-directed. Combustion has its own physics. It is a controlled chemical reaction. Fire produces energy, anger is its vent. I shrink from its bursting flames and heat and I do not know how to put it out.

My rationality goes to pieces when I am frightened. Rab knows this. His anger hooks into my fear. It is a destructive combination. I spend more and more time outside, walking with Maude on the hills. When I come back, we sit apart, each locked in our own silence. We build walls around ourselves. Home no longer feels like home. I am uneasy and restless. For so many months I have kept this truth out of sight, wary of the prying eyes and loose tongues of others. Cristall's eyes alone watch me turning inwards and remaining silent, preferring solitude and the hills. These days are fraught and isolating.

I can feel the multicoloured threads of our relationship being picked apart. They are daily strewn all around us. It is hard not to trip over them, for all Rab's assurances that it is just in my mind. Love only breaks down when it is neglected, uncared for or cast aside. Gradually, we stop spinning and weaving our life together.

I glance across at him. I want to hand him a strand, to wind us closer. He is sitting beside me, but he is not present. His face is fixed and, even though I can feel the warmth of his body, he seems distant and does not reach for my hand. I wonder where he has gone, and when it was that he went. I cannot quite bring myself to ask with whom.

Love is a rhythm, a reciprocity of pulse. I feel its loss like a pain in my chest. Words, laughter and kindness become scarce. Loneliness creeps in. We are unable to comfort or sustain each other. The years of difficulty and stress have brought us both to our knees. In the end, we are unable to give each other what we each want or need. Some things that should be so easy to nourish or grasp remain cruelly just out of reach.

Later, I take Rab's hand and touch his fingers gently with mine. 'We had it all, you and I.'

'I know,' he answers. Both pairs of eyes fill with tears.

The moment is fleeting.

'But you wanted more,' he says angrily.

'Yes,' I say. 'And was I wrong for that?'

He looks away quickly and lights a cigarette. We know what we both wanted, longed for. A child is a gift that others take so easily for granted.

I want to understand. I want to ask him, 'Were you also scavenging, in your own way, to survive?' I want to position his infidelity as a manifestation of a desire to be more honest. It is hard to do this, but I try. I tell myself that it is an act of survival. A bid to belong to something or someone that is not me. It is difficult to acknowledge that.

'At least you were honest in what you did,' I whisper. 'At least you knew what you needed. Even if you went about it in the most devastating way conceivable.' But I am unable to ask, 'Was I really not enough? Did she, and even others, give you what I could not?' In his eyes I see my own reflection. It is always a shock to see ourselves mirrored in another's eyes.

Rab's dark secret makes those last weeks of the early summer infinitely more difficult. We live separately within the house where once we loved. I have lost the babies. I talk to the GP. It is a relief to be able to talk. 'We cannot go on like this,' I say. I am waiting for a crisis. I can feel it looming. I do not share my fears with others. In a small community, some things are too hard to share. In the end, we construct our own truths and lies.

We have been arguing. I can feel an unsettling volatility in the room. As I turn away, I bite my lip and taste adrenaline and blood on my tongue. It has a dull, metallic tang, a scorched bitter taste around its edges. It tells me what I know inside. It says, 'Get out now, get out while you can.'

As I turn to leave the room, Rab screams, 'Don't you turn your fucking back on me. Come back here, you little bitch!' I carry on walking, unsteadily. I feel a strange separation in my body, as if inside I am ablaze, but outwardly I am frozen. These weeks have been different, with an outsize stress and darkness all of their own. There have been episodes I try not to think about. It is the silence that frightens me most of all.

I know not to say anything. Words are not just words when they are words of hate. They carry an import and meaning that cut deep into your skin. I feel the barbs of those whispered so low I have to strain to hear them as acutely as when they are pressed right up against my face.

I have messed up. I have left a coffee cup on the windowsill. I freeze when I see it. It is wet on its underside and it will stain the wood.

'If you do that again, I will kill you with my bare hands.'

His voice is soft. I am unsure if he is joking. That day another line is crossed. I do not feel safe to go to sleep at night. There is no lock on my door.

I watch, listen, wait. I want to mark that line we have stepped over, so I know how far we are moving from each day's new starting point. But it is hard to draw a line with shadows. I do not want to look up, in case suddenly I find I am right on the finishing line. I do not want to be there. It is enough to bear being where I am. I do not know what to do. If we are ghosts to each other, sometimes I wonder why he should not seek someone else to permanently help him inhabit his own skin. Perhaps this will free him to know himself again.

One night, I get drunk. He gets drunk. Everyone gets drunk. We are at an island wedding in the hall. Some are drinking for the joy of it, others to escape. There are those who drink to hide the cracks in their lives exposed by others' hopes and dreams. I drink to numb my fear. I drink to hide my pain. I stare at Rab. He is talking to a woman. They are standing close, whispering to each other. For a while I watch them. When I cannot stand it any longer, I walk slowly across the room.

'This is my wife.' He meets my eyes, but nothing registers. It is as if he is looking right through me. I cannot read what he is thinking. But I can sense a glistening sheen of volatility. It makes my heart start racing.

'It's time we were leaving,' I say.

'Yes, you see, this is my *wife*.' He says it again, only in a way that makes me feel unseen, dirty and worthless. And then, inexplicably, he laughs. 'At least, that's what I think she is.'

I look at him. I try not to show him my pain, but I can feel it pulsing out at him. Tears jump into my eyes. The woman turns and looks at me. She turns back to Rab and smiles softly. And then, all of sudden, she is laughing, too.

I reach for my coat, desperate to get home. I struggle – it is difficult to put a coat on with one arm in plaster up to the elbow. I cannot see through my tears. Someone comes over to help me. I do not know this stranger. I wish I did, because he is kind. 'Are you all right?'

I nod, and then I shake my head. And then I nod again. 'I'm OK,' I say. Only the way he looks at me, I know he does not believe me. I do not believe me. It is such a long time since I felt OK, I cannot remember it. It makes me want to cry.

'You look after yourself.'

And I think, yes, I can do that. I am used to doing that. I am still thinking about the kindness of strangers as I step outside. Two people are standing close in a way that tells you they are not just friends. And then the cold air and the shock hit me simultaneously. They stop my breath, steal the blood from my heart. I walk past them and say loudly, 'Rab, it's time to go.'

I long to feel the warmth of kindness, strong arms wrapped about me. It makes me realise how long my arms have been reaching into empty space.

In the car, we do not talk. We shout, a year's fierce silence bellowed loud.

Anger beats in two hearts that are silent, impotent, raging. In one it stems from an assault of trust. It comes from feeling tiny lives vanish inside me, all their beautiful lights gone out, like sudden-dying stars. I watch this rage. I meet it and then I try to fend it off. I try to hold it even as I shrink from it. And it is confusing to feel that bond still beating between us. A bond is something that belongs to you. It is yours until it breaks.

When we get to the cottage, Rab furiously pushes ahead of me. He is beyond any rage that I know. Something tells me not to follow, but I do because it is too late to go anywhere else and I cannot drive with my hand in plaster. I go inside because this is still my home.

There are two doors to open, since the boot room was added outside the kitchen door. I keep my broken left hand shielded. It is weighted by the plaster and falls heavy to my side. Somehow your body knows to do that. It is as if it knows what is coming and instinctively tries to prepare.

I meet the first door head-on as it cracks hard into my face. I cannot see because it hits me square across my brow. Stunned, I lose my thoughts and breath. I crumple and stumble and, as I trip, I put my right hand out in front of me. I am falling forwards and I cannot stop. All I know is that, as I am falling, the second door is already whistling fast towards me to meet my face again. It slams on to my fingers just before I crash into it. I stagger but I do not hit the floor because I am pinioned to the latch. My fingers are trapped, crushed under the full weight of wood. When I hear a voice howling, I do not recognise it at first as my own. It is a sound that screams not just of bones broken. It is the sound of hurt unleashed.

As torn, bleeding skin is prised off the door, Rab's face is pale and livid. He insists it was an accident. His eyes are dark with a fury that scares me, and something else I don't recognise. When a neighbour arrives at the door, it takes a long time to calm my screams. I cannot speak for the pain of the injury and the realisation of what we have lost. I would like to take flight into that dark empty sky. But now I have two broken hands.

Sometimes, when the world no longer feels a safe or a beautiful place, we learn to function differently. The mind helps to block memory until we are strong enough to hold it. We call it shock. But sometimes I wonder if it is a kindness we give to ourselves at times of crisis or need. It has been three weeks since that terrible night. I stand alone in the kitchen, my eyes fixed on the door. I have just watched it slam for the very last time. I listen as an exhaust rattles noisily, diesel fumes belching away up the track. My eyes are glazed, disbelieving and glistening with tears. I want to cry because I am glad he is gone.

It is hard to acknowledge that it is over. But it feels as if it is only the beginning of fresh troubles. I look at my hands. There is nothing I can do with them. My left hand is still solid up to my elbow in plaster, and my right is freshly encased in a rigid three-finger splint. I am still learning the limits of this extreme handicap, and each day shows me more. It is difficult to dress, to wash, to eat or go to the loo. I am thankful that lambing is over but it is beyond me how I will cope on the croft alone. I tell myself not to think that far ahead. It is enough for now just to be standing here, between these four walls, with Maude.

The quiet is deafening. The silence of a permanent absence somehow has a different quality from a temporary silence. It seems deeper for the lack of tension and anticipation. I fix my eyes on the clock on the wall. I watch its hands moving slowly, minute by minute, from the hour to the half past. Turning to the window, I stand and wait for the boat to leave the island and to tie up on the other side. Then I watch the seconds click by, around and around the dial, until another hour has passed. I pick up the phone and ring to check that the ferry has pulled in. I go outside and look up, cautiously, taking quick lungfuls of the clean, fresh air.

When I come back in, I am shaking. I call for Maude. It is soothing to feel her next to me. I look again at the clock. After an hour has passed, I ring the station, and am told the train for London has pulled away. I keep staring at the clock. I cannot take my eyes off its face. It feels risky to look away, as if somehow those minutes passing might start ticking backwards. But after another hour, I let go and at last give in to a wave of exhaustion.

Suddenly, the day feels so simple. When you are tired, you lie down. So, gingerly, I kneel on the floor and then lie down, curled up in a foetal position. It is reassuring to feel the stability of the solid earth holding me. I close my eyes. I tell myself, I will just lie here for a moment. I will get up in a minute. I feel numb, but a calming sense of quiet solitude engulfs me like a great wave of water, falling soft about my body and over my head. I let myself breathe quietly. And then I close my eyes. And gradually my heart stills.

Some hours later, I become aware that Maude is beside me. I open my eyes and she lays her head next to me. When I look at the clock now, I see that the London train will be pulling into Euston. I blink back my tears. I am too tired to get up off the floor, so we just lie there together, listening to the clock ticking away the hours. I rest my head gently against my dog and study the amber eyes shining back at mine.

'It's not what we ever hoped for,' I tell her. 'But sometimes, life has to work its own way through.'

We stay there, lying on the floor together. And after a while, sleep overtakes me again. And it is a relief to feel the weight of that silence and to close my eyes.

ACT II

1

Hands

I T IS LATE, some time gone midnight. My hand hovers awkwardly over the keyboard. I hold my breath. I almost hang up. Then the screen connects and Cristall is there.

'What's the matter? Is the pain bad again?'

'I'm sorry. I just needed to . . .' My voice falters. And I wonder, how do you say that sometimes the long evenings out here in the islands can feel so quiet? That sometimes you just need to hear another voice?

'I just rang to say goodnight,' I say.

And then I notice that Cristall is not in bed. She is still fully dressed in her skirt and old blue cardigan, sitting downstairs, alone with her dog. She looks tired, and yet unwilling to go upstairs alone. And that is how I know that she understands why I have called. We look at each other carefully, avoiding direct eye contact. 'Have you looked up and seen the sky?' she asks quietly. 'The moon is so bright tonight. It is hard to sleep sometimes, when the world is so beautiful outside.' And then she smiles and holds her arms out wide. 'Goodnight, dear girl. This hug is for you. Sleep tight.' She blows me a kiss.

Now I am glad I phoned. When Cristall smiles, she smiles with her eyes. The kind of smile you feel with your heart. I want to tell her, this is why I called. You are why I called. But suddenly I feel shy. I look down at my broken hands. 'Goodnight,' I say, as I try to wave back.

I never realised how important hands are until I lost the use of mine. Nor the value of friendship. Friendship is, in the end, so simple. It is having someone you can count on, someone you trust, someone who can be all that matters when everything else starts breaking apart. The truth is I am not coping. And I am blinded by fear. I know Cristall knows this, too. The complex fracture in my left hand has not yet healed and the hand still feels dislocated at the wrist. The pain is crippling. It remains encased in a hard, solid cast like a dead limb. I wrap my arm in a woollen shawl. When your bones are broken, you crave something soft against your skin. I hold it close to me like a baby, as if I might rock it gently to sleep.

I am exhausted and know I must sleep. But even getting ready for bed is a challenge. Sometimes I want to cry with frustration. I feel so helpless and alone. I cannot even undress myself, so every night I lie down fully clothed to try to sleep. But the pain keeps me awake through the early hours and sleep does not come. Later, three orthopaedic consultants will say that it is one of the worst breaks they have ever seen. One is speechless and then angry: 'I have never seen such a mess before in my life. How can you function like this?' I worry all the time that if I am not able to sleep, my hands will not be able to heal. Without my hands, I cannot work or support myself. I cannot play the piano, or work creatively, and so it is harder to express myself, too. Without my hands, I cannot do anything.

I will never forget the day Cristall found me after Rab left. The island was sweltering in a sudden mid-June heat, but inside the kitchen was winter-chilled in spite of the bright sunshine outside. Old stone houses can keep the warmth out and hold the cold in, so that when you step outside, it seems like a different world altogether. That day is a blur to me, but I remember the look on her face as she knelt down beside me on the floor. The touch of her hands as they smoothed my face. The soft wrap of a blanket, its reassuring plaid weight. The close weave and scent of her cardigan, scrunched under my head. Her arms cradled me and rocked me gently like a child. 'Ssh, it is OK,' I heard her say. 'I am here now. You are safe. Don't cry.'

I stared at her, eyes wide, uncomprehending. I was not aware of tears. Just of a fatigue beyond anything I have ever felt.

'I am not crying,' I whispered. She looked at me with such pity in her eyes.

Some weeks later she asks me: 'Tell me, how long were you lying there on the floor?'

And I am puzzled, because I am not sure.

'An hour or two, a day or two, no more than that,' I say.

'I want to know.'

'One minute I lay down, and then you came, and everything was fine.'

We sit quietly. Because what else can I say? I am not sure of the sequence of events or the precise details of that day, or of those leading up to it. Even now I find it hard to talk about, simply because I am still trying to make sense of it. Sometimes, I want to say, when your life starts to unravel in an overwhelming, inexplicable way, you hold more closely to your own instinct than to linear time. When you are fearful, your body learns to live by a different pulse; it learns to be vigilant. That day, as I looked at the clock and watched each minute pass, all that mattered was knowing that the ferry was pulling away. Time concertinaed and fragmented in ways I cannot fathom. I do not know how to explain this, and so I am silent. I stare out at the sea.

'It hurt me to see you like that,' Cristall says. 'It was like the light had gone out of your eyes.'

'I'm sorry,' I say. 'I was just so tired, I lay down.'

I wish I could tell her how it was strangely comforting to feel the silence wrap gently round me and hold me. How I knew that if only I could lie still, just breathing and barely moving, time, and this feeling, too, would quietly pass.

'I want you to know that I am here.' Cristall holds my arm gently. 'From now on, I'll be looking out for you, and you'll be looking out for me.'

I smile. And then I reach out so that our hands are touching. 'That's a deal,' I say.

You have to be tough as a woman living here in the islands. You learn not to wear your heart on your sleeve or to show any sign of vulnerability or weakness. The trouble is that you get so used to the strong persona you must inhabit and to protecting that soft heart, you sometimes forget to listen to it beating.

Every morning I wake feeling lost and alone. I know it is better this way. But I miss the familiar rhythm of the life that we shared. Some days, I even miss the hurt of it. Everywhere I feel Rab's presence. I hear his voice. I see his face. I try not to think about my broken hands but sometimes they catch me unawares. The memory of seeing my left hand lying inert, swollen, bruised, broken, discoloured on the table before it was bound makes my stomach lurch and sets my teeth on edge. It is hard to avoid your own hands, but that is what I attempt to do. When I go through a doorway, I angle my body at ninety degrees, sideways, as if there is only half of me in the room. I am so scared to knock it, for fear of any more unnecessary pain. I shrink from hard edges. I wear several shawls thrown loose about me, to keep it out of sight and to keep warm. Pain makes you colder than usual. It makes your blood run thin. And I don't know why, but sometimes seeing my hand makes it hurt even more. So above all, I try not to look down.

If I do notice it, I close my eyes quickly. If you ignore something for long enough, usually it eases, even if it doesn't go away. This, though, is an altogether different pain from any I've known before. My wrist is twisted within the plaster at such an angle it makes me wonder if it will ever lie straight. The edges of the scaphoid bone, trapezium and radius grate against each other. The wrist feels separate from the hand. There were so many fissures and cracks on the X-ray, it was difficult to see if there was any place left where the pins might go. 'We can't take the risk,' the consultant told me, apologetically. 'I am sorry, but there was nothing left to pin it to.'

We looked at each other. Then he looked away. We both knew this was an excuse, a half-truth. The X-ray department was closed the day I fell, and it was one of several minor emergencies where things were missed. We did not mention how two GPs and a team at A&E insisted that it wasn't broken and sent me away. If the complex fracture had been correctly identified I would have been flown to Glasgow straight away for surgery. 'It's just a slight sprain, a bit of light bruising. Nothing that a day or two won't fix.' I tried to convince them, but they told me, 'Come back in a week or two. If it was broken, you wouldn't be able to speak for the pain.'

I was sent away with two paracetamol. A week later, when it was flagged as a complex multiple break, it was too late for it to be properly set. These days, I am not sure what to feel. I am relieved that the plaster cast is rigid, but I am terrified it is not rigid enough. I know this because I am painfully aware of the shattered bones moving with every breath I take.

I clench my teeth and go to the place I have found where you can feel nothing inside. I think this is called learning to dissociate, but I call it swallowing pain. Wherever it is, I am starting to like it there. It is peaceful and quiet, like being underwater, or floating on a dark, silent, cold sea.

More than anything, I am exhausted. My marriage is over and suddenly I am living alone. I blink in astonishment at the beauty of summer on the island, at the long grasses and thistles growing on the croft whilst I am feeling something inside me start to fall apart. I stay indoors more and more. I lie with my broken hands against my chest. When sleep eventually comes, I welcome it. For a few hours, I am free. Cristall alone is here for me, and so daily life is made possible. I am grateful for this – for her, for our friendship. Because without it, I do not know how I would cope.

Each day I listen for the sound of her car, an ancient, dark-blue Peugeot called Bluebell, rattling up to the house. The exhaust is noisy, tied on with baler twine and fencing wire, so you can hear it coming from a distance away. It smells of the diesel that leaves a viscous pool below its undercarriage where she parks.

I hear her wrestling with the stiff latch. The door suddenly jerks open, even before she has knocked on the glass. Her voice is bright, crisp and clear-sighted. It brings a sudden rush of fresh air into the stifled room. She piles Tupperware boxes on to the countertop, reading off the felt-tip labels stuck on to each lid. 'Broccoli and stilton. Lentil. Pea and mint. Cheese soufflé. Chestnut and brussels sprout bake. Don't eat them all at once. These can keep.' She prises off a lid and pulls up a chair. 'Now, let's see how strong you are today,' she says, tying a tea towel around my neck.

Gently, she helps me to pick up a spoon. It is difficult. I have no grip or strength in the fingers poking out of the cast. I narrow my eyes, hold my breath and concentrate. Halfway to my mouth, my fingers slip and the thin handle twists. The soup spills everywhere. 'Take your time,' she tells me. 'Rome wasn't built in a day.' On the third attempt, the spoon falls to the floor. She sighs, exasperated. 'No point in wasting good food.' She bends down and picks up the spoon, wipes it and dips it expertly into the steaming bowl. 'Dear girl. Here, blow on it.' Then she spoons homemade soup slowly into my mouth. It tastes delicious. I am hungry. 'See, you need to build up your strength,' she says, positioning the spoon lengthways in my hand. 'You've got to put this behind you, and with the summer ahead of you, it won't be long till you're back on your feet.'

Later we go to her house. Her bath is lower-slung than my deep cast-iron metal tub, so is easier to step in and out of without hands to balance. She helps me to undress. Buttons are an impossible task, as is lifting a jumper over my head, or sitting down in the bath without stumbling or slipping into the luxurious hot water. And I am astonished, as I always am, sitting there naked and blinking, trying to keep my hands above the water, how difficult simple tasks can be. I think about how friendship is about actions as well as words. About being there when there is no one else to help. About reaching out to someone before they stumble, so they can trust they won't fall. My friendship with Cristall is all of this, and yet it is so much deeper. It feels like a promise. Often it is like a relationship between mother and daughter, a friendship richer than any I have ever known.

I remember the promise I gave to Cristall's husband Anthony three years ago, on a cold afternoon in December, that time of year when the island is burned raw by the wind, all life stripped barren, pared down, desolate. A pair of buzzards were wheeling silent in a low-lit gloaming sky, that liminal time when day and night are distinct and yet inseparable. When light bleeds into darkness, and the sharp, chiselled edges of the mountains run deep into a restless sea. It is at times like this you feel you can speak of more delicate, fragile things, perhaps because these wilds are strong enough to hold them.

Gently, I took the hands stretched out to me. I knew and loved these hands. Even in the glow of the bedside lamp, the skin was grey, translucent, paper-thin. I knew that the Macmillan nurses had done all they could for Anthony. The room was warmed by a low-voltage storage heater, but despite the freezing cold, the window remained propped slightly ajar. There was no way round acknowledging what was happening: these were dying hands. Resting in my fingers, they felt waxen, cold, as if his life was slowly draining out of them. Cancer bleeds the life out of you until there is nothing left. Once the body is not able to eat, it starts to sleep and its muscles and strength begin to waste away. But even then, the mind can still be strong.

I swallowed, felt the muscles of my face set rigid. I looked fiercely into Anthony's eyes. He was cool-eyed and clear-sighted, wearing a faint smile, of amusement and tender concern. I bit my lip, working hard to blink away my tears. Beyond anything, I wished to make this goodbye as easy as possible for him, or at least a graceful thing. Because this was someone who had lived a beautiful life. He had lived with an open mind, a generosity of spirit and a fire for searching for all that life might give, not just for his own enjoyment, but to help others experience it, too; his family, friends and all those he had known and loved. I had known him as a man committed to the guardianship of the earth, of the wilds, of nature; a man who planted trees and shared his passion and knowledge of them. And for this I will be eternally grateful.

We sat there in silence, listening to the clock tick. I ignored the scratching at the door and the murmur of voices downstairs. His family were gathered from the furthest reaches of the globe to spend these last days close to one another, together and alone. Death brings you into stark proximity with your own life, with your loved ones and with those you are about to lose.

Somehow the dimming light and darkening night sky outside made this farewell a more difficult ask than I had anticipated. No one wants to say goodbye in the dark. He said softly, 'I will miss you. It has been my great gift to know you.'

Waiting for death involves sharing a deeper degree of candour as you dare to express all the things you will never again be able to say. It is also a time of keeping silent when you long to speak, because you know that, for all your effort and love, no words can help. Outside, the wind was picking up and, in the distance, I heard the raw-edged cry of the buzzards slicing the darkness. Anthony smiled again and raised an eyebrow. His eyes showed me he was listening intently. There was a concentrated, faraway look in them. I waited. Listened. Held his hand.

And then, out of nowhere, came a burst of light. It was dazzling; luminous, fierce and beautiful. Wordlessly, we lifted our clasped hands together and held them up in the shaft of sunlight streaming through the window. Mine were dark shadows, solid, dense, opaque. His were otherworldly; I could almost see straight through them, the flickering veins a blue-pulsing, soft-beating grip on life. And then the young spaniel that had been whining and scratching furiously at the door barged into the room. It was Isla, an adolescent pup who wouldn't be separated from Anthony by something as insubstantial as a wooden door. And we laughed in spite of ourselves. Because life and love are beautiful. And sometimes, if you do not laugh, something will break inside. This was no time for the indignity of tears. They cannot help to mend that which is tearing open. I turned to leave, still grasping his hands tightly. It was hard to let go. As I flashed him a last look, his eyes locked on to mine. His voice was clear, but with a hard edge. It cleaved the space between us, so stark and uncompromising. 'Promise me you'll look after her when I am gone.'

I nodded. It amazed me how someone facing death so bravely was still concerned with the care of others. How can you prepare? I wondered. I cannot imagine how this feels. Knowing your life is slipping away, not knowing what lies beyond, if anything. Death asks of you a surrender and a courage greater than any I can conceive of. Outside the buzzards wheeled in silence. For a long moment we both watched them through the window. We both knew what the other was thinking. That these magnificent birds pair for life.

And then I left the room.

When someone dies, their spirit is free. But no one is free that is left behind. When Anthony died, Cristall buried herself, and I remember how helpless I felt, because there was nothing I could do. Sometimes it helped to be there, sometimes not. Grief is like soil. It is heavy and clings to your skin, even when you come up for air. And sometimes, even after you think you have brushed it off, it is suddenly there again, miring you in something heavy and dead and weighted and dark. It took Cristall a long time to come back; to sit in the sunlight and fresh air. I know some part of her is still buried under that soil. I did not lose my husband in the same way that Cristall lost Anthony, but I lost him all the same. And it occurs to me how so often life runs full circle. And how, three years on, someone I promised to look after has ended up looking after me.

'Can you feel this?' I try not to wince as Cristall gently touches the fingertips of my left hand. I nod. It is a relief to feel something.

Physical pain is at least a connection to myself. Inside I am still numb. My fingertips are all I can see of my hand. I try to picture how these hands and fingers will be once the plaster cast is off. 'As good as new,' Cristall tells me. But in my heart, I don't quite believe it. And, by the look on her face, I know she has her doubts, too. I close my eyes. Take a deep breath. With an effort, I clench my jaw while she washes my hands. When I open my eyes again, she is watching me closely. She rests her own hand next to mine.

'Try not to think about it,' she says. 'Beauty is on the inside. Look at my hands. Yours are a thing of beauty next to these ugly old roots.' But I do not see that. Hers feel solid, warm, and strong. As she turns them over, I feel the pulse in her fingers beat softly against mine. We sit like that for a while, our fingertips resting together. I cannot imagine my life without her. I smile at her and then, on impulse, I lean forwards and kiss her hands. And for a minute, I cannot see.

2

Foraging

IT IS JUST past midday, or what is called the forenoon in the west of Scotland. It is nearly time for the post, which comes off the late-morning boat, and always used to be a hopeful time of day. I am in my dirty overalls, picking brambles with difficulty at the end of the rough track that links my house to the world, where the van drops off my mail. The single-track road is quiet, so I know the rush for the ferry will have passed and soon the boat will be in. There is an unusually warm wind stirring, and the barometer has been falling, signalling a drop in pressure and a change to the skies. It is a time of year when you look to the clouds more closely and try to predict when, and from which direction, the late-summer storms will blow in from the Atlantic on to our shores. Weather can be fickle out here in the islands.

A friend appears, making her way down the cracked asphalt road on foot. And because I haven't seen anyone, or heard my voice, since yesterday, my heart lifts. I try not to admit to myself, but these days I am often lonely.

The road is so quiet that her greeting sprays like gunshot into the air.

'You know, we wouldn't be friends if we didn't live here,' she says, without preamble, the words flaring out of her mouth.

'I'm sorry?' I reply as the rooks and crows start a riotous, clattering alarm call. Initially, I stare at her mouth moving, because when you hear something unexpected, it can take a second or two for your eyes and ears to synchronise. With a flicker of confusion, I look at her eyes.

'Well, it's the truth, isn't it?' She glares back, and then repeats herself slowly, enunciating each word. 'I said, if we weren't on this island, you and me wouldn't be friends at all.'

There is a long silence. At first all I can hear is a long, beautiful blackbird note, suddenly snared in a mire of briar thorns. But then I hear the hard ring of truth in her words. I do not like conflict, so I think quickly of all the good reasons not to fight. It is too easy to be sensitive and, these days, I have few friends. On an island where everyone lives together within such a small, tight compass, you need as many good neighbours as you need friends. For a long moment, I just stare at her.

'I know,' I say eventually. 'Just think, we might never have met if we didn't both live here.' I try to imagine all the people I might never have met had our paths not crossed by chance. And then I think of all the others I have still to meet, and that is a welcome, intriguing thought. So I smile at her hesitantly. She does not smile back. There is a distinct tightness about her eyes and her lips are pulled thin. I can feel a tense, reflexive pulling about my own. I wonder, what is happening when a smile is not a smile? And then, ever so slowly, she shows me her teeth.

'That is not what I meant,' she says softly, folding her arms. Is this really happening? I ask myself. I can feel my eyes narrowing and my muscles tensing. I notice how she won't catch or hold my eye. It gives me a hollow sensation, as if I am waiting for something bad to occur, something I know is long overdue.

This feels surreal and primal: two females, of different ages and status within their social hierarchy, standing outside, baring their teeth at one another. The day goes silent. I can no longer hear the birds or the wind in the trees. And suddenly I feel vulnerable, because it is just me and her alone on the road.

I know I do not have the emotional strength for this today, so I turn to her and lightly touch her arm. Sometimes physical contact can achieve what words cannot. 'Look, aren't the trees beautiful today?' I say. She just shrugs and roughly shakes my hand off her sleeve.

Even though I don't want a row, I know I must stand my ground. I tell myself I'll just ask her straight out why she is doing this. But as my mouth wraps itself about the words, my question comes out differently. 'How did we get to here so quickly?' I blurt. 'Why are we fighting like this?'

And then I am furious with myself and furious with her.

'You want to know?' she calls to me, her voice rising.

'Yes, I do.'

'OK, I'll tell you,' she yells. 'You've no right staying on now he's away.'

And there it is. A clatter of words, like carrion spraying out of the treetops. The birds whirl away above us, round and round in their own slipstream, moving at speed but not going anywhere. It is strangely calming watching that insular, circuitous flight. Gradually they drift into the trees and leave us in silence.

'But why shouldn't I stay?' I ask in disbelief. 'I live here. This is my home.'

'It's selfish! It's too big for you! You can't even have a family of your own. Why spoil it for someone else?' she screams at me. 'That croft needs a young family to work it properly. You've no business staying here, keeping it all for yourself!'

For a moment I am stunned. I want to ask her, how is a croft not worked properly when I am out all hours, breeding and running my ewes, tups and lambs? Why does that not count in the scale of reckoning? And I think over all of that effort and love – does that not matter at all? What of the other, invisible, unspoken years of heartache? I tried for a family, I want to tell her. I gave my all. But I don't because no words I can find could ever come close to expressing the struggle and the pain of that love beyond all other. So I just shake my head, upset and incredulous.

'That's a shocking thing to say,' I tell her quietly. As I turn away, I wonder, how can such white, blinding heat come out of nowhere? And I am struck by the sheer futility of this exchange, as if the heat of anger could shift the very cornerstones of life. A minute ago, this was an ordinary day, calm and peaceful. I am bewildered at how swiftly we have reached this point of no return.

'There is so much you don't know,' I say quietly. 'And one day, I will tell you. But not now.'

'Yes, you do that. Why don't you tell me, and all of us,' she shouts, 'so we can understand why you're still here!'

But already I am walking away. This island wind blows differently from any other wind I know.

It is not always easy to live quietly where the skies are so big and the wind blows free, brave, thrawn and fierce, wrapping itself about its magnificent landscape and impelling us to strive to match our small lives to its grandeur, in anger as well as in love. Maybe the sheer scale of the landscape dwarfs human emotions to such an extent that the voices of its inhabitants become more pointed, brave, magnanimous, generous, cruel or unkind in an effort to make themselves understood.

It is a beautiful world of stubborn pride, hatred of difference and fear of change. In many ways, it remains feudal, with its own unique honour system that is quick to take offence and slow to pardon. Forgiveness is a quality that is as hard to disinter as the rocks in the soil.

Until this moment this woman and I have skirted our differences, sharing easy thoughts on walks, or waiting for the ferry. When you are outside, sharing that fresh air together, it is as if there is more room to breathe. I never believed I knew her more than superficially, as is often the way when very different folk are flung together. Like the sea, a friendship's smooth surface can lull you into thinking those are calm waters glittering offshore, without considering invisible currents or rip tides. Now I realise I do not know her at all.

It seems I am being punished for staying on at the croft alone. During my time on the island, I have seen how rarely women step up to farming the land solo, unless their 'menfolk' die. In such unfortunate situations, they are treated kindly and supported by other males in their extended families, or in other alliances, and have their unconditional help and support. No other woman on the island runs a croft or farm alone by choice. I think I understand why. I have no family or alliances here, and superficial friendships are structures like fences or gates: they can be closed as well as opened. When those gates close I am left to fend for myself. Beyond my own walls, I must learn to protect myself from the wolves and darkness. Your instinct alerts you to this, like some ancient script still wired from older times.

Throughout history, in any traditional society, family or extended kinships are the main refuge from conflict. There is safety in numbers and they provide a better chance of survival, through a shared interest in each other's flourishing. But when things go wrong, it is the patriarchal shepherd who stays. This island's culture is rooted in a landscape where soil dominance and ownership are paramount. In common with so many ancient tribal cultures, its gender division evolved with shifting agricultural practices. In ancient times, men were first hunters, then herdsmen, while women were the goddesses, totems and cultivators of the soil's fertility and crops. It is only in relatively recent history that men took over the plough, and with it dominion of the soil, while women were subjugated to the house, to domestic chores, management of the family and lesser employment. At a stroke, societies flipped from matriarchal to patriarchal. This division of labour was swiftly naturalised, perpetuated and enforced, and is still apparent in rural communities around the world.

On our small island, this social norm remains widely accepted and unchallenged. Matriarchy is family, children, handicrafts and baking. Patriarchy is its husband: territory, graft, progeny and succession of grazing and land. There is a Gaelic saying that the childless woman is helpless. Without children, she is valued on a sliding scale of decreasing worth. As a lone woman working sheep, without kinship or connection, I am one of a rare breed of its own kind. My working the croft and tending its soil singlehandedly is a guardianship that is increasingly seen as a challenge, a threat and a risk.

As I walk away, I pass one of the sheep fanks, where a cluster of farmers are gathered about, drinking after a day at the tup sales. They fall silent as I go by. The tension vibrates in the air. I ignore the voices that start up again at my back and walk faster. As brave as I want to feel, I don't want trouble here. It is a shock to any small community when traditional bonds are broken. Tradition is a wearisome, coercive thing. It is woven over generations, its threads pulled tight to lend cohesion and structure and design. Unhappiness is no justification for pulling apart the fabric or snapping the yarn. Threads that stray, tear or break are an anomaly in the pattern, giving rise to fear, rancour, bitterness. It threatens the stability of other threads. It might cause them to unravel – or to seek to unstitch themselves. I have no children. I have no husband. I no longer fit the design.

Walking up to collect your post once a day from the box at the end of the track is not a big task, but sometimes it can feel overwhelming. Just opening and stepping out of the door can be surprisingly difficult when you live alone. The invisible border with the outside world becomes harder to cross if you let it. I force myself to get up and out. Each day I hold to the sky, watch the clouds passing and the light smirring. Small pleasures like this can help. They remind you of a bigger, gentler, braver universe. I value small interactions, exchanges, kind words, or just a smile or a greeting. Words can be a vital source of nourishment, and going out and seeing one other person might be your only human contact all day. Kindness can make or break it.

I talk to my horse, sheep, dog, hens, and even the wild birds and mammals I encounter. I miss my old cat, who has died, but in her place I have two young rescue kittens. I fill my world with nature, and that feels strangely more peaceful than seeking out my own kind. But still some days are too quiet. Some days, some weeks, can be so quiet you can forget the sound of your own voice. The days that are not like this become fewer and further between. Day-to-day survival is visceral and frightening.

Even kindness can be double-edged. It may be offered freely and genuinely, or it may be laid with a tripwire and a snare. I am wary of accepting favours and help. Kindness that comes with strings attached can be subtly coercive. It creates its own debts, dependencies and bonds. Gratitude, its reward, has its own fragile weight and springs. You think its soft feathers are harmless until it flexes and draws you in. I am careful. I am becoming more adept at anticipating when I am being drawn in. Whenever I hear 'Not much of a place for you now your man's away,' I swiftly change the subject. Even if it means just making small talk about the weather, or what is or is not growing in the garden, it is safer than being led, unwilling, into a forensic battery of questions or a minefield of loaded speculation. I try to keep conversations light and to restrict them to generalities.

Sometimes it seems odd that no one asks about my hands, even though one is still strapped for comfort and the other, whilst out of plaster, is held in an unwieldy protective brace. But these days nothing really surprises me.

I hunt for small gems that lift a day, gleaming, like the morning an elderly woman talks of the beauty of rainbows, or a young child excitedly tells me where the mackerel are feeding. Small moments of no consequence to others, but which I cherish.

One night I make myself go out. I go to the ceilidh dance. I want to hear music and I have not been to a large party in over a year. It is the usual set-up: a room with a raised platform; a shelf where you put your bottle with your name on a sticker affixed to it. Tonight three musicians are tuning up – accordion, fiddle and pipes. I get drunk, and I am happy because my hand in its brace is slowly mending. It is still not right, but I think, to hell with it, and I dance. It is the traditional reels and jigs, which means you dance with others. After a dance with one of the farmers, I am breathless. He shakes my free hand and then, unexpectedly, reaches out and touches my cheek.

'So pretty. You are so pretty,' he says.

It is too intimate a gesture, but his tone lulls me. It sounds kind. So even though I draw back, I smile.

'Thank you,' I say as I start to move away.

Only he reaches out and, ever so slowly, traces my cheek again with his finger. 'But your skin, so dirty . . . so dirty.' His clear eyes harden as he smiles.

I have no words. I hate that sinking feeling that comes when someone punches you like this. And suddenly I have tears in my eyes. There is nothing I can do to hide this from him. I turn quickly. But he sees and catches my arm lightly.

'You see, you are different from us. You think you are the same, but that,' he nods at my tears, 'gives you away. We are family, if you get my meaning. You do not belong here. This island will never be your home.'

And instantly all of that music and laughter drains out of me as I watch him walk away, feeling like I am six years old, picking myself up in the playground. It hurts how hands still reach for those same tired stones.

Race is something that is not spoken about out loud on the island. You only catch it, like a cold wind that makes you draw your neck in close to your ears.

Some worries keep you awake at night. Hunger is one. So is debt. When one starts to feed another, that is when things get complicated. For a year and a half, maybe longer, I have been in the eye of a perfect storm. In that time I have lost unborn tiny lives, my marriage – and with it my trust – and broken both my hands. It is unsettling how quickly struggling to make ends meet can become a struggle to survive. I have tried to keep working to stay afloat, but there has been no time to recover from each disaster before the next has come rolling in like a wave.

I have heard that grief is stored in your lungs and mirrors the slow decay of autumn, and that's how it feels. Three months after Rab's departure in the early summer, my father dies, shockingly, and my mother is diagnosed with Alzheimer's. As the colder season shutters me in, it brings with it an insidious, devastating grief. It is harder to say goodbye to the things you love which have all your life been remote, strictly conditional or emotionally absent. Death robs you of your voice, of reconciliation and forgiveness, with such crushing finality that it can be overwhelming. I find comfort in the low-burning husk of winter slowly rising over the mountains. It irradiates the croft with light and helps my tears to flow more easily. But winter is long, and some mornings it is hard to find that bright sun.

Then I lose my voice. It starts off with a bout of laryngitis. It is strange trying to talk when your voice doesn't work as it used to and no longer sounds like your own. I force it, because it is easier to try to speak than not to speak at all. Others expect you to make that basic effort. The only problem with this is that the muscles of the trachea and vocal cords become even more inflamed, and then one day I open my mouth and no sound comes out at all.

Next I start coughing up blood. I am diagnosed with a respiratory illness in my lungs, weakened by the physical effort of trying to function and cope with so much grief. With it comes a paralysing fatigue and an immune system that is compromised and struggles to recover. As the weeks and months pass and my voice doesn't return, I retreat into silence. In some ways it is a relief to be quiet, because talking is exhausting. After a while I get used to the silence. Later I wonder at how grief can strip you of a physical feature like your voice. One day I find a young bird in the garden who is mute, and I am moved, because I had never thought that a songbird might not have a voice. I wonder what it might be like for a bird never to be able to sing.

It is easy to underestimate how debilitating grief can be, and how powerfully a shattering break-up of your old life and dreams can hit you, physically as well as emotionally and psychologically. I am ashamed that I, like so many others, used to think of it in such simplistic terms – OK, so you grieve, and then it is over. As if it was easy to roll up your sleeves and carry on as before. I had precious little idea how hard it is to pick up those dropped threads and start to weave substance into the hole where your life used to be. We are so silent on the subject of grief that we render death invisible, yet all the while we know that life is just a fleeting pause, a beautiful, brief intake of breath, before death embraces us all. I wonder how it is that we can bear this contradiction, and why it is that we are so immune or resistant to another's grief, or simply unable to cope with it. Is it because we are trying to avoid facing our own mortality? Do we become defensive instinctively when we see another's weakness, for fear of opening wide the door to our own vulnerability? It shocks me how we do not make room for sharing another's pain.

I quickly learn that trauma is different from grief. Its physical, emotional, psychological threads are infinitely more subtle and complex. Trauma is an ambush that waits patiently until long after the catastrophe that precipitates it is over. It is like being bound, gagged and having your head held underwater. It makes you panicky and lightheaded. You can tread water for only so long before you tire of struggling. And there comes a moment when you think how peaceful it might be not to have to fight to breathe.

Once the lambing begins I have no choice but to endure the raw, bitter weeks of early March. When the ewes start pressing and their lambs start coming, there is nothing you can do to delay those lives from being born. It is difficult and painful working with those crushing contractions whilst still trying to protect my slowly healing left hand. There have been complications due to the bones having been incorrectly set and the muscles have atrophied. Lambing requires two hands and, with no other assistance, I have to use both of mine. I am in constant pain, and still wearing the protective brace, but there are times when I need to work freely and have to grit my teeth and remove it. It is a relief that my right hand is improving, daily becoming more mobile, although, in the damp freezing conditions, the fingers that were so badly hurt still ache and are often stiff and sore.

I try to take comfort in the knowledge that winter is ending and spring, a time of renewal, is on the way. But in April the weather is shocking – hailstorms, snow flurries freezing, torrential rain – and the days and nights blur into one another. I am out all hours with Maude in icy hail, wind, rain and plummeting temperatures. I create a small billet for Maude and me in the barn, a few blankets folded into a bed and laid on to clean, fresh straw, where I can curl into her warm fur and sleep for a few hours, the two of us wrapped deep in blankets in the soft-breathing darkness, our own breath steaming in the cold air. On the nights it is raining, it feels beautiful and quiet inside, listening to the wind and water hammering against the corrugated-iron roof. I doze alongside my sheep, waking in the early hours to the restless bleating of the ewes as they strain, heads back, turning and pawing the ground, with the first pains of labour. There is a bone-clicking sound as jaws clench and breath is stifled; as nostrils flare, flanks heave; and then the sound of gentle panting. And then I know to get up, to move slowly to help ease a tiny, slippery, warm life out on to the straw and to clear its airways. And afterwards, when the lambs stagger to their feet and I have checked the flow of colostrum to teats, and they have sucked, I go outside, wash my face and hands in the water butt and gaze up at the sky.

At dawn, I get up and warm my stiff body by jogging across the croft. There is no hot water because both the oil and the money to pay for the tank to be filled have run out. The house is cold – the temperature inside reads just seven degrees – so it makes little difference to my comfort to sleep in the barn. Those mornings after only a broken handful of hours' sleep are a struggle, but that early run kick-starts my system. I run fast, as fast as I dare without risking falling, in the hope I will not need to gather up any cold bodies lying lifeless on the ground. I dread seeing those dark-blue, unseeing eyes.

If we find a lamb that may be saved, Maude gently licks its face and then I place it in the warm range, or under a heat lamp hung over a box filled with straw, and wait for its mouth to warm from blue to pink. I drink strong, hot tea, shivering as my hands and face thaw. It is a strange relief to feel the pain of life returning. My hands are still so weak that I have little grip left in my fingers or arms. I try not to think back to the events of last summer. It takes time for the body to heal, I tell myself. But I know this work is strengthening, and all these sensations are good. It is heartening to feel that scalding brew propelling the blood around my body. It makes me appreciate how cold those small lambs must feel, waking to the world outside. A lamb is thin-skinned, with barely any fleece for the first few weeks after birth. It is a wonder they cope in that bitter, cold wind.

Once the mucking-out, feeding and watering is done, it is time to start the rounds again. Hours later, I wash my hands and face under a running tap, lay fresh straw, wrap up in thick blankets and prepare for another long night.

On still nights, you hear things differently. Sound amplifies under a quiet black sky, the cries of screech owls and the wind in the trees like a roaring sea. Those first five weeks of lambing are relentless – feeding, watering, fighting the elements, desperate to keep those new lives living. There are those that don't make it, lambs that are stillborn or premature, an umbilical cord snapped too early, a caul smothering an airway, tiny lungs drowned before they reach their first breath. It is tiring, heartbreaking to see the waste of those perfectly formed, motionless bodies.

This year I am grateful because there are no losses, but there have been plenty of years when I have had to grit my teeth and just do what has to be done. When a lamb is stillborn, or dies shortly after birth, there is no time for regrets. You learn to desensitise and to put your emotions and tears aside to get on with the sometimes brutal work that may be required. I may need to take a sharp blade and gently remove the lamb out of sight of its mother. I do not wipe it or wash it, but take it immediately outside and skin it.

You have to cut through the joints of the knees and the elbows, then make an incision under the jaw and slice the skin in a straight line down the chest to the umbilicus. You grip the lamb, head down, between your knees, draw the tiny fleece and skin over its head and drag it down its back. It is important not to cut too deep when you prepare the lamb for skinning, otherwise you will also draw off tissue and muscle which, after a few days, will start to rot. The hardest part is pulling the last of the fleece over the haunches and tail.

When I put the carcass into a bucket, it looks like a dead skinned rabbit. Later I will bury it, and give thanks for its short or unborn life. Skinning is a hideous task, shocking to witness as the sun comes up first thing in the morning. But the reality is that this skin, tied on to another newborn lamb, will give another struggling creature a chance to be twinned with the ewe. Lambing is a tightly drawn bow string, a tightrope walk between endings and beginnings, life and death.

I feel better for a while afterwards, as if the battle to deliver those tiny cries into the world has invigorated my body. I fight for each and every one of those lives I deliver. This year my ewes produce triplets and twins with only two singles. At the end of the cycle there are 110 lambs out of forty-eight ewes, and I am proud of this achievement because it matters. It matters for my livelihood but it also matters fiercely to me to hear that first wailing cry. I think of my own little ones, who I was unable to help; who, too many times, slipped away into darkness inside me.

And then my lungs give way again. I wake one morning struggling for breath and, once more, I am coughing up blood. I tell myself, give it a bit longer, and that is when the ambush takes on a different shape.

139

It is hard to fight shadows, but that is what it feels as if I am fighting. Shadows and a silent, creeping fatigue.

I start foraging when there is nothing in the fridge and no money to fill it. I have barely been able to function for long spells when I needed to be working to full capacity, my scarce funds have gone, and still the overdue bills keep coming in. There have been too many false starts and enforced stops due to ongoing pain and complications with my hands, and my situation is made all the more precarious when my lungs relapse and my body surrenders again.

'If it's so hard, why don't you just pack up and leave?' a neighbour asks me.

At this low point of my life, I only wish I could. But when a marriage breaks down, there is often an extended period when you cannot equally share the financial load you previously shouldered together. In short, I am broke. It is overwhelming to feel so financially out of my depth. The thought of a move is more than I can cope with. It is hard enough to exist, let alone to make and implement such a big decision. I wish I felt stronger and sufficiently mentally resilient to deal with these logistics.

But whatever my own fallibilities, there is no way of escaping an irrefutable truth: I cannot leave because the house is not finished and there is no certificate to confirm that our ambitious, and as yet unfinished, renovations have been satisfactorily completed. Without that vital document, it cannot be sold. I could seek a comfort letter, but I have no way of covering the three-page list of work still required by the building control regulations before this could be issued. There is already a worrying backlog of bills from the still-to-be-completed extension that was added on to the original tiny cottage years before. I do not know how to begin to pay these.

Sometimes it is tempting just to dig a hole and bury all your debris. It's what happens out here when there is no other way of disposing of all that is redundant, unwanted or undesirable: graveyards of rubble. Walking the croft, I notice how the rocky ground is freshly covered with thistles. It makes me consider how sometimes you have no option but to tough it out, kick the soil over and put down whatever shallow roots you can. Sometimes all you can do is just hold on.

I had such dreams for this home when we first arrived on the island. Initially there was only one bedroom, but I had always imagined that one day this might be a family home full of children to love. Now there is just an empty house with two more unoccupied bedrooms. Nothing is finished – some parts are not even started – and sometimes I wonder if it will ever be signed off. One of my biggest immediate worries is that so far, this year is one of the wettest the islands have known, and there is no guttering in sight or any rain-water drains laid around the house. The rain falls unrelentingly and there is a three-foot-deep tide mark on the exterior walls. When the rain occasionally stops, that tide mark is a cheerful livid green, a glistening, viscous reminder of the threat to the house. On wet days – which are most days – water sits stagnant in pools all around the cottage.

As the months pass, it will turn darker as soil splashes back and seeps into the cracking whitewashed walls. If I look closely, I can see living things growing there: small, gleaming slug-like whorls like molluscs, clumps of tussocky moss, pallid white and then dark, browning mushroom spores. I pull out the shoots and plants growing from the lintels, and every few months I scrub at the walls. Often I worry that the house will become so damp it will start to crumble and fall down. I have piles of unopened post in a box by the door. I throw any mail that is not a letter into this box of bills. At first I tell myself that I will open them later; after a while it gets too scary to look. It is amazing how a pile of bits of paper can feel as heavy as a millstone around my neck.

In the end it is simple. Everyone needs to eat, I reason. I am hungry and I do not have enough food to eat. When there is nothing indoors but stone walls and floors, the only place to go is outside. One day, standing in the garden, I hear my stomach churning and cramping with hunger. I reach out and snap off a small handful of greenery. I examine it, and then peer a bit closer. I find myself wondering how it would taste. I am shy of eating leaves at first. It feels too feral, desperate. But the advantage is that there are plenty of them. It is a reassurance to know that as long as the sun keeps shining and the rain keeps falling, this is one source of food that will not run out.

I turn the leaves over, holding them up to my nose to smell. I strive for words that will help me identify the plant. Fresh, green, herbaceous, a hint of citrus, I think as I rub a leaflet between my fingers. But these descriptions are too general. They could be applied to most plants. This makes me cautious. The leaf leaves a green stain on my fingertips, which I hesitantly lick. I want to be sure it is not poisonous. Plant identification is critical: you do not mess around or take a risk. Many years before, I studied herbal medicine in London. I have kept my old notes and materials and over the last months I have made my own practical quick checklist. I can tell that this plant is rowan. The leaves are long and oval, with a tooth-like rasped edge. I know it is safe. So I take a tentative bite, gnawing first at its edges, and then folding it over and crushing it in my mouth. It feels abrasive, like biting into rough paper, but I persevere. After a minute of running it over my tongue, I start to chew slowly so that its flavour comes through. It tastes bitter, acrid, sour in that first rush of sensation; a moment of doubt tinged by its sharp tang.

'Here,' I offer one to my dog, who is watching me closely. She sniffs it, licks it inquisitively and then turns away as if affronted, the look in her eye one of disgust.

'Oh, come on,' I tell her, 'it's not that bad.' And then I look over my shoulder, quickly, and back the other way. Because it feels somehow savage, standing in my garden, cramming raw leaves into my mouth.

It takes a surprisingly long time to eat a leaf picked fresh off a tree. The thick sycamore leaf is the toughest. The beech is soft, ruckled, with tiny hairs like a downy skin. Blackthorn pricks your fingers on its jags if you are not careful, whilst the hawthorn is as coarse-textured and dense as the silver birch is thin and slippery-cool. Tasting those first few mouthfuls feels strange, like an illicit secret in my mouth. But it is more than that. It is a relief. I am ravenous, desperate for food. So the next morning, I get up early and go out furtively, this time with a deep basket. I make a promise that day to take only what I need.

Back in my kitchen, I crush hawthorn leaf with a stone pestle. It tastes nutty, sharp, tangy when it is pulped into a pesto with freshly picked ground cobnuts from my hazel trees. Some days I forage for nettle, chicory or the young shooting tips of beech, birch or oak that can be eaten raw like salad leaves. Out of season, when berries are scarce, wild raspberry leaf is high in nutrients, rich in natural iron, manganese and calcium. In the autumn, I go to the woods and short-cropped hills for chickweed and puffball. I am not sure of mushrooms. I read up on them but still I am wary of picking the small cups, ceps and apricot chanterelles.

In the winter, I raid the barn – there are some tools left behind in Rab's workshop. Inside a chest I find a small, sharp knife. I make a sheath for it out of sheep fleece and take to walking with it tied about my neck on a leather strap. I use it to cut thin strips of sapling oak, just a few centimetres thick, removing the outer covering before slowly cutting along the length of the bark. The outer coating of the tree is tough, gnarled, denser than you might expect. It tastes coarse, like unshaven wood chips, and dents my teeth, so I leave it to one side. But I know bark is sustaining, so I persevere. Underneath the wood is paler, white like skin. I shred this and chew a piece. Its sap tastes sweet, like birch. At home the kitchen is full of steam as I slice it into strips, boil and strain it. As my cupboards empty of conventional supplies, they start to fill with these other different, wilder foods.

It is one thing picking wild food to supplement your diet. It is another trying to live off the land. For months home-grown cabbage and fresh herring, porridge oats and soaked lentils are my staples. In the summer there are store potatoes and sweet greens, and other vegetables and fruits in the garden, but there are always gaps, due to failed or spoiled crops – casualties of the increasingly unpredictable weather – and my own lack of knowledge or experience of preserving and safe storage to maximise each crop's longevity. Trial and error can result in wastage and the loss of a whole, carefully prepared batch.

My food crisis is heightened by a fifteen-day power cut to the island's supply. Two years' worth of meat, butchered on the croft and stored in the chest freezer, perishes. There is no compensation. Now I have no choice but to live off what I can forage and cultivate to survive.

Cultivation is a learning process, and harvesting and storage skills are as important as knowing how to plant. I dig holes in the dark soil and make natural storage pits lined with straw and fleece for my vegetable crops. I know they will keep safe here over the winter. The earth is not reliant like a freezer on mains electricity and it will not add to my box of bills.

There are failures as well as successes. I wait months for potatoes to grow, digging trenches, shoring them up. When I dig them up, I put them in a box, place it in a shallow pit I have prepared, filled with straw and grasses, and cover it over. But when I check on it some weeks later, I realise the store was too shallow. The potatoes are alive with white grubs and larvae, and spoiled by the hay and grasses, which are now riddled with weevils. It is a shameful waste of all that time and effort, and of a reliable staple crop on which I have been depending.

Foraging, too, takes practice. Initially, I walk too quickly and my eyes register only what is immediate or obvious. Not all of what you first see is edible or good to eat, and at first I am cautious, picking only the familiar. You have to thread your way through the wild orchids, harebell, wild scented grasses and flower of Parnassus, sitting shoot by root beside clouds of thistle, bramble barbs and blackthorn spike. I discover wild herbs – thyme, fresh sorrel, mint. When you look properly it is amazing what you can find.

One day I come upon a goose egg. I take it home and boil it. Its yolk is a rich orange-yellow, the albumen white and frothy, different from the eggs laid by my three elderly hens. It is a gift, this wild food. It reassures me that although I may be lean, I will not starve. With this wild land, the sea and the loch on my doorstep, gradually I start to feel a fresh affinity with the earth and air that teem with life. Each day I give thanks for what I have to eat. I make my own rituals, filling the emptiness with meaning that seems to offer renewed hope. It is strange to feel stronger, for my skin to toughen and hands roughen, as I learn not just how to live but how to survive. Wild foraging teaches you so much more than simply what you can and cannot eat. It teaches gratitude, resilience.

This wilderness is generous, forgiving; kinder than folk. When I think back to the woman on the road, and her anger, I am glad of its heat, for what it has taught me. What it may have taught both of us. It helps to burn the anger away and to look at the world again with love. To evaluate and re-evaluate friendships and acquaintanceships and to know which to hold on to and which to let go.

3

Auction Mart

THE AIR IS oppressive, humid and stifling. It is late October, late in the season for the lambing sales, and storms are threatening. I have caught an early ferry to the mainland and arrived ahead of the hordes, to ensure I am in good time to find the auctioneer and show him my lambs. But when I get there, it is not the one I know, and he is deep in conversation with others I do not recognise. As I come in they look up, but no one smiles, and I feel momentarily uncertain and awkward.

'One hundred and six cross mule lambs – is that you, then?' a stockman shouts across, swinging through the pens towards me.

I nod. It is a relief to know they are safe in pens. My lambs arrived late off the Oban boat after a rough crossing and it has been a rush to unload them. I wipe my hand quickly across my eyes and glance at my ticket. It marks receipt of my movement document, which means I am legally permitted to trade, but even so I feel as nervous, jittery and skittish as the livestock straight off the lorry. My left hand is still strapped to hold it steady whilst the tendons and ligaments strengthen. It has visibly wasted so the orthopaedic surgeons have conferred over the results of detailed testing of the bones, fascia and nerves. The results confirm what I have known all along. Having been set incorrectly, it has remained dislocated all this time since the fall. It will be difficult handling my lambs because it is still weak, and simple movements are still difficult.

It doesn't help that I have never sold my own animals alone before. Last year, after Rab left, not only was I too unwell, but my father's death coincided with the lambing sales and, in the aftermath of that awful summer, I was too stricken with shock and grief. The large auction mart lorry collected my lambs at the pier and the auctioneer sold them, unattended, in the ring. My absence was reflected in the prices they fetched. You never make as much for your lambs if you don't present or show them in the ring yourself. This year, I promise myself, will be different. I am ready to take ownership of my livestock. It is important not just for my self-esteem and confidence, but to demonstrate my capability and credibility. Yet for all my determination, I am inexperienced.

'Right, move it!' the stockman yells to the lambs, flapping his blue apron skirts. 'Come on, move it!' He starts hissing through his teeth. I hear the crack of that fabric, like a whip. And then his stick whistles down, hard edge flicking on to a soft back. 'Don't,' I say urgently. 'They are not used to it.' But he is not listening. I see the dark pools of the animals' eyes glazing over with adrenaline, and some inner vigilance switches on its tense glimmer as they dart their fear at me. You have to push those thoughts away, I think. The auction mart is no place for the fainthearted. Meat is meat.

It is a whirl and a blur as we flow, fast-moving as a single body, stepping swiftly down the narrow metal race, cold aluminium ringing loudly as pens are slammed open and closed on either side. The air is close, thick with the scent of stressed, perspiring bodies, hurly-burly, heavy voices shouting, and above everything the rattle and scream of the tannoy in the ring. At last, we are in a larger pen, with two adjacent smaller ones ready to take the separated males and females.

'Hope you can tell a ewe from a wether,' the stockman winks at me. He nods at the bright lights to my right. The noise coming from the auction ring is deafening. 'Fifteen minutes, no more, and then you're in.' As the gates are clanged shut he strides away. I stare at my lambs. I am trembling.

The annual auction is something the crofting year runs forward to relentlessly. It is the only time of the agricultural year that I dread. I love the lambing, working closely with my sheep and immersing myself in the land, seasons and weather. Yet I would wish for a different end for the livestock. One that was gentler, with animals dispatched quietly by a skilled, licensed handler who might come to the island, involving less stress, less travel and less rough handling. In the old days, animals were led calmly to a barn they knew, and meat was produced as needed, rather than butchered on a mass scale.

The pen we are in has already been used, so there is no hay or water. The sawdust is thin, sparsely scattered, and sticky underfoot where it is drenched in urine. My boots fall hard on to bare concrete – in the places where it is not slippery with brown splashes of dung. An animal that is relaxed sheds hard pellets; these droppings are thin, sticky, wet with fear.

It always takes a few minutes to separate the lambs according to their sex, and it is harder now they have had no time to settle. Some trust has been broken. They scent the air rapidly. Their jaws are clenched and a thin, glassy film dulls their eyes like an inner lid closing, a combination of exhaustion, adrenaline and fear. It makes me realise we are no different from each other. We are all animals, lit up by an instinct that tells us when to feel at ease, when to feel wary or afraid. Every creature knows when it is safe and when it is not. I hate the market for this reason. It forces me to witness and to contribute to the animals' fear and stress.

There is also a deeper, human struggle that gives rise to different emotions. Each year I work hard to integrate with the farming community, to be part of it and, now that Rab is gone, to become accepted in my own right. It is not getting any easier. It feels as if there is always a fine line to tread, and not just because of my gender. In seeking to be part of the system and community, it is difficult to walk this shifting line whilst keeping my identity, beliefs, thinking and voice intact. I am surprised and dispirited to find that, as I gain experience and show myself capable in my own right, this balancing act seems to be becoming even harder.

Working as fast as I am able to sort the lambs, I fear my inexperience and my handicap show. In the old days, Rab would have been standing here in my place. There are never any other women in the great auction hall as the livestock arrives. The few women who attend usually turn up later and sit in the gallery overlooking the ring. They rarely go into the makeshift café where their menfolk are gathered, clustering over rounds of steaming coffee and hot rolls, gossiping about the likely day's trade. I know this because, mostly, I used to sit up in the stand, too.

As I work, I notice a white printed sales sheet discarded on the floor. I pick it up and pause briefly. The sale card, which lists the pens to be sold, is something you keep. It is not just a memento but a working document, used to make scribbled notes of each day's high and low prices, pens inspected, sheep to watch or to beat. Today is the first time my name will appear in print as the registered sole keeper of the croft. I run my finger down the list. My lambs are marked Pen 56, but next to the entry, Rab's name is typed. I think of all the cold, frozen mornings catching my ewes, or waking in the barn, stiff, at dawn.

'Excuse me,' I gesture to the steward apologetically, 'I think there's been a mistake. My name is not marked on the sheet.'

He points at the sheet and corrects me, 'That's it right there, next to Pen fifty-six.'

'That is not my name,' I say. 'It should be the same name that's listed on the crofting register.'

'Why does it matter?' he asks.

'Because it does,' I say. 'Because I am the keeper, and it matters to me.'

He shrugs. 'Well, your last name's on it. That's still your name, isn't it?'

As the lambs press about my legs, I take a quiet breath and try to explain.

'It's my last name, but it's not my initial. He doesn't live with me any more.'

'Oh, I see. It's like that, is it?' he asks, folding his arms.

'Please, is it too late to change it?' I ask hopefully.

He points at the sheaves of white, crisp paper folded and tucked into each metal stand. 'Now, be a good girl, and don't make a fuss.'

I stare at him, flushed with annoyance.

And neither of us moves or says a word. How can I tell him, I wonder, all the reasons it matters that it is my name marked as the shepherd of Pen 56 with 106 lambs? I want to say that when Rab left, I was not just a woman alone without a husband but that my very identity had been stripped away. How can I tell him it is because otherwise I am faceless? That even though I have been windblown, drenched in the seasons, this, the agricultural year, does not even know my name?

Eventually I sigh and turn back to the lambs. 'Thanks, anyway.'

'Who looks after your sheep, then?' he calls after me curiously.

'I work my own sheep.'

'You'll be needing a new shepherd, then,' he laughs, heading off through the pens.

For a moment I feel strange and lightheaded. I take a breath, put those feelings aside.

'OK,' I say quietly to the lambs in the pen, 'let's get this done quickly.'

I take hold of the next one, sliding my fingers under the hard, bony ridge of the jaw as my left arm lightly slips over the back. I bend over the lamb, soft wrapped, loose heavy over its body, so I can feel its flanks panting, its breath beating fast into mine. 'Ewe lamb,' I breathe, still bent over, willing her forwards, as I gently feel her rear end to differentiate her from the nearly identical young males. Over my shoulder, I am aware of a few loud voices telling derogatory jokes.

'Looks like you know what you're doing,' comes a call.

I keep going and do not look up, yet instinctively my skin tightens, suddenly vigilant at this easy yet mocking tone.

Then I hear the metal pin of the gate click.

'There's no harm in a helping hand!'

Without warning, legs press up against me and there are hands on my hips. I struggle fiercely to twist around and stand upright but I cannot move, pinned down by the heavy weight of those hands.

'Get off me!' My voice sounds high-edged and panicky. With my head down and arm flung over the ewe, my shout is smothered, buried in her fleece. I can picture the ridiculousness of the scene, like one of those sick comedy moments, but one that crosses a line. It only takes a few seconds, him pressing me and the ewe forwards, driving us into the pen, and then it is over. His eyes gleam as I stagger, brace a knee and then heave myself up, breathless with the effort.

'Not bad, lass. Not bad at all,' he throws back at me.

My cheeks are burning livid, and I feel nauseous, giddy. 'You fucking bastard,' I whisper. I want to scream at him. But I cannot. I do not know why, but my voice is gone. And in some place deeper, there is a cloying feeling of humiliation, of having been muddied, shamed. Hot angry tears spring to my eyes. 'Don't ever touch me again,' I snap at him, trying to mask my fear. And he sees that. And then he sees the brace on my hand.

'It's just a joke, lass,' he shrugs, suddenly unsure of himself. 'Didn't mean no harm. Don't be stupid, mind,' he rallies. 'Call it your penny luck today. Call it a bond, paid in advance.'

Luck money is an old tradition. It is a goodwill gesture offered by vendors to buyers at the end of a day's sale or other transaction. He is one of the sheep buyers. To my dismay, I realise I will see him later in the ring.

I do not like loud voices or rough hands. Violence is an assault. In childhood, when one parent is rough and the other, who should step in, ignores it, it is a double blow. You silence your own voice, over-react, seek safety by seeking approval, or retreat inside yourself. This triangle of complicity brings with it its own paralysis, whichever side of it you stand. We are all children within, and although I try not to, sometimes when I am scared or feel threatened, I swallow my fear and bury my anger in silence. I tell myself that our experiences make us who we are. But inside, a fighting spirit ignites. Perhaps that is why the auction mart makes my eyes shine fierce.

As I press on with separating the ewes from the flock, a young farmer opens the gate quietly. I look up. I am sweating, still upset by the earlier encounter, and my arms are struggling to hold a young male lamb.

He watches me for a moment and then steps in to help me. 'You're gonna have to be faster than that.'

I recognise him. His family lives in the south of the island. He moves easily, arms working lightly through the stock, making soft sounds and talking quietly to the sheep. We concentrate, working fast together in silence. When we are done, he shakes his head and smiles.

'Sometimes it's better to take the help that's offered,' he suggests. 'It's easier. Why make it so hard for yourself? You make friends that way.'

'But I hate the way they're so rough with them.'

'Ach, don't know what you're worrying for. They'll be dead in the morning, for all your care.'

He is right. We are both right.

I am grateful for his help. But it matters to me that this last passage and transit is as low-key and calm as possible.

'You shouldn't be doing this if it hurts so much,' he shrugs.

And then, all of a sudden, we are on. Two mart stockmen stride into the pen as my number for the auction ring is called. I have been waiting for this, but it still comes as a shock. They are big, burly, thickset, striding past with arms flapping hard against their thighs. They give me a curious, dismissive glance. I am the only woman in the pens. The sheep try to scatter but there is no room for manoeuvre other than to be driven forwards. Ahead, the tannoy blares a deafening drone. There is no stopping this sound and motion: feet moving, fleece skittering forwards, boots sliding on wet sawdust, a slip of brown fear as we work our way closer to those hard bright lights. The drone becomes an intensely urgent, staccato yelling, abruptly followed by the crack of a hammer. There is a lingering pause and then it starts up again. The roar of the mart is one gate ahead of us. I swallow. Adrenaline is surging through my body like the lightning jolt of a high-voltage current, my heart pounding, mouth clamped down as the final gate slams shut.

'Should've worn a skirt,' the stockman winks at me. 'Good luck. Smile at them. You'll get the best of the day.'

I step on to a ledge as the lambs are weighed. Afterwards, I take the white printed slip and feel the soft weight of fleeces and warm, panting bodies pressed close against me.

I sense how every moment has led to this. They are big, muscular, beautiful animals. In those strong bones the struggle, beauty, and all the brightness of the sun; the rain, dew, snow thick on wet fleeces and all the wild flowers and heather closing as a pale moonlight drifts. Standing with my sheep I feel a sense of pride, and a keener-edged anxiety. As gates clang all about us, for a brief minute we are quiet, back on those hills.

There is a screech of metal as the huge, weighted gates to the ring are flung open. And I am moving into the blinding lights and treading sawdust. It is like stepping into a goldfish bowl. Self-consciously I walk across the ring and hand my white ticket to the auctioneer on the far side of the gates.

'One hundred and six cross mule lambs. First pen of four.' And then he smiles at me and says, 'Let's get you a good price, shall we?' I smile back gratefully. He leans forward and says conspiratorially to the crowd: 'A nice-looking pen this, take a closer look. Come on, don't be shy. This one is high-class, pedigree. I'm not sure what I'd rather be selling. A flock of cross mule lambs or this lovely-looking ewe.'

'No,' I protest quickly, 'my ewes are good enough.'

He sweeps his hand at me. 'Ssh, now. Come on, lassie, be a good sport. If you're after a good price for this pen today.'

I stare at him in disbelief. I feel a sickening in my gut. I shake my head, but he just laughs and shushes me. And then his voice starts shouting over the tannoy, drowning out everything else. 'Come on, best in show. What'll you give me for her?' he cries. He raises his hand and starts the bidding. 'Thirty pound, thirty pound, thirty pound, forty pound . . . I'm looking for more than that. A young one, too. Come on, now, let's see how high you can raise it . . . and a pen of a hundred and six lambs thrown in.'

A sea of faces is pressing hard up against the rail. For a split second, it occurs to me to walk out, but I kill that idea instantly. It is unthinkable: it will be misunderstood as cowardice, humiliation, rage or shame. No one leaves their animals once they are in the ring. And more than anything, I do not want him to win on such a cheap point. To hell with him, I think fiercely. I will show my sheep professionally.

Only the crowd picks up on my discomfort, and the heckling begins.

'Lovely gigots and hocks!' someone shouts. There is a roar of appreciative laughter. A few low calls and whistles. 'Let's have a feel of her, make sure she's as good as she looks.'

A louder shout from the back: 'A fine-looking ewe!' And then, as the tannoy crackles with the rising voice of the auctioneer recording the bids, the atmosphere changes. The fine skin on the back of my neck shivers and my shoulders tense. I recognise this feral, predatory undertone. I know that no harm will come to me and yet I feel intensely alone and vulnerable. But I am determined not to let them see it get to me. Eyes glittering and cheeks burning, I stay focused in spite of the hot anger kindling inside me.

The two stockmen are in the ring with me, banging sticks on the ground to control the sheep. One gives a crack to a back and I shout angrily as the lamb's skittering body leaps forwards and its head strikes the metal gates. Each time the stockmen come near, I drive the sheep the other way. We swirl round and round together in a kind of grotesque dance. The bidding seems endless, but at last it is over and the hammer slams down. As the final bid is marked, the auctioneer hands the ticket to me. 'Well done, you're a tough lassie – now that was a good girl.' I do not look at him. I do not shake his hand. I just take my ticket. I know my voice will be unsteady. But I cannot leave without saying something. I have to force myself to address him coolly.

'That whole performance was out of order and unnecessary.'

'Ah, but you got a good price. So don't tell me you're not happy with that.'

I turn away quickly, so he doesn't see the hot tears in my eyes.

That burning anger stays with me all day, stoked by a rising sense of injustice and of the auctioneer not having played by the rules. I feel both humiliated and compromised: by accepting the buyer's cheque my hands are bound. My lambs command one of the top prices of the day, but it is a bitter bargain. The words I really want to say only come later. I promise myself I will never sell my lambs in this ring again.

Later, on the ferry home, the farmers make a joke of it. So I ask, 'Would you have treated your wife or daughter the same?' They dismiss this with the same old argument. 'You got a good price, what more do you want?'

And in their own way, they are right – at the auction, it is a man's world and meat is meat – but so am I.

I am glad of the peace and stability of the croft. It teaches me to watch over my animals ever more diligently, through quiet observation and gentle handling. It toughens me up as, with the hardening season, the grass gleams silver and cold glitters across the fields. Walking the croft at nightfall, you learn always to have one eye ahead, even as you heed, at your back, the weather and skies darkening. In the waning light, the croft's boundaries blur, becoming ever more indistinct, and you are aware that you must commit to memory the run of those march lines. I know I will have to keep my wits about me if I am to hold my own and earn my rightful claim to this fistful of soil, and my place in the farming world, in the long, gruelling winter months to come.

4

Dead Grass

IN THE SMOKING dusk, the grass is fired with strange lights and shadows. Below the horizon, the wind stills as the sun glows a deep afterburn, so the raw skies are lit with an eerie portent. It is always this way when an empty moon is rising and the tides sink low. It is a time when you can glimpse the moon's darkness facing the earth.

As I approach, the wrestling shape on the ground before me is beautiful and startling. Its plumage is soft and tawny and moves fluidly with a lithe grace all of its own. As it lifts and falls, it appears to dance with its own shadow. All the other roosting birds are silent, perched safe for the night. For a few minutes, I am transfixed. It is a strange creature, larger than a crow: a single body made up of four wings.

I look on as its component parts cleave together and then separate. It is hard to distinguish if this life is struggling to be free or struggling to be held. I guess it is a female buzzard feeding her fledging young, still grounded. Yet it hurts to watch, because she taunts the chick. There is a cruelty to the encounter – feral, primal and unsettling. The older bird forces the younger to flex its wings, to fight for regurgitated scraps. As soon as the fledgling is airborne, just a few feet off the ground, the parent lands against it heavily and knocks it down. There is something I recognise in this battle. The young bird is desperate for food, visibly exhausted by the relentless baiting and beating down. But it gets up, again and again, and takes what it needs to survive.

I blink blearily as the window is suddenly floodlit by the dazzling bright glare of headlights in the yard. It is late, some time gone midnight. I have been woken abruptly from a deep sleep, my arms wrapped about Maude in front of the cold fire. I am exhausted. The winter and early spring months are typically a time of rest before lambing, but every day, I am busy from dawn to dusk. Working outside is something I can do with my hands now they are slowly healing. Cutting back, washing containers, lifting plants or filling pots are all actions that strengthen the pincer movement between fingers and thumb that I have lost, and which the orthopaedic surgeons are unsure will ever properly come back. 'Let's give it some time before we think about breaking your hand again,' they say.

The headlights switch off. Then I hear a car door slam and heavy footsteps walking over the rough stones. There is no time to react; no time to turn off the lights in the house or close the curtains. Normally when this happens I have time to hide upstairs. The next second a man is standing inside my door. He is middle-aged, stocky, with a pale, waxen face. I stare at him, startled. It is not that I don't know him – on an island, everyone knows everyone. It is just that I do not want his company. This is something I often do battle with. The proud tradition that lights in a window signal open hospitality, and you do not refuse entry to anyone who comes to your door, is one that is too often abused.

Tonight I am too tired to deal with this. 'I'm sorry,' I say. 'It's far too late – I'm just on my way to bed.'

He smiles and shakes his head slowly. Then he falls heavily into an empty wooden chair, as if his legs have suddenly given way. A bottle of whisky is placed on the table. It is already close to empty. His eyes are watchful, glittering.

'Always time for one last dram before bed,' he slurs. 'Now, let's be having you. When's this man of yours coming back?'

I choose my words carefully. 'No, really. Please, you have to leave. I'm so tired – let's leave this for another day.'

As soon as I say this I am kicking myself. I am trying to keep the atmosphere light, my tone courteous, civil. But this open invitation is one I did not intend to offer. He knows this.

'That's not much of a welcome. Come on, don't be so . . .' he searches for the word he wants, then says it slowly, '. . . tight.'

He smiles mirthlessly. Then he reaches back and tips a glass off the counter. He picks up the bottle and angles its neck towards me. 'Want a dram?' I shake my head and watch as the amber liquid sloshes halfway up the glass. It is a quadruple-sized shot. I know as soon as it is poured that I will struggle to get that chair to empty.

'Not much hospitality here,' he mutters. 'You're all the same, you incomers. No sense of community. Slange!'

He knocks the drink back, then his hand reaches to fill the glass again.

'No, that's enough,' I say. 'I really think—'

'Better be leaving?' he cuts in. 'Like that, is it? I'll go when I'm ready. But I'm not ready. I'll tell you when I'm going. It's not just yet.'

It is a challenge. Wearily, I pull up a chair. Arguing only creates more problems. Hostility is easier to deal with when it is soft-handled. So I sit there and watch him drink. I am at a loss to know what else to do. I cannot physically remove him from the table. Drink can make a person prickly, sensitive, quick to take offence or start a fight. I do not want the atmosphere to deteriorate further. It is like treading on egg-shells. These days, I feel something brittle inside me is breaking, too. I keep an invisible momentum, angling him towards the door.

Drink is an unacknowledged problem on the island. This croft sits on what used to be a well-worn drinking track. It was different when Rab was here, but now that I am on my own it is unnerving to hear men outside the door at night, their hooting voices slurring – even when the house is in darkness. More than once, I have been woken by a group crowding through my door when I am asleep upstairs. The sound of someone in your house when you have not asked them, after those tense last years in London, always scares me. I lie there, holding my dog close to me. A few calls up the stairs, then they give up and I hear the door slam.

Another time stones are thrown up at my window. I have never hosted after-hours gatherings at my house, yet in the months after Rab left, even without an invitation, they came. It is easy to be caught off guard because these incidents are sporadic. The door is not locked – no one locks their doors on the island. It is a source of pride that in this small community, everyone knows everyone. The man in my kitchen tonight is not a regular. But it does not matter. He is still here uninvited and, when he is asked to leave, he refuses to go. Eventually, he departs of his own volition and, as I watch the headlights trail into the darkness, I wonder about fixing the lock.

These days, wherever I go, I have the sense that I am constantly dogged by a shadow. It has different voices, aspects, personalities and faces. But I know its shape and it knows me. That quick step and flicker of movement behind me. Sometimes I catch it out of the corner of my eye, or in a glance; other times, I can feel its arm silently wrestling me. When you start trying to avoid a shadow, daylight begins to feel brittle, ragged, sharp-edged; you become more vulnerable as you feel your own outline and shape, your confidence and trust, gradually disintegrating. In those early months, if I'd had the use of both my hands, I would have felt braver and stronger. I don't know if sound hands can stop whispers or shadows, but they can at least make you feel capable of fighting back or keeping yourself from harm.

One day I am challenged on the ferry by a group of local men. It is a simple but loaded accusation. It is a relief to hear it so that I can confront it head-on.

'Are you happy now you've kicked him out?'

I wonder how much to say or not to say.

'Just wanted the croft all for yourself?'

I blink, because it hurts not just to hear this, but to know that someone wants to wield that sharp blade. I am at a loss. These men were not even friends of Rab's.

And then they use that word again. It is a basic, abrasive form of name-calling, but shocking none the less. It doesn't matter how many times you hear it, it always feels like grit in your eye or a stinging slap in the face. 'Bitch.' I know that word, with its sharp, upright letters. Not only have I heard it used of me before but, two months after Rab left, it was sprayed on to my walls in sheep-marker spray.

'We made a decision. It was the best thing for both of us,' I say. And then I am silent. I stare out of the window at the beautiful flowing sea. It is calming and somehow helps wash that deep hurt away. I do not say, 'It was the only way.' Sometimes there is no point in trying to explain.

Besides, it is still too raw to speak or even think of what happened all those months ago. Cristall says I am still recovering. 'Recovering from what?' I ask.

'Shock and a longer lack of love.'

In my heart I know it is this and not this. Fear takes a long time to settle. Some memories cast a dark cloud that blocks out the sunlight.

Sometimes I stare for hours at the horizon, thinking everything I might ever need is waiting for me out there.

It is restful gazing into a wider view. My eyes learn to lift and seek out the wilder birds and the mountains. I listen to the beautiful, haunting cries of the buzzard and eagle as they soar in the high passes, flexing their wings. It is strangely uplifting to journey with them. I imagine a pale sunlight streaming through feathers in a cold rush of flight. It is reassuring tracing the dependable, solid contours and rugged faces of those peaks. I draw strength and inspiration from their uncompromising, weathered profiles. The realisation that the landscape no longer overwhelms me is startling. Instead it holds me. It gives me strength and the courage to walk away from social structures I no longer need and which no longer have any sway over me.

The decision to start afresh is never simple. But when it is time to give up my job at the school, I know. I leave with a sense of relief as well as a bittersweet regret. I will miss the children. But there are other factors that make it easy to go. A voice calls after me: 'So you're off, then. Well, it was a fine wee job for you when you thought you could still have children.'

I do not rise to the bait. I merely turn and smile. Experience has taught me when to stay and fight and when to just walk away.

And I do miss the children. Life feels barer without their daily contact and laughter. But it tied me to a stale recycling of my own heartache, which I know is unhelpful and which I have to break. It is liberating to bind myself more closely to the croft, my spirit free to embark on the journey ahead of me.

I have made a new friend. It has beautiful tawny plumage and a hook-curled beak. I love to see it whilst I am working on the croft or walking on the hills. It is a delight to hear its call. I stop, straining to listen to the edge of its high-pitched mewing. It is a juvenile, and its cry is quite unlike that of a mature-sounding buzzard – shorter, with a repetitive staccato flow, rather than a single, yearning call. It is a sound that shears the air and slices into your thoughts. Perhaps that sharp quality is characteristic of a young bird. I love to watch its tentative fledgling flights. I seek it out and it watches me back. Over time, it lands lightly on fence posts and sits, eyeing me beadily. I talk to it and grow used to its company. It remains wild and vigilant, yet it starts to follow me closely. Its wings drift in my shadow, so that as I turn, often I see it overhead or alighting in the trees close by. Some days I hear its call when I wake. It makes me glad to open my eyes.

Gradually it claims the croft as its territory. I try not to worry about what this means. Any bird of prey settling on to a territory will inevitably pose a risk to smaller birds and other darting, quivering lives such as voles or mice. But one day it does not come and I miss it. It is a shock to realise that I am unwittingly in its thrall. The next time I see it, I am unsettled by a look in its eye. It swivels its head and fixes its gaze on a small starling on the windowsill. I make a sudden movement to distract it and it lifts away. And I am shaken, because in its keen eyes, the cruel curve of its beak and its unblinking gaze, I saw the face of a predator. For all my observance, its feeding is invisible to me. I see only a fragment of this bird's daily life, whilst its clear, sharp eyes see everything.

*

It is a bright day but I am sitting in my house, resting with Maude, watching the birds bobbing on the windowsill. A rose wraps around the frame. I have made soft string ties and hung the wire support of the beautiful climber with simple bird feeders. Every morning I fill them with suet mixed with fresh berries and seeds. One bird is different from the others. It seems shy and sits apart, reluctant to feed with the other birds. The others recognise its difference. As it is quietly picking seeds, the resident starling colony descends and mobs it. I watch as a noisy scuffle unfolds. The solitary bird tries to fend them off but soon takes fright. For several minutes the starlings engage in a feeding frenzy, and then, as rapidly as they arrived, they are gone. It is only then that the smaller bird returns. I smile as it dips its head and starts to pick at the seeds again.

Suddenly, a familiar dark shadow hurls itself against the window. Sharp talons grip the bird, tearing at its chest and throat. The assault is so swift that I am rooted to the spot, looking on in horrified silence. There is a faint fluttering and an agonising shriek. Afterwards, I stare at the empty feeder as tiny feathers drift to the ground.

That spring I make up a new tradition. I designate the end of lambing as the turning point of the year and mark it with my own ritual. It has been a hard, lean winter. As the sun rises high above the mountains, I set light to the old dead grass of the hayfield and the rougher, fallow ground. Its desiccated stalks are wind-dried and frost-burned, holding scant nutritional value for the horse and sheep. All that remains of the beautiful green flowing grasses is bleached white like the old bones of the land. Their brittle stems are hollow, the precious seed heads scattered long ago.

In the old myths of regeneration, the dead land was purged of all that sucked it dry. I am forging my own future, erasing years of crofting hardship on this pyre. It is a still day, yet as the fire catches, the heat scorches my face and arms so I beat it with wet cloths, setting new boundaries for the crackling edges of those smouldering flames. Sometimes you have to cut yourself loose from the dead grass of your outworn existence. I know I need to make and break my own rules. I watch as the fire incinerates those dark memories, burning them to oblivion. Witnessing my old life disintegrating is strangely liberating and brings a new perspective on some things I am still striving to make sense of. I wonder what exactly I will need to do differently in future in order to free myself from the island's rigid strictures and start to live on my own terms.

Yet for all my determination to break new ground, I do not know where I am heading. Sometimes change forces your hand, and comes to find you before you are quite ready for it. Life is always a struggle. But there is one thing I know for sure: every time you are knocked down, you get up. Every single time.

5

Swallow

I HAVE MISSED YOU,' Cristall says.

'I have missed you, too,' I admit. 'I am glad the lambing is over for another year.'

We talk as we work. Somehow it is easier to talk about important things out here in the fresh air, our fingers snapping pea pods off budding plants entwined around willow canes. The sound is cool, crisp, rasping. The air is heady with the scent of broken sweet peas. Where the dogs have scurried, the earth smells rich, of shadows, tousled ears and soft wings.

'Tell me, is it still so hard?' I ask quietly. I know some days are worse than others, and that those days are a struggle for her. I try to offer some comfort, but I am lost for words. I have been busy and it is difficult to know how to help. And then her eyes fill with tears. 'Oh, my dear girl. I miss him so much it's as if it happened only yesterday.

And yet it is so hard to talk about. It is somehow shocking to say how I feel.'

Grief is still too close to both of us. It has been two years since Anthony died of pancreatic cancer. It was a shattering loss, a life over in a matter of weeks. Something felt so deeply, some bond torn away so brutally, that it left only half a life behind. Cristall tells me how, in nature, it takes a greening plant two or three full seasons to heal a deep incision, longer still if you cut off a limb or a leading branch. She tells me that it takes time for a notch to grow, and longer still to bud, before it can start flowering again. How sometimes the branch just dies, and then it is only a matter of time until it must be cut back entirely.

'I sometimes think the life in me has died,' Cristall whispers. 'I miss him so much, I wish that my life would end so I can be close to him. So I can be with him. Are you shocked? I wish for this every day since he died. Some days the feeling passes. But some days it stays there. Maybe it never goes away entirely. But I know it's wrong to think like this. So each day, I wake up, force myself to get up, and get on with life.'

And in my own small way, I think I understand. My own suffering is written deep into my body, in all the subtle ways only a kindred spirit can intimately know. 'Don't give in to it,' she tells me. 'Keep taking one breath in and one breath out. Keep holding on to the small things and the usual small routines. Routine is important when you live alone.' I know what she means. I try to keep busy when I feel that tightness constrict me like a bird in a snare. Loneliness can catch you off guard. It is like balancing on a high wire waiting to slip.

Outwardly we both maintain we are fine. We each put on a well-rehearsed, near-perfected front. She glitters. I stay vigilant. But when you sit with a friend so close, out here, there is no hiding. We are both tired of being brave. 'I am so alone that sometimes I do not know myself,' I confess. Cristall understands that sometimes I find it hard to explain how that feels. It is as if I am cut adrift, as if I am lost or have been left alone in the dark. Some days I cannot move. The weight in my heart is too heavy.

We work on in companionable silence. A shared solitude is one that comes of a long, trusting friendship. When she next speaks, her voice lifts light as a bird's song. 'Life is all about finding a slipstream, a safe passage. If you can do this, then things will start to steady again.' Our conversations often go like this. The last difficult years pared back to just a few words. 'And you know you always have me.' She reaches out and gently takes my hands.

'Promise me you won't leave me,' she says quietly. 'Family is so close in spirit, but so far away. What we share is a special bond. Promise me, if anything happens, to one of us or both of us, that we'll leave this island together. I couldn't bear to stay or to leave without you. I don't want to be alone.'

'I will go wherever you go,' I say solemnly.

'And promise me if, God forbid, anything happens to me, that wherever we are you will look after Isla. She knows you and loves you. I would feel happier if I knew she could stay with you.'

I nod. 'I give my word.' She squeezes my hand.

'I cannot imagine my life without you,' I tell her. And then I take a deep breath and say it again, only this time looking straight into her eyes. It matters to do this. There are so few times in life when you really say what you mean. We hug tightly. I want to hold on to this moment. I feel so happy it almost hurts.

Then we are laughing, the wind blowing on our backs, Cristall's dog Isla springing about us ecstatically. It is a release, when you have been talking of real, serious things, to laugh out loud. To feel the elation in those racing paws whirling circles, the peeled-back ears and panting breath. To feel that wilder, joyful self come alive inside. And suddenly it is easier to breathe, because life is a beautiful, simple thing.

The next morning, early, I am in the garden. Cristall goes past on her way to the ferry. She is waving out of the window of her battered Peugeot. 'Toot toot!' she calls. I smile and wave back. I watch her go and then I think, I wish I had told her I love her, that she is like my family. It is there in my heart, but I wish I had said it out loud.

'I love you,' I call after her. I shout it again, louder. 'I love you!'

But already she is gone.

Later, in the afternoon, I go to catch the ferry. It is my first trip in many months to the mainland. I am going to meet Cristall for tea at the small hotel that sits at the top of the slipway facing back over the sea to the island. She has been for lunch with her brother and sister-in-law, who live an hour's drive away, on another island further down the coast. As the ferry throttles its way over the water, I let my head rest against the glass of the window. I blink at the sunlight refracting off the sea. It is a beautiful afternoon and a quick crossing today. The sea is rushing out at turn of the high water. The seals are basking, wet viscous pelts glistening heavy on the rocks. Sandpipers and curlew are already wading through the upper shallows. Sharp beaks stab into the first low pools left behind by the tide.

Back across the water, the island rests in its fierce tidal channel. It is brilliant green in the bright sunshine, a tiny Hebridean jewel. And suddenly I catch a strange feeling flickering inside me. It is as if my heart is smiling. I look up at the swallows rising and falling above me. And I think of how the season is turning, and how perhaps life may change for me. For a minute, I wonder, is this happiness? It is so long since I have known happiness, I cannot be sure. But it is a different feeling, and that is enough. I am grateful for it.

I remember the promise I shared with Cristall. It somehow connects me to the landscape in a new way, as if I have close kin and a sense of belonging here of my own. I feel rooted by the strength of that bond. As I breathe in the sunshine, it is as if summer has sped in from behind the mountains and lifted all the grey from the world. I smile as I recall how she greeted me as she drove past in her blue car so early this morning. And then I think of all the ways she matters to me. We have looked after each other so closely that we have woven unbreakable ties.

As I step off the ferry, I smile at the ferryman. I walk up to the little hotel at the top of the slip. This is still a working pier and already the fishing boats are tying up. Baskets of fresh langoustines, crab and fish are being unloaded and packed. It is so different from my London life. There is a simplicity to each day, and yet it is busier and fuller in more ways than I ever remember experiencing in all those years in town. I step into the bar and restaurant. It is a treat to sit at a table and order a freshly made coffee. Strange how such small things can bring such pleasure.

An hour later, I am standing by the hotel window, watching the sun dip behind clouds. I stare out through the glass. Oystercatchers are high-stepping the low tide, bills bent low, bright orange eyes darting into the wet gullies and ebbing pools. Powder-white gulls soar the clear air, harsh cries tearing the high reaches. I blink and try to steady myself, to take in all the things Cristall so loves.

She has not yet arrived because there has been an accident, two cars in a collision, and the road has been temporarily closed. And then the receptionist is beckoning me, holding up the receiver of her phone. I listen in disbelief as she tells me, 'A doctor wants to speak to you. It is your friend Cristall in one of those cars.'

And suddenly my feet are running across the floor and my heart is beating so fast it feels like I am floating.

'Is she OK?' I ask immediately. 'Is she hurt?' My voice is sharp, anxious.

'Please don't worry. She is OK. Everything is going to be fine.'

I heave a sigh of relief. The doctor needs a telephone number for her daughter who lives down south – the others are in New Zealand – and I kick myself that I don't have it to hand because I have left my phone at home. But I am grateful, and touched, that he has thought to call her, so that she can come as soon as she can. 'That is so kind of you, and she will need that,' I say. 'Someone to help me look after her.' And, I think, Cristall's daughter will want to visit her, if she has to go into hospital. I give him the number of someone on the island who I think may be able to help, and then I reassure him, 'OK, I'm on my way, I'll be ten minutes,' because I know it will take her daughter some time to get here. And I know Cristall will want me with her.

He sounds distracted. 'No, better to stay where you are,' he says firmly. 'There's a long queue of traffic, and you won't get through. It's all cordoned off by the police, and they don't know you.'

'But she's OK?' Anxious, I press the point.

'Yes, she's OK. Just stay put so I can ring you straight back. Trust me, everything is going to be fine.' Only suddenly the line goes quiet, until he says hurriedly, 'I'm sorry, I have to go.' And then there is just a flat tone. He has rung off. It is only when I go back to my table and sit down that I think, why does he want to speak to her daughter personally, if there is nothing to worry about?

I will ring for a taxi and go straight to her, I resolve, the instant he calls. But the phone doesn't ring. I grow more frustrated as the minutes pass. I know I must sit tight but I am desperate to get moving. The doctor did not say if she was hurt. I try to push the thought out of my mind, but it refuses to go. I realise there will be things she needs, so I try to distract myself by making a list.

An hour later, the phone rings again and a paramedic is talking to me. His voice is calm, low, measured and professional, so I know this is more serious than I had ever imagined.

'What's happened?' I ask, my heart going cold. And suddenly I am frightened.

He tells me carefully that it was a head-on collision. That Cristall is still conscious, but she is trapped inside the car and they cannot get to her. 'It's a mess. The fire brigade are cutting the roof off the vehicle,' he reassures me. 'It is the only way they will be able to free her. The car is a wreck.'

When he says that I know that Cristall would want me there. Because I know she will be frightened, trapped in her mangled car alone. I am so sure of this it makes my throat catch. And in that instant, all I can see are her beautiful sky-blue eyes. I am already picking up my bag to leave, and he knows this. He is trained to know this. 'Please stay where you are,' he tells me. 'We're doing everything we can for her.'

After the line goes dead, I find I am still clutching the receiver, white-knuckled, hanging on to it as if to a lifeline. I hold on fiercely to every word he has said to me.

I feel so helpless.

I stare through the window at the gulls clustering around the fishing boats out on the water, wishing I was a bird, able to stretch its wings and fly swiftly across that open skyscape. I make a quick calculation of how long it will take me to reach the hospital. As my eyes follow the ferry disappearing into the distance, low clouds scudding across the water, the sun dips behind the mountains. Home is still there, only it is suddenly in shadow.

I wait. I do not move. I stay because they tell me to stay. I listen. I trust. It's OK, everything's going to be OK, I tell myself over and over again. As if by repeating something you can make it true. It will take me years to understand why I stayed put when I should have been with her, and still longer to forgive myself. I cannot retrace the footsteps I didn't make.

Authority has a way of making you less brave. Trust is a subtle, dangerous thing. You hand over your voice, tether your instinct. That sickening realisation comes suddenly in a wave. I do not make it outside. I run to the ladies' room and then I am not sure what happens, because time unravels. All I remember is that hard floor and my fingers white, clutching the rim of the basin.

I am standing shakily back at the reception desk. The bar is empty. There is no one in sight. I walk past the bar into the small restaurant. A waitress is folding napkins.

'Have you any news? What has happened?' I ask her, worriedly.

She looks at me, uncomprehending.

'The car accident.'

Her eyes widen as she understands. She carefully puts down the napkin she is folding. And then she folds her hands.

'I'm sorry, but she didn't make it.'

I can see her lips moving and hear the sound of her voice, but I can't make sense of her words. I stand there, lost, staring into the blinding sun.

'No, that can't be true. The doctor said she was fine. He told me himself.' But suddenly, I am panicking. 'Please, tell me what has happened. I need to know,' I insist. 'I am close to her.'

She shakes her head, very slowly. 'It is true,' she says, 'the old lady died. It is very sad.' I stare at her, stricken. And then comes that awful moment when it hits you that the world is not as you know it. And that it will never be the same again.

Behind the waitress, through the glass window, the swallows are whirling, diving, soaring. But now that pale-blue sky hurts my eyes. I am lost, my heart searching for that life I love, careering through a sky raining blue swallows, white sunlight, rushing air.

I scan her face desperately, but she looks down at her hands and quietly sighs, then returns to folding the linen napkins. She is called Ana and she comes from Romania. I know her casually, in the way people recognise each other but know little of each other's lives.

The room closes in. I just stand there, sucking air. Weaving life into death. Silence into sound. Swallow wings and a blue sky. Trying to make it bearable, comprehensible. This is one of those pivotal events you know will always hurt. One of those catastrophes you know you may never understand.

What is a life? And where does it go, when it is so shockingly, abruptly over? I close my eyes tightly. Every time I open them it hurts to be in the world again. I feel in that blue sky a cruel contradiction, that something so beautiful can bear witness to something so terrible.

'Please,' I whisper. It is not a question, more a cry for help. As Ana starts to speak to me, horrifying images fill the gaps in my consciousness. I can smell the burning tyres, dark tracks on scorched tarmac carving a hole in my mind. A broken fence, metal flung in sheets over the road and two cars abandoned at awkward angles, like toys tossed aside. One is inverted, like a broken bone piercing through ragged, torn skin, the other is concertinaed into a tree. And then there are the crumpled bodies, shadows slumped over a wheel. Suddenly it hurts to breathe. Some things are too much to imagine.

I blink, stare out through the window. I know Cristall is out there somewhere. All that is separating us is glass. I can feel her. I can feel her so close, I can sense her breath. She is in the wings of the swallows, wrapping her arms about the sky. I can hear her voice, see the sky blue of her eyes, feel her laugh ringing.

All I can do is open and close my eyes. I cannot cry. 'Stay with me,' I whisper. 'Please don't leave.'

I can feel her in the blinks of light on the window, small fragments of a rainbow. One life exhaling its last beautiful sigh. So I touch that light, place my hand over it, as if I might hold it for ever, but when I lift my hand, it is gone.

I turn to Ana. My eyes cling to her face. 'Please help me,' I whisper.

Our eyes meet. We are both embarrassed by my naked vulnerability. She has brown eyes. Golden orbits around the iris. They look at me for a long moment, long enough that you know, at some point, one of you will have to consciously look away. I gaze across the distance between us, my eyes pleading, 'Do you see what I see? Can you feel what I feel?' She is the one who looks away. We are standing so close together, I can see her pulse beating in the soft hollow at her throat. I think, someone will have kissed her there.

We sense another's need and desperation. Why can we not feel another's pain? Why, when someone dies, unless they are loved by us, can we not feel even a fraction of that grief? Is it because it is too much, our brains too small and our hearts too fragile, to hold more pain than our own?

Ana shakes her head. She sighs, distracted. Then she glances at her watch. 'It was a bad smash. The road will be closed for hours.' She has a beautiful voice. She stares hard at me and then fiddles with a ring on her finger. For a long minute, we both look at her hands. Then she shrugs matter-of-factly. 'I am sorry. I thought you knew.'

Moments like this, you need someone, something to hold on to. But there is no one. So your heart just keeps running after what you have lost, as if love alone, and a voice crying out a name, over and over, can bring it back. And so I whisper, 'Please. Do not go. Stay with me.'

Ana hands me a glass of water. My hand is shaking. I spill most of it, so I put it down.

'Please,' she says. 'You cannot stand here. Service is about to start.'

She reaches out then, uncertainly, to put her hand awkwardly on my shoulder. It feels small and unfamiliar. Instinctively, she does not take my hand, so it flutters between us in suspended animation. I feel for her and I feel for me. Two strangers, forced momentarily into intimacy by a random tragedy.

'I am sorry,' she says quietly. 'Truly I am.'

I sit waiting for the ferry. The skipper is early. He sits down next to me but does not look at me. It is strangely comforting to sit in silence, just to feel another body there beside you. He stares at the sea. Then he says, 'Aye, it's shocking news.'

I know that he knows I know. For a moment, we both watch the gulls. And once again, those birds give me an inner strength to ask, 'Please, tell me everything you know.' I am desperate to fill in the gaps, even as every cell in my body is screaming that this is not happening, can't be real. Taking courage from the landscape, I brace myself to listen, all the while fixing my eyes on the water as an extraordinary sunset irradiates the skies. And that light is so exquisite, I am grateful for it. I do not blink, even though it is dazzling, as I hear of the small miracle that Cristall survived the impact, was conscious and able to whisper her name. Only when they cut her free and lifted her out did her body begin to collapse; it was the metal that was holding her together, keeping her breathing. How she died in the helicopter on the way to Glasgow A&E, up with the swallows in that beautiful blue empty air.

I drive up the island but I cannot see the road through my tears. I stall the old pick-up in the yard and abandon it there, keys still in the ignition. I walk in a slow stagger across the yard. Shock drains you suddenly after its adrenaline high.

My house is empty but still my hands reach out to hold someone, something. I crouch down and hold the soft green leaves, stems, flowers, plants. And then I kneel and tug at the grass. I rip out huge clumps and hold them up to the sky. I lift my head and call out, my voice lost in the blue as I scream her name. I am sobbing so hard that I cannot recognise my voice. Inside I feel hollow, my pain blowing through the dark ragged hole of my mouth. No words come, but if there are any I want them to be hers, not mine. I know she is still somewhere close by. And so I wrap myself in a blanket and sit under the darkening sky. I listen and cry until I fall asleep, my wet cheek on the grass. Hours later, I have no voice left. And then I am silent. My voice has turned to dust.

In the morning I wake stiff and cold. It is a beautiful day. When I go inside and wash my face, I do not recognise the haggard reflection in the mirror. I am an apparition, with tufts of white hair at my brow line where there was none before. Later, researching in medical books, I learn that this can happen in extreme instances of acute stress.

That day, Isla comes to stay with me. I curl up with her on the floor, pressing my nose against her soft ears and inhaling the smell of the wind in her coat. She sighs and licks my cheeks. Her tail thumps – she is waiting to go home. Later, I take her there. I have to find Cristall's passport, documentation – all the small threads of a life. The family needs it for the procurator fiscal. It is too much to go alone. So we go together, Isla and I. To say goodbye.

I start crying when we get there and cannot stop. I switch off the engine and sit clutching the steering wheel. Isla licks my cheek then burrows down into the seat and refuses to move. I know she knows. It is difficult for both of us. In the end I put her on a lead. I open the gate, and we walk slowly into the house. It is like walking into a different world. A world that was yesterday. A world now gone.

Everything is as Cristall left it: a half-drunk cup of coffee, a jumper draped over the back of a chair. The space is so quiet, all its life spirited away. We sit in there for hours. Feeling the heavy weight of furniture without the hand that moves it, that brings it to life.

It is difficult to look for the documents. I do not want to open drawers or hidden spaces. They belong to a life that is not mine. It is only when we get up to leave that I see a swallow sitting watching us on the inside of the window. I cannot understand how it got in, because the doors and windows are all shut. But it helps to have this small life with us in the absence of another. The bird hops on to the cold stove and looks straight at me with inquisitive, beady eyes. It opens its beak as if it has something to say, but no sound comes out. And then it ruffles its feathers and hops to the back door. I open the glass panels slowly. It looks at me again and then it flies away. When she sees it go, Isla gets up. She walks to the truck and does not look back. And that is when I know she knows Cristall is dead. That this is no longer home.

The family arrives. We grieve together and alone. We do not bury Cristall but scatter her ashes as she asked, returning her to the wind, mountains and skies.

Her ash is soft and fine. I try not to breathe: I want her to be free on the wind, not stuck in the hard grief of my lungs. I dip my fingers slowly and take a small handful. It clings and sticks to my fingers so it is hard to let go. It feels strange to hold her in my hand – a life so loved reduced to a grey, soft powder. The ring of her laugh, the bright blue iridescence of her clear eyes. These are her thoughts. Her heart and song. I walk with her and take her into my garden, and to all the favourite places on the island that she so loved.

There is a secret part of me that wants to keep some of her in my pocket. To sit again with me beside the fire. To play cards, chess, to cook, garden, talk, drink wine. But I do not do this, because I know where she would most like to be. We say goodbye quietly together, Isla, Cristall and me. I do not dig a hole – it is too dark and damp in the soil. Instead, I brush a handful of her ashes gently over the trees and plants we once planted together, years before, as tiny shoots and seeds. Each leaf, each plant, each place is a memory. The rest I scatter into the wind.

After her house is cleared, I fill my home with her belongings, surrounding myself with all the things she loved. All the clutter, debris, bric-a-brac. Furniture, books, Tupperware boxes, salt and pepper pots. Paintings from her walls. I can barely move for this physical collateral, my home and I both steeped in grief. It seems strange to others, but I need to have her near to me in these things. How we experience grief is unique and intensely personal. Sometimes I think I can hear her in another room, but when I look the room is empty. She is there, but always out of sight.

You do not get over death. It simply becomes an intrinsic part of your own fabric. Whenever I scent the sticky buds of the balsam poplar, it always makes my heart sing and grieve. And I stop. I look for the swallows. I turn my face into the wind. I say her name in my heart. And slowly, over time, it doesn't hurt to breathe. And I am able to start to talk of her.

It is nearly seven years before I find a kind of peace. I meet for coffee with a firefighter, a local man, who talks to me about how he was the first to arrive at the scene of the accident. The first to find her there. He recalls how, as he knelt down, she slowly opened her eyes.

The wonder of this. The miracle of life. He tells me how for him that image is still as vivid as it was that day. How she was able to whisper her name. How she smiled, a trembling flutter across her face, as she fought to stay conscious, to stay alive.

Listening to his words is not easy. Afterwards they find me, even when I am not seeking them. It is so hard when you do not get to say goodbye. It leaves some part of you adrift. You have to find those words of farewell, in silence, alone in your heart.

I am here. I am there. I want to know. I want to know all and all and all of this, and why it ever happened. And why anything like this ever happens. His kind voice, and the hurt I can see in his eyes as he recounts everything he can remember, makes me so glad that he was there for her. It comforts me to know that she died with kindness and love. It brings me a sense of closure I have been searching for all these years. It helps me to understand that the love you have felt will never leave you.

6

Tup

I AM NOT ready at the door until close to midnight. When I glance at the clock, my jittery fingers start dropping the things I have gathered: ropes, tools, a full-size body bag, gloves and a head torch. Some jobs are better done quietly at night. As the door clicks shut behind me, Maude whines softly, but I steel myself even as my heart flinches, appalled at the thought of what lies waiting for me to unearth. A skein of sweat prickles on the back of my neck and scalp. All my fears and doubts are jostling as my brain desperately seeks an alternative, but my instinct insists: 'It's now or never.'

I snap on the head torch, which flickers a dim, wavering beam, then pick up the shovel, and start walking quickly over the fields. I didn't plan it this way but I daren't go back on my new-found resolve. Tonight is Hallowe'en and I am raising my own dead. I am digging up my beloved tup, buried six weeks ago, and then I am going to drive him on the first early boat to the Oban mortuary, and on to the Glasgow veterinary pathologist to find out what killed him.

It is hard to walk fast when you are carrying unwieldy kit. As I cross the croft, I prang the shovel and its metal edges fall clattering against a rock. It is unsettling how far the sound carries. An owl screeches then silently drifts ahead of me, wings sculling towards the grave. It is a beautiful night with low cloud cover, wisps of scudding light that show the wind is up over the sea. Already there is a dim glow behind the mountains. As the crescent moon rises, these fields will gleam with a crystalline, silver light. And then there will be no place to hide.

I am dreading the thought of uncovering him, but each time I tell myself, just let it be, my instinct quivers. It is an awful feeling when you are unsure if something that has happened is just an unfortunate accident or a natural occurrence, or if, as my gut hints, a possible injustice or wrongful deed has been done. I want to know, but I am torn. I hesitate to start digging as I wrestle with a growing sense of crisis. Time is of the essence: every minute my tup is under the soil, the natural process of decomposition will make the result of any scientific testing harder to read. Finally I make my decision, and I am strangely relieved as the first cut slices wet into turf. With each thud of earth I edge closer to the grave.

Before he died my tup was in prime condition, still braw and beautiful after winning a clutch of fluttering rosettes and prizes at the island show, including the coveted Purebred Sheep Champion silver cup. His success followed another auction where my lambs reached top prices in the commercial sales, and were commended amongst 10,000 livestock heads passing through the markets that day. On the island, they are marked for breeding rather than simply sold for meat. But when the lambs were sold, I was mocked and undermined by local farmers who made me doubt the quality of the lambs and my own ability to raise them. I had not planned to continue with commercial lambing, only I felt trapped, and unable to relinquish it. If I give up my sheep, I am scared I will lose the croft. It has happened to others. Whispers can facilitate this; a croft needs to be worked. Its grass cries for its own livestock. When a piece of soil is so coveted and its history is alive, still rippling with older disputes and grievances that pre-date our arrival, I know to ensure that every blade is grazed. This year's lambs are the first offspring of my tup's huge pedigree. It is incredibly rewarding, having invested my all into this daring venture. They are the finest I have ever bred, with his beautiful conformation and strong, noble head.

The last time I saw my tup alive, he was feeding quietly from a bucket. Afterwards he nickered to me, rubbing his beautiful great brow gently against my legs. It was utterly shocking to find him dead the next morning. I stared dismayed at his lifeless body. It was heart-breaking to see his eyes glazed over, unmoving. I tried to close them gently. As I wrapped my arms about him, my own eyes filled with tears. Yet even in my distress I was puzzled by where I discovered him: face-down in a shallow ditch, hidden out of sight – a narrow space against a fence immediately behind his freshly laid covered stabling. It made no sense to me, because at night he always slept inside with sweet summer hay and a bucket of clean water, sheltered from the wind and weather. It hurt me to see his beautiful head soiled in the mud, so I washed his face. Afterwards, I dug a hole, laid it with fresh straw and buried him. It did not occur to me not to bury him. And I did not tell anyone of his death. You do not think straight when you are in shock.

All the fight was punched out of me that day. That night, after I covered him over with soil, gently trod it down and arranged the turf over the grave, I wrapped myself in blankets and I sat out on the hill.

I stayed up all night, gazing upwards, until the skies lightened. Even though the sky was clear, it was hard to see the stars. Ever since Cristall's death, I had desperately needed to see those hard blinks of light. I kept searching but that night the darkness was impenetrable.

The day of the show had been overcast before the rain began to fall. Watching my tup standing, ears pricked and densely muscled after careful feeding, I felt a surge of pride. He was solid at eighty kilos, every ounce a pedigree, and I was nervous and excited to realise that we stood a chance. At last I felt my time had come to join hands with the farming community in solidarity and mutual support. I was determined and hopeful that I would do this without compromising my own voice. It's time to show what we're made of, I resolved, as I smoothed his newly clipped fleece with a soft cloth. It was a thrill to feel ready for this challenge. Initially, the atmosphere was bright, but predictably it deteriorated steadily as bottles were emptied, and hooves and boots spattered mud. As the mood shifted, I started to feel uneasy. In the ring, my 'pet tup' was mocked, and I was derided for entering him. A woman assisting with scores was angry and refused to wish me luck. 'You've no place here at all,' she said.

'But I was invited.'

She glared at me. 'You shouldn't have come. It's man's work. The ring is no place for a woman.'

I kept moving. There was no time to be downhearted and this was no more than I was expecting. 'You and I, we can do this,' I told my tup quietly. I had worked hard to get here, practising daily for nine months to handle him safely after being charged and brutally knocked to the ground. It had taken courage, commitment and effort. I suddenly realised how much today mattered to me, and how much I had learned. All the same I was astonished as each category class my tup entered, he won. At the prize-giving I was elated. We had done far better than I'd ever dreamed possible. As well as being awarded Champion Purebred Sheep, we were given an overall First Reserve, a string of rosettes and two silver cups by an independent judge. If only I had known how quickly those bright toys would lose their shine. Sometimes, when I look back, I wish that I had never attended that show.

This felt like such a premature end to his life. He was only three years old. It sickened me all the more to remember the awful sleepless nights caused by the stress of the thinly veiled threats after the show. 'I can't do this any more,' I swore bitterly. 'I am having nothing more to do with farming or sheep.' Perhaps it was because I was so hurt, grief-stricken and confused that I kept his death a secret. Yet I also felt a churning sense of anger, aware that it might delight others to know he was dead. Knowledge is currency on the island, and it is a gleeful cold wind that rushes in to blow tall poppies down.

Yet something about the circumstances of the tup's death left me disorientated and uneasy. Call it a hunch, but whatever it was, it just did not sit right. Animals die, sometimes for no apparent reason. Yet mine were sheared, dosed, wormed, inoculated, fed on herb-rich pasture. My ewes and lambs, in prime health, had also been commended at the show. I checked the field for any possible toxic plant, but there was none apparent. It was all the more mystifying to see the companion lambs in full health in the same field. My suspicions grew as small things bothered me: gates found not as I had left them, other details that didn't stack up.

Some weeks later, all those small details and others came together and I blamed myself bitterly for burying my tup so quickly. A chance remark someone made left me shocked and suddenly alert, questioning. Rumours do not start with no tinder and no fuel. Those words stayed with me, causing me to wake sweating and anxious in the night, and afterwards I followed up that lead with a longer conversation that is witnessed by a friend. Pathological testing to ascertain a cause of death is standard good practice, especially in the case of a pedigree animal. I realised that I had acted in haste.

Quietly, I did some research, talking to breeders, veterinary practices and animal health departments as well as poring for hours over fact sheets and medical reports. 'The only way you will know is to exhume him,' the advice came back. 'But you need to be quick, because the body's own autolysis and process of rotting and degradation will destroy the tissues needed to establish a cause of death.' At first, the thought of such a drastic course of action appalled me. Instinctively, I turned from that horror and chose to leave him to rest in peace, reasoning that it would be impossible to lift or drag him out of the ground.

Only later, I changed my mind. It becomes imperative to act when a creeping sliver of doubt persists, because uncertainty is acidic, corrosive. It burns into the connective tissue of your own thoughts, eats away at your peace of mind. That is when you need an explanation to put you out of your misery.

Tupping is a ritual still regarded as the province of the island's men. My lambs, commanding top prices in the markets for both meat and breeding, have helped me earn my right to my own fistful of soil. But by raising a tup I have been playing with fire. The ram is seen traditionally as the bringer of life to the island with its insemination of the ewes, and its newborn lambs, anchoring the cycle of the seasons, marked by the church, that drives the farming year. Its essence is the sacred phallus that procreates its seed – a symbol of fertility long since wrested from the ancient guardianship of the matriarchal goddesses and priestesses – which continues to be protected by the men with vigilance and circumspection.

I knew it would ruffle feathers to encroach on this domain and that I would need to tread carefully. Yet to carve my own rightful place in this fiercely competitive territory, I also knew I would have to dig deep and discover for myself my own inner strength. It felt important that I was able to finally draw my own boundaries and establish my own set of rules and values for my own practice, if I was not just to continue getting by, but to be able, at last, to thrive. I thought of all I had endured and lived through, in all the years since I arrived, to create a livelihood and viable home.

Healing comes sooner with a salve than by leaving a wound open. It is strange how whispers flicker. You can feel their heat at your edges, even if you cannot see their flames. Lying awake at night, I have looked at the stars and wondered what they know. It is like that with all that lies buried.

My father once said to me: 'The stars are always watching, even when you think nothing is there. They are always there, even in the daytime, when all you can see is clouds. When I die I shall be a star up there. One small star, shining its light over the world.' His usually troubled eyes were radiant, his whole being fired with an iridescence not, as it often was, fuelled by alcohol. So I know there would have been times when he, too, needed to find a bright light in those skies.

I asked him, 'Why a star?'

I will never forget the sorrow etched into his face. 'Because when you are a star, you are free of the earth.'

I think of my father whenever I look up at the stars. But the truth is, he is everywhere. He is everywhere I am and everywhere I look. My father is the light in my eyes and my darkness. He is the fierce, warm sun and cold, dark moon. His death was as disturbing as his life. Even though he died three months after Rab left, I can still feel his presence. I want to say, I forgive you, for your love, anger, despair and violence. I want to break that cycle of trauma that was always yours – a six-year-old child growing up in a tin shanty hut in the townships, condemned forever to watch his own father, in the Apartheid years in South Africa, hacked down before his eyes. I want to say, it is time to lift that soil that smothered us both. I would love to free myself of him, so my life can move on.

The night my tup died, his words came back to me. I did not want to think that anything might have happened to my beautiful ram that was unnatural. And yet I did not know what to make of the threats thrown at me or what it might mean to 'silence one in our midst'. I startled at the slightest sound, shadow or movement, my skin prickling with fear. The vulnerability of being a woman living alone suddenly felt real and palpable. As I lay awake at night, I watched the moon waxing a stronger luminescence, gaining in presence and light. It was calming to witness that silent transit, like a rite of passage. It made me dream of living differently. I knew what I had to do.

I am relieved that my procrastination is behind me. I am sick of its shadow. I am ready to lift my own dead and to free myself, at last, from all that lies under that dark, weighted turf.

Above my head, a thin sliver of moon is rising. At first the soil is dark and crumbling, but it gets wetter the deeper I dig until it is like a sodden pit. Mud clings to my legs and feet, so it feels like I am sinking. The blade shears away with a slow, sucking sound as it cuts into the soil, until it catches the edge of something wet. A matted clump of fleece comes away on the edge of my shovel. I put down the shovel and gingerly move closer. There is an awful, sickening smell and for a minute my whole body retches and I have to turn away. I know I am going to have to tie something over my mouth, cover my nose, so I do not have to breathe in that hideous odour. It is impossible to describe. It is rotten, like damp leaves, but also sweet; a frightening, bitter, horrifying stench. In short, it is the smell of a dead body that has been under the ground for six weeks.

It is amazing what happens as all that dark organic matter draws life out of death. The tup's flesh is exposed in places. It is too soft and gives way. It is difficult to lever my shovel under his great weight, to work sacks and thick ropes beneath him. The main body structure is still intact, held together by a smear of sodden skin that tears and wet, mired wool that sticks to itself, but it is visibly disintegrating at its extremities. His legs are still tucked neatly beneath him as if he is sleeping, but as I put the shovel under, I shudder as a dark, cleated hoof separates. It is shocking to witness the decaying mass of this once beautiful organism.

It feels too intimate to touch him, even through my gloves. As I heave and roll him over, there is a low sigh as gas releases inside his organs and rumen. To my horror, his body ripples and moans, respiring from its own slow-shifting fluids and liquefying pulp. I turn away, compulsively clutching at the soil above me. I can take only short gasps of breath and hold them until I have to turn my head to gasp another. After a few minutes, I gag. The cloying scent has a nauseating familiarity.

I construct a winch with ropes tied to my truck's solid towbar and steel frame. The decomposing body is heavier than I expected and as the winch lifts it, my truck churns its wheels. And then he lies still in the dark clarity of the moon. It moves me to see him so exposed and, to my surprise, I can see how this aspect of death is fiercely beautiful. It is stark and uncompromising. I know now that death is not just when the heartbeat stops or the brain ceases to function. It is not just when there is no next flutter of breath. It is not when the skin chills, the blood congeals and the vapours and fluids of the body stop moving and assimilating. It is all these things, but it is something else besides.

As I raise my tup, I force myself to go through with what I have started. He is so big that the veterinary bags do not fit him, so I wrap him in the full-size body bag provided by the mortuary. I know I am probably too late to find answers to his cause of death, yet somehow now it does not matter. What matters is that I have done everything I can for him. I drive him on to the early ferry to Oban, stopping at the mortuary for fresh body bags, and then I do not stop until the police pull me over in Glasgow. 'I'm sorry – I got lost,' I say as they take my details. I have been kerb-crawling, asking passers-by for directions, and someone has reported me.

'Is this your vehicle?' they ask suspiciously. And after the documentation is checked, they examine the rear. They prod the body bag in the back of the truck. 'What the hell is that?'

And suddenly I feel weary. It is a lot to explain, and halfway through, I begin to wish I had kept it simple. 'It's OK,' I tell them, 'I have all the proper clearance.' I show them my exhumation licence and government-approved permission of transit. In the end, they escort me, with lights flashing, to the veterinary site. I have an odd sense of déjà vu: this feels just like going to see my father in the morgue. Pathology, just like the hospital mortuary, is tucked away from view, with little signage. It is little wonder we avoid talking of death if even in its own rightful time and place it is always hidden out of sight.

The police wait outside nervously until the body is unloaded. 'I suggest you drive slowly,' one of the officers advises. 'If you've been up all night digging him up, you're probably more tired than you realise.' And then they escort me back to the motorway.

When the results come through, it is as I feared and expected. The tissue degradation is such that it is impossible to establish a conclusive result. The unit suggests we take the next step and run an autopsy on the vital organs, which may still remain fresh as they take longer to decompose. 'There is still a chance we may get lucky.'

But ultimately we have to accept a dead end. 'Even if we had a better sample, it would be difficult to give an accurate cause of death,' the pathologist sighs. 'There are an infinite number of ways a sheep can die. And it becomes even more complicated if it is by a poison. You need to know exactly what you are testing for before you start to get a true result. You could kill a tup just by injecting it with Savlon.' It seems there is an infinite number of toxins. Almost as many as there are stars in the sky. I draw a line, and accept what fate has decreed.

I have done everything I have asked of myself. I have tried. His exhumation feels important for other reasons, too. Hallowe'en is traditionally the day when you walk between the dead and the living. It is a liminal time when you do not look away, or rush to breathe life into the dead, but accept that we are all soil in the end. It helps to witness this, to know that over time even memory fades and becomes insubstantial.

7

Wild Cry

THE GEESE ARE calling in the half-light. As a shivering mist drifts through the window, I draw the blankets closer. I listen intently as a dense silence falls over the leaden horizon before a lone voice journeys on, straining. It makes me wonder at its solitary, sky-bound struggle. The sound of its broken cry is disquieting. It expresses a yearning, a hope, fear and something more. In its call I hear an echo of my own. I have a splinter in my heart. Every now and then it quivers, contracts in a spasm or flex of a muscle. I think, how is it that a bird knows when and where to go if there is nothing to follow?

Loneliness makes you search others' eyes, like a moth seeking a light. I circle, ever closer, drawing as near to that flame as I dare. I am hungry for warmth, kindness, companionship. Not just a passing smile or nod or words about the day or the weather, but words that have meaning. I long to hear my name spoken with love. Need makes my smile too bright, my eyes too wanting or hopeful. I don't know how, but others sense if your confidence is fragile or broken. They keep a wary distance. It is something we learn to watch for as children. Loneliness frightens even the birds away.

One day I force myself to go out to a small gathering. I am sober and clear-headed. I know it is time to leave when arguments start to flare. I try to keep out of the fray, but it finds me.

'You think you're better than me.' It always starts in the same wearisome way. These words are flung as an accusation, not a question or even a statement of fact. I do not know why this particular unwarranted challenge is invariably chosen to pick a fight. But I am learning that it masks some fear or insecurity. I have given no provocation. I am simply trying to reach the door.

'Please, I am just trying to get past you. Will you let me?' I ask. The man's eyes are glazed, but radiating anger. I remember that sour look. As the memory floods back, I feel something snap inside me. I want to tell him, you had already decided to hate us, even before you met us. Long before I entered my tup into the show. I think of those early bitter resentments; the whispers of a longstanding dispute. We hoped those feelings would slowly dissipate but instead they have festered like an old wound. I bite my lip. It makes no difference what I say.

Perhaps he reads my eyes. Whatever it is, something acts as a trigger. I hit my head as his hand lunges at me, pitching me back against the wall. As I stagger, he comes at me again, and it is only then that I realise how drunk he is. Suddenly I am screaming, 'Get your hands off me!' and he is yelling back at me. And then someone shouts, 'Hey, that's enough – no fighting in here.' The atmosphere is thick, with a palpable upsurge in tension. Suddenly I am struggling to tear his hands off my collar, and as the room closes in, I twist and free myself. Recoiling, I make my escape. It is a relief to sense the cool air and quiet fields outside. I welcome the darkness, but after a few paces, it unnerves me. I can still hear his voice in my head slurring that word again. 'Bitch.' I start walking as fast as I am able home down the road.

Violence is not always predictable. Drink gives it licence. Sometimes it just happens because it can. There is too often trouble and no one wants to hear of it. 'It is yours, a private quarrel' is the island way. But with no help or support, I feel unable to deal with it alone. After that night, I start to avoid community events. It means I am all the more isolated. But it feels safer.

I miss Cristall. Every day, the ache of her absence hits me anew like a stinging slap. Our daily lives were so intertwined, I still feel her shadow moving about me. When she was alive I did not seek others, simply because she was everything to me. I worry it is too long a grief, but grief has no timetable and no notion of social norms or etiquette. It is a wave that breaks over your head and rolls you under slowly, holding you down.

Absence teaches you to look harder for glimpses of what is remembered deep in a heart. It is impossible to forget. Everywhere I go I am surrounded by her. I walk daily through woodland where her ashes rest, under trees she gave me and planted with me. And I am grateful that she is everywhere; in the garden, shoots and roots that we nurtured together now provide shelter for wildlife and birds. As the balsam buds, its scent makes me sense her passing by. Sometimes I talk to her, and it feels natural to do that with Isla at my side. It is a daily reality, at times bittersweet and at others a source of comfort. The truth is, I do not move on. I look for her in everything.

And there is a beauty in this. It feels as if the landscape is alive with her spirit. Some days, I feel she is so close she is in each flitting wing, or drift of light, or rustling leaf. I try to cope with my grief, but each day that wave keeps on rolling and breaking. Each day it gets harder to face the empty horizon alone. Drowning is easier than you think. It can happen slowly, in full consciousness, with your eyes open. It can clamp weights to you, so that even as you fight, you lose your buoyancy, slowly tiring as they drag you down.

Listening to the lone cry of the geese as I lie in bed, my body feels heavy, cold, inert. I feel myself caught in the muffled snare of their wings. For some minutes, I struggle to move, but I can't. Move! I tell myself. And then I say it out loud, and louder, again and again. Eventually I haul myself out of bed.

The next day, I set my alarm. As I open the door, I whisper to Maude, 'Will you help me?' Sometimes you just need a friend to stand by you. I pull on my boots and we set off on a sedate jog across the croft. From that day on, I start running every morning, and sometimes in the evening, too. I run in the dusk or dawn, when the island feels softer. I run to force a warmth back into my heart. And it feels as if the landscape throws up its bright gifts to meet me. When you run in darkness, or in the gloaming, the wildlife is less timid, stiller, so you become more aware of its presence. The glistening rocks, wet grass, or rasp of the rushes against my legs make me feel whole, connected and present. Outside, in nature, I notice that I do not feel lonely.

At first I cannot run far so I stop every few hundred yards, bent forwards and gasping for breath. Maude waits patiently, her amber eyes watching, willing me on. I have never liked running, but running with a collie is different. We move together, to our own rhythm. Every day I stretch myself a few breaths further, marking distance not by minutes, but by a target – the next bush or a far gate. Each breath hurts, but I am grateful for its sharpness. The pain in my heart eases as my limbs lighten.

One morning, I go out later than usual and pass a small group of women on the road. They are out on a walk together, sharp-eyed and gossiping. When they see me running towards them, they fall silent. Coolly, our eyes meet and then glance away. It is awkward but afterwards I am glad of this brief contact. It is one small step forwards. When I get home, I wonder if asking if I could join them on a walk might help to bridge the divide between us. The next day, I send one of them a message making this tentative suggestion. About a week later, the word comes through that I can. I am nervous but hopeful. It offers the chance of a fresh start and an end to a weary stalemate.

The first day we walk together, we are guarded. Smiles are worn like shields; eyes are hard and bright. Gradually, as I begin to walk with them regularly, our eyes start to meet each other more freely. One day a ripple of laughter falls like birdsong and at last I feel that we have turned a corner. I relax. I tell myself that friendship grows from small beginnings.

Then one of the women offers a kindness. 'You've had it tough.' She looks at me. 'When your husband left, I felt sorry for you.' I try to smile. I bite my lip as my mouth quivers and then I look away, mortified and embarrassed, as I feel myself start to cry. Sometimes there is nothing you can do to stop it. When you are trying to stay strong, it is often compassion, not hostility, that pierces your defences, especially when it is in short supply. Loneliness is dangerous: when you have been too long alone, any small intimacy can lure you into mistakenly feeling warm, safe and supported. 'I am struggling,' I whisper, fiercely rubbing my face. 'It is hard trying to cope alone.'

I know I should not talk of missing Cristall, of graffiti on walls, of hard eyes and cold shoulders, but I cannot help it. I cannot stop those hot tears from falling or those words from sobbing out of my mouth. Sometimes things so long held in flow out of their accord. I did not want it to happen this way.

Mouths tighten. Jaws clench and shoulders stiffen. We are only a foot apart from one another, yet the distance feels as wide as a yawning canyon. 'I am sorry,' I stammer, turning away, ashamed.

'You can't say that,' one of the women tells me. 'You cannot accuse your neighbours.'

Other eyes skewer me silently.

I say nothing, because she is glaring at me with such anger it makes me feel like something you would scrape off your shoe. I have made myself weaker. I wish I had not spoken. By showing my vulnerability, I have implicitly insulted them. I have dared to criticise the island dream and I will be punished for this. And yet I feel a flicker of anger and injustice. I have lived my own truth for years, regardless of what others deny, or try to silence or shut down. I am sick of tribes and allegiances. I am staring into the softer, unknowing face of entrenched misogyny. I will never make this mistake again.

Afterwards, backs turn and I have no one to walk with. I go back to running alone. 'I can cope,' I tell myself as the weeks go by. 'It will pass.' Only it doesn't. Ostracisation makes you doubt your very existence. It is a new level of silence, more difficult to cope with than the aggression of before. I have no armour to deal with this. Its wound is deeper, more subtle, inaccessible. At first I fight it. I write in a notebook lists of people I love. I make a friendship tree of their names.

At the ferry, I join a straggling line of passengers with familiar faces. I dread that sullen queue yet I am thankful for it, for the slim opportunity it provides to break the impasse. I try to remain hopeful that it will force an adult response from myself and others. An acknowledgement that we all breathe the same air and cohabit on this precipitous rock face. That, even if our views differ, or we do not choose each other's company, a humanity binds us.

'Hello,' I say.

No one answers.

Even a rock face is worn down by a steady cold drip of water. Over time, I feel myself being eroded. Again, at first I endeavour to fight it.

But over time it wears me down. You accept it. You get used to existing as if you don't exist. You start believing that you are nothing. Sometimes I even wonder if I am imagining it. Yet every time I try harder, the harder I am knocked back. One day, as the skipper helps me lift a heavy bag, he says quietly, 'It's hellish, seeing this going on.' And I am grateful for those few words.

Everyone has times when they have no one to talk to or people turn and look the other way. It is one of those cruelties that we inflict on each other, a playground game carried forward into adult life. All it takes is one or two dominant individuals in a group to lead the way and the rest follow blindly. Society builds and dismantles its own power structures using such tactics. It targets the lonely, the unwanted, the vulnerable or the marginalised. I have watched this happening to others from under-represented families or groups. But I am alone, which makes my isolation and vulnerability more acute.

I do not go up my track where I might encounter passers-by. I keep out of sight. I stay close to the hills. And I miss Cristall more than ever. I miss her smile, her laugh, her unwavering friendship, her kinship and trust. As I have no one to talk to, I stop talking. Then I stop coping. I make myself invisible. It is easier to do this alone.

I am losing touch with words. I go to the woods because they offer a quiet sentience that is softer, kinder than anything I know. I press my cheek against the cool bark, rest my head wearily against a solid trunk. I make a rough shelter and bring thick blankets. As darkness falls, I light a fire and stare into its flames. The damp wood hisses and spits, but it provides a warmth and comfort. Maude's eyes are bright lit, glowing in the flames. I am safe amongst the trees. I can feel what is wild and broken inside breathing. I am ready to let go of the world I know, like a leaf curling up and fading before winter. When morning comes, I do not want to leave. And so I stay.

It is peaceful living in the woods with the birds. Some days run anxious and quicksilver fast, while others drag, heavy, sodden and weary.

I sit for hours observing and inviting a closeness with other wild lives around me. Hare shelter in the long grasses as dark wings of owl and falcon drift. In the early dawn and late gloaming, grazing deer flare their nostrils and peel back their lips, scenting the wind warily. The birch trees rattle their limbs, cold branches singing pale as winter bones. Crouched quiet, I sit with other taut hearts, sifting shadows, listening in the hushed undergrowth. Later, I harvest wood for kindling and fuel. I remember how, a few years ago, these woods kept me fed and nourished my spirit. With hindsight, those times of foraging for food now feel easy. Scavenging is different from foraging. It brings a sharper edge to daily life.

Cristall once told me I would recognise my own kindred spirits when they came. One day I notice a tiny, olive-coloured bird. Its fiery crest is golden with a dark-edged crown. It eyes me with a curiosity that is infectious. It opens its mouth to sing, a quick cadence of rising and falling notes that suddenly brings her to mind. In that birdsong and the whispering trees, she is breathtakingly close.

I think about how all organisms are influenced by the behaviour of their friends and neighbours. I recall how, in Cristall's garden, a raw stump shorn back to its bare roots was encouraged to grow new shoots by the empathy of others in its immediate environs. She explained to me that trees either instinctively nourish and sustain others, or incline away from their need or suffering. It brings tears to my eyes, remembering her words. And I realise that true friendship is given freely. It does not have to be reached for, expected or sought.

When I think of the island women, I see how we have each played out the roles demanded by the political imperatives of these simple rules of dominance and submission. How the interest of any society or community in ensuring that it prospers is almost its sole purpose. The families bound together on this island are fundamentally no different from the trees: rooted in a tiny patch of soil attached to a small tidal rock.

I do not belong. And it is clear to me now that, in trying so hard to fit in, it is sometimes easy to lose sight of, or even disown, our own needs. It is time to forge my own kinships. Even on a tiny island, the sky is wide and the sea is deep.

Listening to the tiny goldcrest, I am in awe of its beauty and brave resilience. Barely the weight of a twenty-pence coin, it has flown alone across a wasteland, and an ocean, from the wilds of Russia and Scandinavia, relying on nothing but its own instinct. I know I must find a different compass. As darkness falls, sitting quietly by my fire and shelter, I wrap my arms about myself and whisper, 'I am myself, just as I am.'

8

Raw Element

I T IS ALMOST daylight. My feet stumble on to the ragged shoreline as a
  sullen glow rises in the east. I have pushed myself until I can go no
further. The island is at my back; ahead of me is dark, shifting water.
The waves are breaking hard on to the glistening shingle and the wind
is whining through skeletal trees. I know this place, and it knows me.
It draws me irresistibly to it, always when I feel most alone. I watch as
the sea rushes in and sucks itself back, fiercely caressing the hissing,
wet stones. It is a fleeting time of year when the sun and moon glow
low in the sky together. It makes me wonder at the beauty and strange-
ness of life, and I almost falter as my heart whispers, if it doesn't break
you, it might heal you. But I cast off all distractions and force myself
to strip.

Cold slows you down, but it makes numbing thoughts feel weightless inside. As stuttering fingers clumsily unpick buttons, I wonder if

it will ever be possible to pinpoint all those moments that can shunt you to a crisis point of despair.

Alone in the early hours, my inner voice was raw and wretched, mired with questions, hopes and uncertainties that I dared not express to anyone, least of all myself. All the while, the voice inside was keening, 'Will daylight never come?' I call this time the dark watch. It knows my face intimately and all that lies inside a heart. I long to hear another voice say, 'You are not alone. There is nothing to fear,' and to gently touch my hand. I close my eyes then. Those days and Cristall are gone, and time runs ragged on, different from anything I have known before.

The temperature has dropped below freezing, and the wind chill is searing at a bitter minus eight degrees. Standing half dressed, lifting arms and bending knees, baring my skin leaves me exposed. Sometimes our physical situation can exactly mirror our deeper feelings and emotions. I welcome the cold's sharp edges. I am tired of hiding from my own thoughts; wherever I turn, they come seeking me out. I used to hide, too, from a voice that whispered, 'How dark would it be if a light were to burn itself out, or extinguish itself?', tried to push that soft whispering away. But always, it is there in the shadows, at the jagged lines around my eyes.

I do not know how or when daylight becomes too bright, darkness too absolute and the things you see in silence too frightening to speak of. Loneliness can be hard to express or see. I feel it in my body, and lick my fingers along its points as close as I dare. Isolation is far worse. It is searing, blinding.

As I remove my clothes, I fold them and place them neatly into my torn rucksack. Carefully, I take off my wellington boots and tuck my socks into them. I am not usually so tidy, but today it feels important to do things right.

Routines crumble when you lose hope. The bedraggled framework that holds our daily existence in place loses its cleanliness, its order. Life's small clutter matts together in a pile of unkempt tasks. Even small rituals – eating, washing dishes, brushing teeth or hair – can feel insurmountably difficult. Each day I make myself go through these motions. I wonder, what will happen if I stop? I stare at that thought in the mirror. It scares me to look at its face. Its dark eyes are wide and empty.

Naked now, I gaze at the sea and open my shivering arms to the wind. Inside, a voice whispers, 'Turn back – it is dangerous. There is another way.' But I do not turn back. My heart is frozen, numb, yet it needs to beat. I open my arms to the cold embrace of the wilds that heal the ache of this beautiful world. Only they offer the close kinship which for years I have been lacking.

In the end, it is simple. Everyone needs to be held and to hear their name whispered with love. I look out at the sea rising and falling. I think of how peaceful it will be to dive under those waves. I breathe fast as I walk towards the water. I try not to look at the sky. 'There is no going back,' I tell myself softly. I have not come here to go swimming. I have come to the sea to be held.

It is chilling to look at yourself, your frailties, in all your raw nakedness. To truly understand that life is only a single, fierce, trembling breath.

It frightens me that I have reached this point. I know my life is different from others. I have learned to live each day with less and less. Now I live with so little it is hard to know what is missing.

There comes a point when you know something is not working. That time has come and gone for me, only I have kept on, tiring but struggling. It is like treading water, with the current growing a little stronger every day and slowly, irresistibly, dragging me down. I have just been going through the motions, because we all adhere to one simple rule: you never stop trying. No one is allowed to give up. You can stop, but you can never pass your hand. Each day I have lowered my expectations. It is like a controlled hunger strike. When you starve yourself, you learn to detach from your hunger. Your own body helps you. It is a basic survival mechanism. But ultimately, a stomach is different from a heart. A heart needs the warmth of love and kinship to beat and thrive.

One day my legs started running. It was not like the running I used to know. I trusted a single glimmer of instinct to keep me safe. I opened the door and I let my legs take me wherever they needed to go. I was lucky. They didn't stop running when I reached the water. I kept on, running off the rocks and into the waves, and afterwards, I felt stronger. If not for days, then at least for a few short hours. Once you have been in icy-cold water, anything and everything feels possible. It makes you laugh or cry, sometimes both at once. You feel like a child who is given a promise. The sea is true. It will never break, snap, shatter, die or end.

As soon as I am bare on the stones, I move instinctively, and with a grace that I struggle to find when landlocked. Water flows by the path of least resistance. In the water, I lose all my doubt. Doubt is dangerous. It makes you cautious, so you question. Questions give rise to uncertainty and fear. Fear makes you hesitate, or draw back from what is calling you to it. Sometimes it can stop you from doing the very things you need to. Drawing back from life keeps you trapped inside your own wave, forever pinned to its trajectory, over which you have little or no control. Having no control is the other side of fear: it silences your voice and keeps you a willing victim, locked inside your own restraints. The sea unpicks that lock. It releases everything that is held silent or bound inside. In the fast-running tides, you are free of it all. In the sea you are simply breath. In the sea, there is no place for fear.

We all have our moments of crisis. It is too easy to put on a brave face when really we are well beyond an acceptable level of coping, when the daily struggle goes on behind closed doors. Sometimes even the strongest of us can falter. Ultimately, giving up on life can feel like the only sensible resolution to a grind that has become untenable. I just never thought it would happen to me.

I have come here to take my own life. Today it feels like the only option I have left. As I lay awake in the early hours of the morning, stiff, cold and silent, I felt as if all the air had been crushed out of me, as if I were gagged and tightly bound inside a metal box. It was terrifying. I lay there for some time, unable to move, barely breathing. The bravest thing I ever did was to force myself to get up. There was no thought or reason. I just knew that whatever this was, it could not go on. It was not a decision. And yet I have been building up to it, planning for it. The shadow that has been rising behind me, following me everywhere, is now falling in slow motion over my head, engulfing me.

For all your planning, you cannot know how you will react when that shadow falls. I have thought often enough about pressing a sharp blade to my wrist, dreamed about it, played with it over all those hard years after Rab left. But in the final analysis, it was a step too far. You think of your loved ones first. I may not have children, but I have four-legged dependents. I felt guilty, not only for seriously contemplating finishing my life, but for leaving my dogs to find me.

You try to work it out as best you can. If it's going to have to be like this, you think, it is kinder to be together. I hooked up the car exhaust to run through its interior and we sat in a row together, Maude and Isla and me, in the front seats, looking out through the glass, as if we were going for a drive. The only difference was that the windows were jammed shut, the handbrake on and the engine chugging through a hose. It took me only a few minutes to know it was a mistake. The sky becomes exquisitely blue when smoke clouds inside a windscreen. I switched off the ignition, pushed open the doors, threw the keys into the grass so I wouldn't find them for a while and walked away, retching. And again, I felt anguish, and a terrible guilt. Not over my own life, but for presuming to take others with me without their consent.

No one speaks of the thoughts that can come to find you when silence falls inside and traps you under its crushing weight. I wonder why that might be. I have heard others talk of a light in the darkness, but not of the bleak flipside of that coin. As a child I used to hold on, trusting, to anything that provided comfort. A favourite bear, a toy, a book or a tree that watched me through my bedroom window. When I was very small I used to talk to God. And then I stopped. Everyone needs some irrefutable truth to cling to. When your childhood is bereft of answers, you are like a magpie, hoarding whatever looks bright and shiny on the outside. I am good at nourishing others with those bright pickings but, calm as I am, I have always struggled to nourish myself.

When parents are unreliable and unpredictable, when one looks away as the other harms you, trust, as well as a small body, becomes a casualty. Its integral framework is irrevocably cracked when events conspire to undermine it in childhood. Your tolerance level stretches, imperceptibly, beyond acceptable limits. It takes you into altogether unknown, different territory. You watch, hungry, longing to feel safe, with that guttering hope constantly held in suspension or frozen in motion, hanging on to the belief that today or tomorrow the world will look different. Trust and intimacy feel dangerous. They keep you holding fast to an elusive potential in which your heart is snared. They are addictive.

The world view you develop is distorted. You deny that darkness exists, because your whole being clings to light. Life is a primal tug-of-war of belonging and deracination. You scavenge for bright toys and try to turn your back on the carrion. Trusting in a different truth from the one you know or have created can negate the validity or value of your own life and silence your voice. Fear gives no leeway for uncertainty, so you mask your own questions and hold fast to an impossible rainbow. The life you grow up believing in is unrealistic because it is constructed of hope and shimmering dreams.

Here, on the rocks, there is nowhere to hide, no shelter or buffer. Behind me, the island's dark shadow is watching, brooding. I turn my back to it. I am a lone wild bird, estranged at the margins. I call once more for my own kind, but I have been calling for my own kind for so long, my voice is cracked. When at first they did not come, I learned to turn to the gentle and broken things in nature. As I lost my own fear of the raw wilds and elements, trust and love came to me from a different source. I have stood many times on the edge of these rocks, my hands crying out to the sea. Today, it answers and starts softly calling me.

I gasp as I step into the icy water. It stings and slaps against my shins. I cry out as it splashes over my chest and shoulders, but I keep walking. I do not drop my eyes. I know that the harsher the cold outside, the gentler the sea will feel. Diving into the freezing water brings me a peace unlike anything I have ever known. Cold gives no space for thought. It threads your heart and head beautifully together and binds them to each present moment. I feel safe, protected and warm. I reach out to the sea's silver scaffold and weave myself to its soft steel frame.

For those minutes I am in its cold current, and the sea flows through me, I am shell-spun, salt-burned, wind-wrapped and kindled like a broken piece of sea tinder that the light shines through. I am glad at last to feel the pain of the cold. It washes my skin and hurt away.

I am an island. I have a name. A fistful of wind is all my voice. I give to the sea that cold silence inside.

Acceptance is a wonderful surrender that comes rushing in like the tide. As it turns, slipping away, it takes you with it. I go willingly. Its forgiveness is a gift of kindness. These wilds are fierce and uncompromising. The sea is soft and beautiful. The moon is shining, pale and huge. As I look at the horizon, I feel the deeper water calling. So I start swimming, heading into the sublime blue darkness beyond.

Out in the channel the wind has dropped. The silver waves are rippling with a burning silver fire. I start to drift, as the snow, long promised, starts to fall. It is mesmerising watching the thick flakes swirling. A soft kiss brushes my cheek. 'Thank you,' I whisper to the sky.

I feel only peace as lungs start gasping and flesh starts shaking. You go beyond it, so that hard barrier dissolves, becoming of pure instinct. I let my body slip under, let the sea hold me close. The water moves so quietly, I can sense it sighing and breathing. Its breath is so close and intimate, it is soft on my lips. I sigh, too, as it gently unwraps my skin.

There comes a moment when life flickers as a fierce, trembling, singing breath. It breathes of the crueller, darker waters. It whispers that if I continue, I will never breathe or love again. Or know the wind on my cheeks. Or feel sun and darkness shine in my eyes. It permeates my consciousness. It murmurs my name.

This breath calls with a different voice, like a strong-flowing river or grasses swaying under the sky. Like clear amber eyes seeking mine or dark hooves drumming the winter earth. It ignites some pilot light inside me, shearing away the darkness. A wilder voice calling my name with love.

It compels me to struggle. I have been too long in the water. Every fibre in my body is numb with cold, yet burning with a brutal pain. My head tells me to sleep and not to fight. But I do fight. I fight because my heart beats with a powerful urge to survive. There is a point when you are forced to make a commitment. It is not a moment of choice but a moment of truth. I keep swimming because suddenly, I know I do not want to die. Because I still have love to give. Because I understand that my breath is my source, and therefore my most precious gift.

It is never too late. Life can change irrevocably in a single beautiful gasp. There is no warning, but you know it instantly. In the half-light, the sea is breathing. It lifts and falls in a great rushing whisper and swell of sound, jolting me awake and filling my body with a tumultuous inspiration. Each breath is suddenly a jewel to be cherished. I turn back and swim for the shore. For all the love in my heart. For Maude. For Isla. And for a promise: for all I have still to know and for all I have yet to love.

The waves carry me as I tell myself, with each stroke, 'One breath. One life.' My arms are losing sensation. They twitch with stiff, ragged movements that make swimming futile and awkward. Yet the sea is forgiving. If you breathe, it buoys you up. White-hot needles of pain stab my limbs. Prolonged exposure to cold cuts off circulation to your extremities. I am grateful for the pain. It whips my skin into savage, visceral life.

I keep breathing, fingers pulling empty through the water. My throat is raw and my lungs are gasping. I keep my eyes, blinking salt water, fixed on the dark shadow of the island that suddenly, even after everything, is the only place I want to be. Above me the blue moon is shining pale and huge. Dark silhouettes of birds are flooding in great numbers through a moonlit fissure in the sky. My heart joins that wild dedication to survival, wrenching each hard-won breath from my aching lungs.

As I finally drag myself out of the water, I cannot stop my body from shaking. My jaw is clattering as my teeth shudder. I am close to delirious, yet inside I am forged differently. My skin is raw, flayed with wonder and the cold, glittering fire of love.

Salt can thaw the hardest ice. Tears can free the frozen voice inside. My eyes are shining, hot tears stinging. At first I rub them away. And then I stop. I let them fall because they are warm and I am blue with cold. I let them fall because they are mine. As I feel those breaking waves inside rising and falling, I promise to follow my breath wherever it goes. I turn to the sea and whisper softly, 'I am an island. And you have carried me home.'

ACT III

1

Water

THE RAIN IS falling. Great sluices of water are carrying clouds of spindrift over the waves. As it spatters my hair, I lift my face to it. It is harder than you imagine to catch fresh raindrops in your mouth. Rain is fresh, sweet and invigorating when washed with salt. My mouth burns, numb and swollen with those icy drops. I look out at the rippling gusts over tide and the grey, furling waves. Each day I throw a few lost hours into the water. Each day it renews my strength, fires an inner resilience inside and gives me a sense of gratitude for my warm breath and beating heart. It is a year and a day since I hauled out, exhausted, after the long, gruelling swim back from the channel from which I had not intended to return. It has been a tough, beautiful year.

I am excited because I am swimming out to the gull-wracked rocks where the seals are slipping in and out of the deeper water. Every day their smooth heads and wide, liquid eyes dipping into the waves draw me to drive myself a little further. I know that pushing the longer distance out to the skerries to join them will be a test of my endurance. It is further than I have ever attempted to swim before in winter. For months, I have dreamed of swimming out beyond the wet sands and fishing creels into the deeper water where the tides cross over and surge, foaming over a barnacled ridge of broken rocks. It is where the wilder, sharp-eyed birds, the cormorant and guillemot, rest after sailing in on the strong Atlantic currents. Their cries mingle with the peeping of a lone sandpiper or peewit, left behind and forced to over-winter on these empty shores.

'You can do this,' I chivvy myself, as the stinging wind whips my hair against my face. And then I take a few fast deep breaths, slapping my arms about myself to get the blood moving in my body. Standing at the water's edge is no time for nerves. I calmly focus on my breath, conscious that I will have prepared sufficiently to meet the challenge.

It is only a half-mile there and back, but swimming in the bitter cold without a wetsuit requires a different kind of stamina. Distance is measured not just by external markers of time and mileage, but also by a more subtle internal measure that requires a deeper understanding of the body's physical and emotional equilibrium.

Swimming in the sea is tough all year round in the Hebrides, but the cold is particularly punishing today. As I dip my jam thermometer into the water, it barely touches seven degrees. I know I will need to work hard to get there and back without losing concentration, or my inner warmth and strength, or I will risk exposure to hypothermia. For this reason, as well as for comfort, I have brought a flask of scalding-hot tea to warm myself immediately before the swim. It will heat my core, providing a few minutes' additional protection. I gulp it down in swift mouthfuls. It is the closest sensation I can imagine to swallowing fire. Afterwards, I am glowing, braced and ready. I lift my face to the pouring rain, and I think, nothing will stop me today.

I have been training daily for this, building up a core strength and endurance to stay longer in the water, pushing myself a few minutes further each day.

Most days I swim naked, but in the winter I wear Neoprene socks and a pair of 3mm gloves to shield my extremities during longer swims. This simple protection also helps me to climb in and out off the sharp rocks that take me straight into the deeper water, rather than wading in through the shallows, exposed to the wind, from the shore. I love the sensation of the sea and the raw elements against my skin, but it is not without risk.

Without a wetsuit, it has taken time to build up to twenty minutes. The half-mile will take me twenty-five if I can keep up a steady pace. Adrenaline warms my body, but the winter bite is ferocious at two degrees outside. Today has required meticulous planning. Given the plummeting temperatures, I have decided to break my swim and warm up on the skerries with a fire. I have a diver's waterproof drybag containing a fire steel and dry kindling, a small tarp, a full-body, zip-up, fleece-lined oil-skin, a thermal hat and a second Thermos of piping-hot coffee. The extra weight will slow me down in the water, but I have trained for this.

The conditions are good and the tide is coming in, so whilst the swim out will be taxing, the return will be easier when I am starting to tire. The thought of an influx of hot coffee and a crackling fire lifts me with a childlike excitement, making me eager to start out. The wind and rain are at least softened by the waves, and it is a relief knowing that at last the thaw is here. It means I can stay in for a few precious minutes longer today, which I know I will need, along with every last reserve in my body. It is invigorating listening to the snowmelt gushing off the cliffs, thundering back to its source.

I never used to like cold water, yet here I have grown to love its shocking, icy embrace. Every day, whatever the weather, I rise early and head for the shore. I tell myself I am not strange to do this, yet sometimes I wonder. I tell myself it is not a compulsion but simply an irresistible call. I have not missed a day, regardless of storms and punishing Hebridean conditions. I have swum in snow, in freezing rain with thick ice particles obscuring visibility, in crisp sunshine and in dense, glowing, amber mists, and once with the wind chill dipping to minus sixteen degrees and the solid, crackling edges of the sea freezing. After a while, I start to think that perhaps it is not merely seductive but addictive.

I know I am not alone in questioning this. Anyone who keeps company with the sea through the winter is in a strange place, gritting their teeth to find a release. After a while I stop kidding myself. The truth is, in those temperatures you cannot distinguish pain from pleasure. Cold-water swimming brings you to the brink of both. In the end, it is difficult to identify your motivation or to know exactly what it is you are seeking.

I used to tell myself, 'Soon I will stop.' Eventually, I realised I didn't want to. It gets me up and out when mornings are grey and the leaden horizon is flat. It helps me to set firm boundaries. Above all, the sea teaches me to trust. It teaches me to commit, not just to my breath but to something infinitely greater. I know that if I can stand bare-skinned in the freezing cold, hurl myself into the waves and keep swimming, then I am winning.

As I return to shore, feet gripping shingle, I feel braver than I did before. Courage is the first attribute you need to confront your difficulties. After my cold-water swim, anything else that happens in my life feels, if not easy, then at least possible. And it is as good a start to a day as any, I think. It tests your limits, stretches tolerances and slackens and strengthens a core fibre that quivers through your whole being, like some inner thread being tensioned. Blood courses through my body like a protective shield against the cold; breath animates every cell.

There is a moment as I step forward, feet sinking into the wet sand, when I leave something behind. I watch as the sea fills my footprints and then washes those bare impressions clean away so that, inside, I feel light as air. It is immensely liberating and forgiving walking into the water. My shoulders shrug off my outer layer, all my worries and cares, the minutiae of my life. Winter swimming tests your resolve and mettle. It asks that you give your last ounce of strength, and then it asks for more. You discover you have more to give than you ever imagined.

The sea moulds you skilfully, shaping you with fresh contours that are able to resist life's knocks. You feel your soft edges, the grace and lightness of your being, more subtly without boots and gloves on, and so even in the colder months, there are days when I like to swim free. When I am standing naked at the water's edge, a braver consciousness animates, firing a steel-blue, unquenchable flame in my heart. It tips you over the wave of your own fear or resistance and recalibrates your inner compass. Whatever it is that drives me, I recognise that it is a force for good. It is only looking over my shoulder at the months that have passed that I realise I am back on track.

At my back, a buzzard is hunched on a hawthorn spire, watching with unblinking golden eyes. 'You and me both,' I smile, noticing how we both have our shoulders drawn up to our necks. The buzzard's presence tells me that soon the rain will stop and the clouds will fracture. My heart lifts, knowing how brilliant the sun will be. The gulls taking to the air, shrugging off the wind, provide further reassurance of a break in the clouds. If the rain were setting in they would be sheltering in the nook of the bay or huddled in the fields.

My feet shrink from the achingly cold stones but I steady my breath and focus. Overcoming each sensation is an opening and a surrender rather than a battle. I have learned to trust in whatever these fierce tides throw at me. These days I am alone but I am not lonely. I am gentler to myself. Solitude, like the sea, draws you to it, but my relationship with it has changed over the years. In London, solitude was synonymous with time out or relaxation, a pause or vital decompression. Back then, it was a rare pleasure to be savoured. Now that solitude is my everyday condition, it is a constant presence. I have to guard against it metamorphosing into loneliness, which can seep into a heart unnoticed.

A ripple of wind is stirring the skin of the water. Cormorants are flying low, their dark-arrowed bodies gliding a couple of inches above the sea's upturned face. As I briskly rub warmth into my stuttering hands, Maude presses her wet body against me before tearing off, excitedly snapping at the waves. It is a routine we have established. Each day we come to a different stretch of water. We give each other the freedom to do what we need to do. Each day we make and break our own rules. Everyone has their own inhibitions, fears or areas of life that are hard to confront. To move forward it is important to step up and face them. Every challenge met is permission to start over.

My toes are pale shells on the barnacled rocks. All about, tiny crustacea cluster like glistening wet flowers. I watch the waves rolling in on the tide. At my back, an otter, wet and sleek, pours its shape off the rocks. Though my body clings to its own warmth – and I do not blame it – I do not think about what comes after. It takes an effort to do this, but so does anything worthwhile. If I hesitate, if I think about the cold, I will not go in. As I step into the rocky shallows, I gasp, but I know not to stop. I follow my legs, wading in. When I dive into the waves, my breath comes in short, fast gasps and my face burns with each arm's rhythmic stroke. My heart beats faster as my salt-stung eyes open wide in the cold.

I have never been scared of water. I learned to swim at three years old. Years later, in London, I used to swim in an open-air public pool in the dark after work. I always went just before the pool closed, to throw off the day. There was nothing fancy about these facilities. They were basic, functional, but they were clean, and they offered a choice of two full-size pools. I would pay for my ticket, slot it into the turnstile and push against the silver metal bar, turn left past the drinks vending machine and the chewing-gum dispenser and head down the stairs into the changing rooms. I didn't bother with a cubicle, I would just peel straight out of my clothes, wrap the locker key on its rubber band about my ankle and wade bare-toed through the foot bath with its stomach-clenching smell of chlorine, trying not to slip on the cold tiles.

Stepping outside into the night air always made me gasp. All about, the throb and hum of London living was itself beautiful, traffic rattling past on the far side of the high walls. It felt incredible to be standing on the near side of these bricks, staring into the beautiful, dark, still water. I would put down my towel and dip my toe over the edge. I'd take a few breaths and gather myself, looking at the steam rising into the cold air. And then that summons that impels your toes to grip the edge of the pool, and your legs to tense, springing up in a long, open arch. A fleeting silence. And then the splintering of surface, a glimpse of the sloping tiled floor and a long ripple of water undulating away ahead. I felt a weight unwind with each slow release of breath. It was my own beautiful blue decompression chamber. I swam endless laps, tumble-turning and flipping slow on to my back every few lengths. The steam wafting from the heated water offset the cold of my breath frosting white. Swimming under the night sky across the heart of the capital was amazing, yet sometimes even that wide vista felt too small.

Now, thinking back, I am incredulous at how, for so many years, I was landlocked on this island. Deterred by the cold, I rarely swam in the sea or the loch. I was happy to dip on hot days, but even then I could not bear more than a few minutes. I am not the only one. Few islanders take to the water. The sea is freezing, its tides are powerful, its currents come off the wider Atlantic. If you are not familiar with its conditions, it is dangerous.

But now I am so glad to know this shore intimately. Whenever the island feels too narrow or small, I run over the hills and step off into the waves. It offers uncharted territory beyond the single track road's binary north and south options and polarised arguments. Sometimes I wonder if living here might be different if there were a circular coastal route, too. Landscape shapes the psyche of its people in so many ways. Perhaps the idea of a third, circuitous way might have taken root in the local culture. I used to envy the birds their ability to lift and land anywhere, on waves or soil. Now I, too, have a limitless freedom. It helps me to redraw my own parameters with fresh, fluid lines.

There is a point at the skerries where the tides of three bays meet and the water rushes in and through from different directions. It can be unsettling at first, but I have tested these waters in the summer months. There is no rip tide or current here. When I look back at the island, the rocks look like great humpback whales. The wind is keen, ruffling the fine down on the exposed back of my neck. It is here, and across my bare shoulders, that I feel the raw cold most intensely. In winter, I instinctively seek the faster water. It keeps me focused, adrenaline singing. Still, calm water is harder to swim in when temperatures sharpen. It lulls and tires, demanding greater concentration, effort and stamina. Always I duck my head under. It helps to regulate my body temperature.

I keep breathing, drawing my hands through the water. Lungs expel air as a gasp and skin whitens. Here, as the waves start to chop, the sea keeps a thin skein washing over my skin. I feel warm and protected out of the sharp teeth of the wind. Halfway across, the water suddenly deepens. I am at the meeting of the tides. A great pulse shimmers, rising up from beneath. As the sea swirls, I am lifted up and borne forward as if on the breathing back of a whale. It is exhilarating to be held and supported. The sea washes into this bay, and so carries me on to the skerries with minimal effort. For those last minutes of my outward journey, I am flying like a bird.

At the skerries the gulls are bickering, jostling and skirling into the wind. The water here is teeming with fish. Silver shadows dart. Further out, a murmuring flock of geese drifts, quietly resting. Birds lose their fear of humans when they are in the water. We glide past each other curiously. I feel embraced by the sea and the sky and connected to both.

Hauling myself on to the rocks, I light a crackling fire. A small tarp tied to the ground keeps my few sticks dry. There is no time to dry off when temperatures are this low, and a towel is raw and burning on the skin, so I just step straight into my fleece-lined oilskin and pull on my hat. It keeps things simple. I keep moving as I gulp hot coffee and feel that warmth filling my core. Back at the shore, there is a sturdy backpack filled with basic provisions that will help me recover after the swim. An enamel mug, a flask of hot soup, a kettle and some tea, a wedge of chocolate, firelighters and kindling, and plenty of dry clothes. You learn routines so that with practice you don't have to think. Your muscle memory goes through the motions. It is important, because cold slows you down.

These days I value my life and I do not take risks. I have learned how to protect myself through experience. There was a time when I wasn't so careful. My knees are scarred with fine white criss-crosses from rock cuts. I know now how to recognise hypothermia. The threshold between severe cold and hypothermia is perilously thin and it is even harder to recognise in yourself when it becomes a real threat. My body is a living testament to this.

I have a souvenir in the form of a small section of frostbite on the knuckle of my right index finger. It will remind me of these beautiful days when I am old. It is nothing much to look at. Just a small smooth area across the knuckle, with no wrinkles or markings, like scar tissue, or a burn. When I first came out of the water it was red raw. I had been swimming in a wind chill dipping to minus sixteen degrees, and my glove had ripped so my fingers were exposed to the flaying cold of the air. You lose circulation in your extremities faster than you realise. The rest of my body was covered by water, apart from my head, which was protected by two woollen hats over my swim cap. The sea was freezing around me, crackling in soft, hissing murmurs. It was so extraordinarily beautiful that, although I knew I should not, I stayed in the water for ten minutes longer than I ought to have done. And I do not regret this, because it was one of those brilliant, crystalline wonders that stay with you – a once-in-a-lifetime experience that will always remain seared into my heart and my flesh. For weeks my knuckle burned with an itching, aggravating sensation, like a boring inside my skin, so irritating that I could not bear to touch it. Now it is a talisman. That day, the sea kissed me and bit my hand, sending its silver venom coursing through my veins. In this brand I feel that the sea will forever be with me.

These days, I always run over the hills to the shore and light a fire there to keep myself warm. I have hot tea or soup before I swim. Afterwards I shower in tepid water rather than hot, to keep my body heat safe in my core. Allowing warmth to move out to the extremities is dangerous, because it robs the core organs and tissues of blood. When you have been overly cold, or close to hypothermic, a flood of cold blood, even once you are slowly warming up, can shock the heart fatally.

Each day, when I come out of the water, after drying and stepping into protective thermals, I wrap shivering arms around Maude's wet body to warm us both. I place a tiny tin kettle on burning sticks, listen to the waves roar and the trees gust. Boiling steam starts to bubble and sing. Stuttering fingers wrap tightly about a mug of hot tea. Often, staring into those flames crackling on the rocks, I wonder, how in the world did we end up here? It is strange to be so alone and yet so immersed in such a beautiful moment. I feel more complete and connected in these wilds than I have ever felt with another human being.

It can be frightening to cope alone when you have no one to turn to, but I feel I have met the challenges I have been dealt and they have been important in shaping the person I have become. I know now that burning out is when a longer struggle gives way to a relentless, unstoppable assault, like a rock's face being worn down by erosion. You emerge with your contours hewn differently and something else inside transfigured. Some of these changes are welcome, but others can leave you grieving for the self you have lost.

Out at the skerries, the light and tide are turning. Back in the water, I grasp a rock to catch my breath. Beyond, the seals are slipping smooth beneath the surface, dark heads lifting, black eyes blinking, reflecting the sky as the water flows slick off cold brindled skin. We watch each other silently until one calls curiously, a singing gurgle, sweeter than a bark. As it dives into the dark depths, I take a lungful of air, slip under and follow into that dark, green-fronded world below. Further out in the channel, the rich feeding grounds are waiting. I am reassured that other, unseen worlds are breathing; that here are as many worlds to inhabit as beating, invisible lives. These days, the sea is no longer an object to me. It has a name and a presence that is loved and intimate. As the sea rises to meet me, I open to its beauty and flowing possibilities. I am discovering how life becomes less complex outside day-to-day human interaction. Its infinitely simpler rhythms allow me to connect deeply to my instincts and a more primal voice. They allow me to reach closer to the sky, the sun, the wind and the moon.

Transformation is regenerative, redemptive and comes with a struggle. For change to come, or to strike out differently, you have to let the rough edge of the pain of all that life throws at you graze your heart. Some days I feel like an oyster shell creating itself from a handful of grit from the inside out. Each day the sea washes me smooth. As it draws back, it reveals a part of myself that is new and subtly different to me. When you step beyond your fears, it takes you into a wilder space. It is not for everyone. I am not who I was, but I am still evolving.

'This is just the beginning,' I whisper to the sea. 'We are just starting out together.' And then I gaze out at the seals slipping under the tide, and I think of how much further I have still to swim.

2

Fire

A HARD PERMAFROST has seized the island. Every morning I rise in darkness and pad down to the kitchen in my woollen kilt socks and thick thermals. An empty flask is waiting for me on the kitchen table, together with other essentials – matches, a fire steel, a handful of dried kindling, a rough breakfast for a shallow pan, and a small tin kettle to warm me from within.

When I return from my swim, I know how important it is to keep moving. Today I fold two large hessian sacks that were once old post bags, still stiff and durable, shoulder a heavy tartan rug and collect a worn saddle as Maude's paws skitter out of the door before my boots scrunch into a brilliant frosted world. At the gate I stop as my voice calls, ringing over the croft. There is a brief silence and then a whinny. Hooves come drumming over the frozen earth, and then my Highland mare stands before me, nostrils flaring, breath snorting. So you feel the beautiful wildness of her.

Fola is dark in shadow but glittering with frost, her long lashes blinking slowly as she nudges the rug and saddle. Her mane is frozen stiff and as she arches her neck her back crackles with rigid ice sworls. 'Are you ready?' I murmur, and she tosses her head, circling and flaring her tail high. I imagine how it might be if we always travelled like this, saddling up at dawn every morning to journey to where we needed to be. Our breath clouds white as I rub her thick coat briskly with my chapped hands. Shivering shards of ice shower us with a white iridescence. Our outlines are lit by a golden glow as the sun starts to rise and the day feels immensely beautiful in its physicality and stark simplicity. I acknowledge, looking out over the land, that it provides me with everything that I need not just to live, but to thrive. The granite mountains framing the horizon are chiselled into insignificance by the otherworldly flaming rings cast by the ascending sun. Below the silver sea is a shimmering mirror of glass.

It is strange how the skies have the power to stir our deep atavistic instincts, drawing on our ancient impulses and ancestral memories to bring some deeper spirit alive. For a second I feel I have been here in this moment before, and that nothing will ever surprise me again. 'I know this land,' my heart whispers, and time feels suddenly such a blink and yet simultaneously hugely expansive.

It is a time of year when you can feel the seasons and the Earth's axis shifting, and something else awakening in your own consciousness. The ground is still frozen, but you can feel soil stirring in the darkness, all the life below germinating, as if aching to reach upwards, to break the crust of the world and to shatter this paralysing cold thrall with the warmth of new growth.

The freezing air reddens and burns the tips of my nose and fingers. Quickly, I tighten the straps of the saddle and girth. It is immensely satisfying to feel the leather slip butter-soft through each cinch, thanks to hours spent rubbing wax into its brittle skin. As I inspect my handiwork, I smile. 'What do you think?' I ask Fola, as she curiously eyes the rough hessian bags hooked on to the fixings saddled to her back. It is a rudimentary device, but it works. Her front hoof lifts and paws the hard ground, so I stroke her and say, 'Walk on, girl.' Her nose blows blue clouds as she pulls forwards, Maude streaking like a shadow behind. We are going to the woods to collect kindling and windfall, and piles of wind-dried furze and gorse.

Winter is long in the islands. With the sun setting at 3pm and not rising until after 9am, every day can feel like crossing a high mountain pass with low supplies. You do not take the winter months lightly. It is important to prepare for them, mentally as well as practically. Winter was known here as the time of the Lesser Sun, its light fallow and pale. The weather can hold sway over your spirits. I love the cold glittering days, when the ground is frozen and snow falls thick on the hills. It is a time of stillness and containment, when the earth quietens and draws its sap. Yet for all its beauty, these long, dark months can drag.

For six months of the year, from October to March, the sea accentuates this closing in. Its tides beat fierce against the island. On quiet nights, a timetable curfew means the last scheduled sailing to the mainland runs at 6.30pm. Every year storms set us adrift from the mainland. When I first came to the island, I was discomfited by being cut off from the rest of the world. Darkness resonates, and it is felt more intensely away from the urban centres. I had not yet become inured to the storms, or acclimatised to lengthy periods when the sea and winds were raging, resulting in cancelled boats, electricity cuts and fallen telephone lines. In those early days, the longer the rough weather lasted, the greater I felt its corresponding emotional deficit and dropping of morale. Cold can injure not just our physical bodies but also our emotional resilience and equilibrium. As well as spurring you to take precautions, such as shoring up provisions and fuel, and being efficient with timing and chores, it stimulates you to reflect on your frailty and your place not just on this tiny island, but as a human being craving contact with others in the universe. There is nothing like a storm to bring to front of mind your own vulnerability and to prompt you to toughen up your resilience.

When I think back to my first Christmas on the island, those years with Rab seem so long ago. We were so young, naive and childlike in our enthusiasm to experience our first island festivities, as if we truly belonged, that we willingly elected to spend Christmas away from our own families. Even though we had so little, we had each other, and therefore so much. Now those times seem like distant echoes from a different world.

My first winter alone after Rab left was the coldest and harshest I can remember. This was the winter when the heating tank ran dry, with the fuel lorry not due for another six weeks. It made no difference, given that I had no money to pay for the oil anyway, so that year the house sat cold until the spring. Sometimes you simply make do with what you have. I wrapped up in thick layers and blankets, lived off soup and slept wearing several coats and hats. When the coal ran out, I burned the kindling wood I'd collected from the woods. I would take a rope and tie up a large bundle. With my broken hands it was too painful for me to lift, so I tied the rope around my waist and walked slowly back up to the top of the croft, dragging it behind me.

That was how life felt to me then: heavy, cumbersome, awkward. But I learned that if you persevere, the load will lighten and your skills and fortitude will strengthen over time. Those hard years are gone and I would not wish for them back. And yet they were an extraordinary and invaluable time. And occasionally I miss them for their raw, elemental edge and stark beauty. Sometimes the hardest years give us a strength we might otherwise never know. There is always a time of darkness in life, but it makes the light all the brighter when it comes.

This year I have no problem filling those quiet winter hours. Lanterns are trimmed ready for when the power cuts out. Matches strike calmly in the darkness. Candles are lit and paraffin wicks flicker brightly. Breaking down the running of the croft into a series of small, manageable tasks makes the day-to-day jobs easier, rather than confronting yourself with an outsize list that can feel overwhelming. Each morning I set myself three goals to achieve by the day's end, in addition to the usual daily chores such as gathering kindling, walking the croft, mucking out, lifting dung and doing the rounds checking livestock. Fruit trees and plants, vegetables and herbs require attention and maintenance all year round. In the long evenings I reach for beeswax and oil the cracked leathers of Fola's tack. Maude and Isla doze by the fire, legs twitching with their dreams. This year a hen sleeps indoors on the back of a chair. I read aloud. I shuffle and play cards. I catch up on mending clothes. I write poetry. Candlelight is soft on white pages. I gaze into the flickering flames.

Fire draws your eyes towards it in darkness. The sensory stimulation of its heat and flames is the great call to life. It ignites a spark of courage or hope. And when you rest close by a fire at night, you are held safe, secure from all that lies outside its flickering glow. You know the wolves are still there, but as long as that light is burning, nothing can harm you.

I am grateful for the help Fola now provides with collecting the stores of wood that keep my fire burning through the winter nights. Loading the dried wood into the makeshift saddlebags takes practice. The weight distribution is important. We make several journeys every day, walking from the woods up to the hills above the loch. The gorse is on an opposite hill. It blazes a golden trail across the hills when all is bare: a symbol of hope. It is remarkably adaptable to its environment and throws its seeding flowers away from its parent plant in order to ensure independent flourishing and self-sufficiency. The prickly spines are too sharp and unwieldy to load into the sacks, so I pick the bright gold flowers to suck. They taste of sunshine, bitter almonds and honey. Later, on the hill, I will boil hot water in the kettle and infuse some into a delicious tea.

I build a fire on the hill. I am practising building different types of fires, and I am planning to spend a full night awake out in the open, watched over by the stars. Coaxing that first spark to catch can be tricky, especially if the day is damp, so I come ready prepared. My pockets are full of dried tinder, moss, lichen, birch bark, twigs, dried grass and straw. When you peel wood thinly with a blade, it curls back in springy curves and smells delicious, like vanilla essence mixed with fresh leaves. I shave away the inner bark so that what remains peels into tiny shreds that catch alight more easily. Birch curls inwards when it is hot, and its flame can quickly extinguish itself, so I flatten it and fold it like a fan, edge over edge, to extend the life of the flame. If Maude is shedding her coat, her thick fur can be rued like sheep's wool by gently tugging at the loose pieces that fall easily into your hands. I gather these into a handful and roll them in my palm to make a small ball that sparks and crackles alight, even in wet weather, with a couple of strikes of my fire-steel flint.

The ability to create fire is an important skill and is a sure way to make yourself feel capable of and ready for anything. I am growing more competent at it and trying out different types of fire constructions. I am also developing my skills in building shelters. It all helps me to think on my feet, and to be adaptable and responsive to my surroundings. It promotes an ingenuity and openness of thinking that builds up practical as well as mental stamina and engenders trust in the world around you, self-assurance and confidence. When you are able to live comfortably in your environment, wherever you are, you can have faith that whatever happens to you, you will be OK.

In the mornings, I light a candle and express my hopes and plans for the day. It makes me aware of my own silence and invites me to break it with sound and movement. I spin round, weaving my body, using my arms to lift and turn. It is liberating to see and feel your body moving freely, exploring a full range of expression and movement, and it feels wonderful. It consolidates the intentions to which I have just given voice. I grow bolder as I experiment with ways to strengthen myself through the daily ritual of forging my own traditions harnessed to work and play.

Each night I walk, in moonlight and darkness, testing my night vision, an exercise that forces me to step out of my comfort zone. I purposely keep away from the isolated twinkling lights of the island as my footsteps tread the dark hills and fields beyond the croft. It helps me to familiarise myself with the island at night, to feel self-reliant and safe wherever I am. When I reach a favourite place I settle. I do not take a torch or other battery-operated beam. I prefer to use natural illumination, such as a lantern, which casts a softer light and allows my eyes to pick out shapes and shadows. It also makes the small wild animals less wary. I listen to owls and geese in the darkness. I am as quiet as the deer.

One day I wrap old cotton rags and lint tightly around thick branches, dowse them with paraffin and lightly spray the fabric with alcohol. That night I set them alight and walk the march lines and perimeter of the croft with a burning torch. There is something wonderfully primitive about carrying raw flame. Its glowing beacon is gloriously anachronistic. It anchors my feet to the soil. It binds my eyes to light. It keeps my heart reaching out into the darkness.

I walk across the croft, burning flames over the land. 'This is my home!' I call to the wind. That night, the fire burns away my fear. There is something I need to confront and I know it is time I did. I know now what I have to do.

The next morning at nine o'clock I knock on a door. My heart is hammering in my chest. I tell myself fiercely to keep the flame in my heart burning. I do not want to do this. But I know I have to.

'We need to talk,' I say quietly as the door opens.

There is a silence for a moment.

'There's nothing to talk about,' a gruff voice pushes back eventually.

'I wish there wasn't, but we both know that's not true.'

And then I say his name. The man looks at me closely, and incredulity flickers in his eyes. But he does not hold my gaze, so I feel his embarrassment. I wish I did not. Embarrassment is dangerous. It lives next door to pride. You can restrain a fire by building walls and creating barriers. I know my flame will be stifled unless I can dismantle those walls quickly. Very gently, I rest my hand on his arm.

'Please,' I say. 'It has to stop.'

And then I see the fear enter his eyes. 'Ach, to hell with it. I'm not talking to you.'

'I am not leaving until we shake hands,' I say calmly. 'I barely know you. I live on my own. I have no one to do this for me. What if someone, a man, was fighting like this with your daughter? You would want that quarrel over.'

He looks at me sideways. And then slowly he rubs his face.

I keep my heart steady. This is just one door. There will be others. But it only takes one to open to start a wave of change.

'I am not leaving,' I say again, 'until we sit down and talk over a cup of tea.'

I wait. I am trembling. It could go so horribly wrong any second. I want to run away. I want to be anywhere else but here.

'Please,' I say.

And then a miracle happens. He shrugs. The door opens and he steps back to let me inside. 'Well, if you're not going, you'd better come in,' he says. 'The last thing I want is a scene.'

'Thank you.'

And I follow, my legs still shaking.

Fire has to flare before it dies. Hatred is like a fire that smoulders and then spontaneously combusts. It is terrifying when it is directed at you. And its heat burns. Over the years, I have tried to avoid this man and those close to him, but it is hard to do this in such a small place. There are times you have to cross each other's path. Every time you meet hatred but do not confront it, it becomes more difficult to act naturally. It thrives on hard walls, separation and difference. It beds down with fear and fear of change. It baulks at the close touch of kindness. But its heat can dissipate if you quench it with understanding. I tell myself to seize this moment and keep talking, that there is nothing to be afraid of. I trust in that bright flame of truth in my heart.

'You think you're better than me,' he tells me, just as he did the night he lunged at me and tried to knock me down. I do not mention that night. I know not to because it will close down our conversation.

'I am listening, but I need you to help me. You keep saying this, but I don't know why. Help me to understand how I have offended you.'

'You ruined the show with your tup,' his voice rises angrily. 'You're a liar, claiming to have won prizes you did not.'

'But the judge awarded the prizes. I didn't make up the scores.'

'Not the first reserve,' he growls. 'You stole that prize, you selfish bitch.'

'But I have the certificate,' I say, and I show him a photograph of it on my phone.

He stares at it and then back at me. 'How did you get that?' His eyes gleam with resentment.

'There was a lot of whisky drunk that day,' I suggest. 'Perhaps some things were forgotten along the way.'

'You're a selfish bitch! Say what you like, but you didn't win it.' And then he folds his arms. 'Always got something to say, haven't you? That's why you get everything else you ask for here.'

My heart falters. I swallow. My palms are sweating. 'Please hear me out. All I did was to turn up, support the event with my livestock and take part in good spirit. I didn't have to come, but I did because I wanted to show willing and to participate.'

'You wanted to win,' he says furiously.

'And what if I did?' I retort. 'So did you, and everyone else who took part. I worked hard to be able to handle my tup. I entered him as a way of proving to myself I could handle him. You didn't know that, did you? That I was getting hurt, getting knocked over on to the ground?'

He does not reply.

'All the good it did you now he's dead,' he says finally.

I look at him squarely. 'Yes, he is dead. And I wish I had never entered him.'

Our eyes lock. I feel cold and sick, and the room is closing in on me, but I force myself to hold his gaze.

'Let's end this now,' I say. 'There are no winners and losers. Not in this room, and not on this island. I live here, and I have lived here for fourteen years. You may not like me, and we may always have our differences, but let us try to show respect to each other. I have as much right to be here as anyone. I have no family and no one to stand in my corner. I may not be your friend, but we can at least be civil and bury this – all of this, the hatred and all of it – once and for all.'

He looks away and shakes his head. 'Ach.'

I wait. I tell myself, don't give up – not now, when you are so close. And then I do it. I hold out my hand.

'Here,' I offer. 'A truce. Take my hand and let's shake on it.'

We both look at my hand, perplexed. When he doesn't take it I just leave it suspended in the space between us, my heart hammering in my chest as the moment drifts. It is excruciating. I wonder if I have compromised myself. It dawns on me that he now holds all the power in this exchange. If he shakes his head and tells me no, I am out of options.

I stand there, hand outstretched in a gesture of peace, trying not to think of all the years that have passed. I try not to think of that first visit to the croft, all those years ago, when two men fell drunkenly out of a tractor on to the ground and a brawl broke out in the yard. I try not to think of those eyes fixed with hostility on mine. I am scared, but I stand fast. I have spent fourteen years avoiding this conversation with this man and others. I have to see this through. I focus my energy and attempt to summon all the positive energy I can muster into this room. I imagine kindling a fire, with all my attention and focus. I breathe softly on that guttering flame.

'Please,' I say, 'won't you meet me in this? It is time for us to end this fight.'

Another minute passes. And then he shakes his head and stares hard at me. 'All right, I will,' he says, and at last he shakes my hand. I am nearly sick with relief. My heart is pounding, and I feel exhilarated by something I cannot quite name. It is a feeling not dissimilar to reaching the summit of a mountain: everything in you is exhausted, but your spirit is suddenly fired with an elation you never thought you would feel.

It has been a difficult reckoning and, for now, there is nothing more to say. In my heart, I am not sure if this will be a lasting truce. Anger can burn out, but only if friendship, or something like it, is nurtured in its place. As I leave, briefly we shake hands. It feels like hope, if not a promise. I tell myself, it is a start.

When I get home, I am shaking. I make some strong coffee and as I stand gulping it down, a thought comes to me with such clarity that I put down my mug. It is time to burn the past, I think. This year I do not want to wait for my ritual bonfire to mark the end of lambing. I feel an urgent need to cleanse the house, now, of all that is redundant. I wrench out a drawer and tip its contents on to the desk. It is full of letters I have kept that I wrote to Rab. They are filled with hope, hurt, love and betrayal. I read a few words, and then a few pages. And then I put them into a box.

I am ruthless, stripping the house. If an object makes me feel sad, angry or weighed down, I throw it outside. Soon there is a pile of old furniture, clothes, boxes of small items, files full of yellowing bills and paperwork. I do not need you any more, I think. It is strange how the weight of the past is suddenly so palpable. In the vacuum, the cottage feels lighter and emptier.

Afterwards, I burn sage and walk through each room, holding my smoking torch of herbs and smudging, or cleansing, the space. I load up the truck with all the debris outside on the grass, open the croft gates and drive across the fields, up a steep grass track, weaving amongst the exposed rocks and boulders, to the top of the hill. Tonight I will build my own fire with crackling gorse, brush and timber, and set it ablaze on the hill above the loch. I will sit with those flames, close to my favourite ash tree, until their embers glow bright in tomorrow's dawn.

It is a beautiful night, clear and with a waxing crescent moon rising over the mountains. As I strike a match, the furze crackles and spits. Crouching, I cup my hands and breathe on its white flames. As gorse spines catch, the flames roar quickly. I pile armfuls of brushwood and broken furniture, letters and photographs on to its back. As the wind lifts, the pyre ignites. It burns with a blistering heat.

Once the flames die down, I nestle five thick logs into the centre in a star shape to construct a slower-burning fire on which to cook a pot of stew. As darkness falls and the skies deepen, I will position two longer logs, with a groove hollowed along the length of each, filled with dried wood shavings and crisp lichen, one stacked on top of the other, with both ends balanced on boulders to raise them off the ground. These will burn through the night. It is a beautiful way to keep warm without constantly having to refuel the fire. Away behind me, Fola glows pale in the darkness, cropping the grass.

At midnight, I open a small wooden box. Inside are two scraps of paper. I whisper their names softly. I read the dreams of long ago aloud. I kiss the shells. I close my eyes. I imagine tiny hands lifting to mine, and tiny sleeping eyes. 'Goodbye,' I whisper. 'We were not for this lifetime.' I stand and gently lift the box up to the sky. I watch as it falls into the flames and those dreams ignite. It aches to say goodbye to them, but it is strangely freeing. I stay with them, their bright gold flames flickering in my eyes.

As the sun rises, my blanket is white with frost. The fire is no more than smouldering embers now. I smooth it over and pile the embers into an old milking pail. I walk with those hot ashes, scattering their glowing life around the croft. I whisper a wish as each spark sizzles, smoking, on the glittering frost. The buzzards are calling in the high passes of the mountains. Their calls echo on the wind. It is the sound of sunlight and all the raw promise of the spring. I blow out clouds of frosted breath. I lift my arms and I let my voice sing to the wind. My heart is light as I call the sheep for feeding. I watch the sun rising in the east as the Morning Star burns bright in the sky.

3

Kin

As I TIPTOE to the door, I hesitate. 'Downstairs,' I whisper to Maude, as she presses excitedly ahead of me. Her bright eyes plead with me, but I shake my head. Her paws skitter away down the wooden stairs. I hear her stop on the bottom step and see her turn around. She fixes her gaze on me and waits, a question in her eyes. This is an unusual experience for both of us: there is someone else in the house. I put my hand on the doorknob and softly push open the door. I don't generally use this bedroom. It is where Rab and I used to sleep. It is my favourite room, in the oldest part of the cottage. Sometimes I stand at the window and gaze out at the garden and the sea. The croft feels so close here, as if the walls are thinner. You can hear every whisper in the low eaves.

Inside, it is sparsely furnished. The old chest with tiny mother-of-pearl flowers, given to us anonymously as a housewarming present, is dark against the peony walls. An elderly woman lies asleep on the bed. Her mouth is open and her long, white hair adrift over the pillow. It is my mother. She is older and more fragile than I remember. She is almost eighty but, sleeping, she looks like a child. Gently, I tuck the blankets more closely about her. My eyes trace her face. It is hard to believe she is here. This visit is a rare occurrence. The last time my mother visited the croft was when my father was still alive, over eight years ago. I am holding my breath, willing time to slow. And then she stirs. I do not want to scare her on waking so I tiptoe back down the stairs.

The table is set with cups and plates, a milk jug and a sugar bowl. I have warmed the teapot, but then I remember that my mother does not like tea, so I put it away. She only drinks coffee. Dark, strong, thick as paraffin. 'My father's army brew,' she used to laugh.

We only have a few days together. I am trying hard to make them memorable, meaningful. I want to fill each moment with a mesh of smaller memories that will bind these hours together and will never break. It is strange how love can run so deep and yet feel so fragile. It is like a thread that has worn, frayed fibres hidden on the inside. One minute you are holding it and the next you are left with two broken ends. I am still struggling to understand the thread that joins me and my mother. I have been struggling to make sense of it all my life. I have spent years trying to weave us closer to each other, but each time she lets go or the ends fray. Every time that thread breaks, I knot it together. 'Here,' I say, holding it out to her, 'this is your end.'

I want to ask her so many questions while there is still time. It makes it hard to know where to begin. The realisation that it is too late only comes when it is too late. And it is harder to unravel a life when memory has its own mind.

These days, I am noticing how memory can be both selective and forgetful. It chooses carefully what it hides. Sometimes I wonder if we only remember those things that are important to us. What is important to us can be different from what others think matters. My mother does not know who I am. When she wakes, I will tell her again. 'Hello, Mum,' I will say. And then I will introduce myself. It helps to know who is there at the start of a day, and to be reminded where it is that you are staying, if the bed feels unfamiliar. Even after I repeat my name, often she will forget who I am a few minutes later. Every day our journey is different from the one we made the day before, but always this is the same. Later, when she says, 'I'm sorry, but I don't know who you are,' we start over, and sometimes I wonder if it is more important for me that she knows who I am than it is for her. But it doesn't matter because, already, I can see from her face that she is thinking of something or someone else, and the moment is gone.

In all my life, I have never heard my mother say, 'I love you.' I know that love exists between us, but I long to hear her voice these words. As a child, I used to have a problem shaping my mouth around them each night before sleep. I had a terrible stammer that came on when I was stressed, which, at home, was often. I think it was born when those words of love did not come: at six years old, I stuttered only on the sounds I, L and Y. 'I love you' is an avowal, but in my heart it was a question. Every time it is meant as a question and does not find an answering echo, it gets harder to say.

Now, when I look at my mother, I realise the sadness of it is that 'I love you' cannot be a question. If you hear these words in response because you are asking to hear them, their significance is diminished. Love is a gift. You cannot ask for it. It must be given freely.

It has been difficult to arrange for my mother to stay here. I have done everything I can to make it possible. At home, in the family house where I grew up, there is a finely tuned list of routines and round-the-clock carers. My mother decided years ago that she would rather stay in the house where we grew up than close to where any of her family were then. We fixed accommodation near each of us, to make it possible, but she refused it all. 'I want to stay here,' she insisted, and that was the subject closed. I have always understood and respected her decision, yet it makes life infinitely more complicated, and her deterioration harder to manage as a family. Yet in other subtle ways, I know it is the only solution, because she has lived in that house for over fifty years. It is her home. It means that even if her mind is not always certain of the finer weave of each day, her physical body knows where she is and where to go. I think I can relate to this. It must be like searching for markers in the dark, tapping your fingers along the walls when the power cuts out. In the darkness, my body is now able to read the physical space of the croft like invisible Braille, and my feet know where they are going.

My sister is anxious. 'Five days, or it will be too much for her.'

'But I would like her here for two weeks,' I say. We argue and deliberate, and it is all the more difficult because we rarely speak to each other.

In the end, we compromise, and she comes for a week. I am excited, and yet I am nervous, too. In addition to her illness, my mother is nearly blind. It means this week we will be inseparable, and I will need to provide round-the-clock care. Not only am I glad to do this, but I know I need to do it to make my peace.

My house is not conventional. It has steps and hidden corners. So I must be always there in case she falls. There is still much that remains unfinished. There are none of the usual cupboards, utensils and furnishings of a modern kitchen or house, but it is honest, if rough at the edges. 'We will manage,' I say. 'I will do my best.' My mother needs help with dressing, daily hygiene, washing, preparing food and being reminded to eat it, alongside the countless small aspects of care.

She can be given only so much leeway before threads fray. When you have Alzheimer's, life's missing pieces can make you vigilant and alarmed. You can spend all day searching for something you sense you have lost. Eyes wide, hunting for whatever will fill that empty hole. Only then you can forget what you are looking for, and why you wanted it. 'Here, take this,' I say, when I see fingers start to burrow in her handbag. I would love to take that bag away from her, but it is like a child's security blanket. It makes my mother feel safe knowing it is there. Sometimes she forgets it is close by, so I have to remind her. It is strange how a bag can feel as alive as a breathing person sitting next to you.

Whenever I can, I give her something to hold. Gently, I wrap my hands about hers. 'Look, isn't it soft?' I say. And then she relaxes, and smiles. 'Yes, it is beautifully soft.' Her hands explore it closely and then look at me in wonder. And together we stroke whatever it is. A teddy bear, a favourite cardigan or a cosy, woollen hat. It unifies us in that moment, sitting there in front of the fire. And I am grateful for this. Because in the end, all we can try to offer to each other in life is compassion. In the end, there is an infinite number of ways to express and know love.

It is not easy caring for someone, but every minute is precious. Washing is difficult, as is brushing her teeth. I wish I could tell her, 'I have not experienced what you have, but I think I understand.' I remember having trouble with all the basic routines. There was a time, when I was struggling with my mental health after so much shattering loss, and the pain and hardships of living in a hostile environment, when sequencing, reading and speech defeated me. My memory was shot. I forgot the smallest and biggest things. I was unsure of myself. Some part of me, ragged and broken, shattered into sharp splinters of glass. I now understand how the most mundane aspects of a life can be not only frightening but desperately confusing. I want to tell her,

'It's OK. We will get by.' But I know to say only what matters. So I tell her, 'I love you. I am here.'

Alzheimer's teaches you to be economical with words; the value of language. I do not want to ever have regrets that I did not try. Each night, while she is here with me on the croft, I know to reassure her. I talk to her, hold her hand, tuck her up in bed and switch out the light. It is like looking after a little child. It fulfils a need in me that has always been waiting to provide these gestures of love. It is baffling to feel so happy and close to tears over something so simple. With my mother, I am able to care for another human being in a way I have always longed to. Such small contacts can forge memories that will last a lifetime.

I must anticipate her needs. The night of her arrival I did not tuck her in, and she lay uncovered on top of the bed all night. It scared me to see her lying there, shivering and desperately cold, in the morning. She did not understand that she needed to get in under the duvet, blankets and sheets. The thick stone walls of the house make it much colder than she is used to. I keep the fire burning, piling it high with logs and coal. The stove sounds like a dragon. A thick heap of blankets and throws sits on the sofa and armchair. I pull them closer to the fire. It is only by reaching out and touching her hands that I am able to check if she is warm or cold. It also tells me when she needs to eat and drink. You lose heat when your blood sugar drops. So every few minutes I hold her hands. It is a link between us. It is a joy to me to have this excuse to hold her. Now that she is ill, she does not pull her hands back. She does not shy away. Sometimes I wonder if she remembers there was a time when she did. This does not matter any more. It makes me sad, but at the same time glad that I have this physical closeness now. And when I realise I do not need an excuse to touch her, it is a revelation. She is my mother and I love her, and hands are made to be held.

I am getting to know my mother as I have never known her before; getting to know the part of herself that she never showed to me. She is so different from the mother she used to be. And that, too, makes me both sad and glad. And confused. I feel guilty because it is illness that is giving my mother to me in ways she was always absent. Alzheimer's can be like that. It can construct a unique present out of frayed threads of the past. Its pattern, its warp and weave, is often different from the one we knew.

Everyone's experience of illness is different. Memory loss is devastating but, for all its heartache, it allows me to talk to her more intimately than I ever did before. It frees her in ways I never thought possible, gives her permission to do things differently. One morning, we are washing up and I drop a mug. My hands are less responsive since they were broken, and I am always dropping things. I practise each day to strengthen them and to master tasks that I used to take for granted, but I know they will never be the same again. Simple actions can still be difficult. Holding crockery, fastening buttons, turning pages or opening lids.

I watch as the china mug smashes into bits on the floor. I do not react. Most of my crockery has chips, or ends up in pieces being used as drainage for potted plants outside. But my mother does. She laughs. 'Fuck!' she shouts, and then she laughs again, as she sings out the word over and over, and starts to dance. She twirls around the kitchen, and suddenly I am laughing and dancing with her. It is a beautiful moment. Afterwards, as we wipe our tears away, I am inexpressibly happy. I hug my mother tightly.

Time has unravelled the last few days. I am out of sync with the routines that normally anchor my life with an easy rhythm. But it does not matter. It is a priceless gift to have this time with my mother, uninterrupted.

It is a benefit to have her here in other more subtle, invisible ways I had not anticipated. Her presence gives me something in common with the rest of the community. They see that I, too, have family ties, close kin in need of my support, and that seems to matter. It makes me less strange. I sense I am being perceived in a different light, one that may lead to the smallest shift or thaw in relations, through simple exchanges, prompted by interest or mere curiosity, when we are out and about or at the shop. 'Is that your mother?' is a welcome invitation to engage, no matter how briefly. Her illness is apparent, as is my care of her. Just being seen at a distance, walking slowly hand in hand with her, places me in a familiar context. I can feel that I am being reappraised. I realise how making this connection may be important to others. And how important their reappraisal may be for me, too.

On our last night, my mother and I sit together, the same as always. We are wrapped in blankets. The house is not warm, but the fire is lit and the stove is cooking a hot supper. I have dug out a cardboard box of photographs. Old, faded, white-edged prints. I hand them to her so she can hold them as I describe them to her. As I pass each small square to her, my mother's eyes light up. For a few minutes, she is lost in the past. I look at each of those strange images, family pictures of my childhood. We stand alert, separate, each in our own space, staring out at the camera. Pale faces; eyes wide, fearful, silent. I know my brother wants to stand closer, but he is wary, alert. He would keep his eyes fixed on the door because when trouble starts, even if it's your sister who is getting knocked to the floor, you run. It makes me feel happy and sad to revisit those days. It is my childhood. At the time you just accept that this is how life is.

'What is it like,' I ask my mother, 'right now in your head? Please tell me. So I can help you. I want to try and understand.'

She thinks for a moment. 'It is like you are living in a world with no connection to anyone or anything. It is lonely. It is like nobody is there.'

I need to understand why my childhood was so unhappy and difficult. Why such a vital bond was lacking. I do not know why it matters after so long. But it still does. I wonder if perhaps it is because, regardless of how much time has passed and how old you are, something inside you will always be the child you once were. With my mother, that part of me still reaches out shyly, arms opening, waiting for her approval and love. Love and validation forever inextricably entwined. It is healing to know that now she will not turn away.

As a child, in the absence of comfort, I used to turn to my favourite tree. It stood strong, tall, dependable, reaching its branches out to me like waiting, open arms outside my bedroom window. Waking or sleeping, I felt it watching over me. It saw my childhood through my eyes. Each night, I would wrap my hands around it, press my lips to its bark and pour out my secrets and sorrows to it. It helped to know someone was listening. It was the first thing I saw as soon as I opened my eyes. It may sound strange, but I am convinced that beautiful presence looked after me. It helped me in ways that adults could not. It taught me the importance of wild nature young. When you have nothing else to turn to, you learn it helps not just to bury your pain. It helped me to look up to the sky and to find comfort in quiet, living things.

I know I cannot ask my mother all the questions to which I need answers. But there is one that I will always regret not asking if I do not try. I have imagined so many times how the scenario might play out. I sit closer. I take a breath. I do not know if she will admit to it. I do not know if she will even remember. It is hard to ask your mother why she looked away.

'I did not know,' she tells me, her eyes wide, staring at me.

'But how could you not?'

'It never happened in front of me. I never imagined he would hurt you.'

My face flushes. It is confusing. The truth is, I can understand how her memory has fashioned a narrative she can accept, because in my head I, too, have erased those sights and sounds.

As we sit in silence, I hear myself say, 'It's OK. We are here now.' My eyes fill with tears. For those few fleeting moments, her mind runs in a beautiful clarity. We look into each other's eyes. I know she sees me and I see her, exactly as we are.

I want to ask, 'What did you think when you first looked at me in your arms?' My mother once told me she was not ready for me, and resented my coming into the world. Those words have stayed with me, yet in my heart I know it is not her love that is in doubt, but her willingness or ability to express it. If I ask her this, it will be a wasted question. I will simply be asking her to express a version of her truth that I can better understand.

I wonder then if I should ask about her relationship with my father. But I do not, because I realise that I do not want to know. Her love for my father is not mine.

I want to ask, 'Were you happy in life?', so I can understand how she sees the world. But she has always been a private person, and I don't want to diminish her by taking away that part of her nature.

The hardest question is the one I cannot ask. The one that is a distillation of all the rest. 'Mum, did you really love me? So if anything were to happen to me, you would stop it, because otherwise it would break your heart?'

In the end, if this is all the time I have left with my mother, I do not need to ask her anything. Because in my heart I already know everything I need to know. When you have your mother back for a few moments, it is too precious a time for words. So I just hold her.

4

Earth

THE GRASS SCRATCHES my bare legs as I lean heavily on the gate. As the latch lifts, my hand sends the bolt swinging. I look back over my sun-freckled shoulders, sweat running into my eyes. The light is flat, so the glassy air shimmers with a dry, crackling heat. It is full summer, the rough heart of the year, and the sun-parched earth is gasping for moisture through its hard crust. Over the past weeks, the shallow springs have gradually run dry. The grass is blackened and scorched beside the baking rocks. Even the silver ash leaves are wilting. I have risen early to gather in the ewes in the fresher dawn for the shearing. But already the heat is intensifying.

As I walk the ewes quietly by the low stone wall that runs along the west march line of the croft, the foliage canopy provides scant shelter. The air is thick with their rasping breath, their flanks panting, flaring nostrils pink and blowing. At their feet, Maude gasps in staccato bursts, her tongue lolling sideways out of her jaws. Forty-six fleeces are to be shorn off these heavy, sweating bodies. Already, the sharp tang of lanolin sings high and a warm, sirocco wind is wafting across the croft, steeping the air in dust, fresh dung and acrid urine. I pour a bottle of water over my head and splash my burning face.

The barn is not big enough to hold and shear stock in these numbers. The fank has always been used for this job, and that tradition has meant I have never considered doing it any other way. But stringing the heavy machinery over a makeshift frame and ensuring that it is adequately supplied with mains power is a challenge, and I need help to do this. The fank is surrounded by tall trees, but, with no overhang, to provide a stable framework I need to use these huge long ladders which have to be dragged out from the hayloft. The resulting construction looks both precarious and magnificent, if only for the sheer enormity of its scale. When it is ready, I pull myself up the twenty-foot ladder to fix cables to the trees so it is safe to switch the power on.

Above my head, the primitive, square assembly frames the clear sky. At first glance it may not look very sound, but I have made sure that it is tied tight with baler twine and secured with double knots. You do not hope for the best at the shearing. No one fools about with razor-sharp cutters once the whirring motor is on: it matters that you get everything right every time. The shearing cables are draped through the trees, connected to the power by a black cord snaking to the fuse box in the barn. The engine is old and cumbersome, but it starts smoothly first time.

At last I give the thumbs-up to the young farmer standing below. 'All set,' I call. He nods, rummaging through the heavy bag at his feet. Carefully, he pours oil on to the sharpened cutters and combs. I appreciate his help. I would love to do the shearing myself, but it is a highly skilled craft which I am not trained in and cannot manage. Sometimes you have to recognise what you can and can't do. For years this was difficult for me, because I felt I had to do everything. It is a relief to lay down that burden and to feel able to turn to others, to offer and accept help in equal measure when and where it is needed, as those who work the land have always done. These exchanges still usually take place within families or other close associations, but I always pay for the help I receive. It makes it easier to ask for assistance and sets firm boundaries. Good fences make good neighbours.

The farmer shearing my sheep for me today has been away working on the mainland, and has come back to the island armed with some refreshingly open-minded ideas. He is diligent, reliable and used to shearing hundreds of sheep in a single morning. His relaxed manner and broader outlook have made it easier for me this year to make arrangements for the shearing.

With the platform assembled, only the last mechanical checks remain. I watch as strong hands expertly position the comb guards so that they are slotted into the handpiece ahead of the cutters. The gleaming blades are clean and sharp, dangling from the machine suspended above the shearer. As he wipes their edges, he reaches into a bag and throws a container on to the earth. 'Tar, for spraying nicks,' he explains. I already have my own supplies of tar spray in a bucket, but I am touched by the care he has taken. However skilled the shearer, sharp blades occasionally wound soft skin. Tar spray covers the bleeding gash and stops blowflies sucking the blood and laying white eggs in the open flesh wound.

Catching a ewe under the chin, I steer her into the central pen. 'Ready?' I ask. The farmer nods and then, gently, he crocks her, swiftly turning her neck and pushing down her rear end, so she sits on the rubber shearing mat. 'All right, lass,' he says quietly to the ewe. 'Let's get this heavy weight off you.' I watch as he settles her, tenderly stroking her face.

'What?' he laughs, as he catches my surprised expression. 'They notice when you are good to them. They behave sensible.' I am encouraged to see how the sheep are responding to his quiet handling. It is one of a few welcome signs lately of how the island is slowly changing. 'Pull!' he calls. I tug the cord and instantly the engine starts whirring. It makes a low, purring sound. And then I relax, looking on, mesmerised, as the thick wool spills like water away from the skin. I give my full attention to this important ritual of stripping the fleece from a breathing animal. Watching that wool tumbling on to the shearing mat, I can feel all the months and years falling away.

Shearing is always an eagerly anticipated date in the farming calendar. The ewes struggle to carry their fleeces in the heat, especially this year. My legs are weary and aching from walking the croft four times a day to check for any tipped over, or 'cowped', on their backs. Counting sheep is not just for children or for trying to get to sleep. I count mine diligently to be sure none are unaccounted for.

I am glad to see those thick fleeces shorn and the ewes spared the risk of heat exhaustion. It is a release for us all from a sense of heaviness, and it heralds a spell of rest before the lambing sales. I have no tup, but, to my surprise, I still have six lambs. Although no gates have been left open or fences breached, somebody else's ram somehow found its way on to the croft. I keep quiet and simply integrate the lambs into the flock. My sheep are no longer sold for meat. I long ago stepped off that track. These days, the shearing supplies me with raw wool for handicrafts. There have been criticisms that I am wasting the croft by not lambing, which does not seem to me entirely coincidental to the arrival of the lambs, but I show by doing, not talking. Change takes time to be accepted, but I am confident that one day acceptance will come.

Shearing is an old dance. It tests stamina, skill and resolve. The ewe rests back into the shearer's body, carefully braced against his legs and arms, her four legs raised above the ground. The soft, close curls that fall from the belly, shorter, denser than the main fleece, are discarded. Once the abdomen and haunches are clipped, her head is tipped back and the cutters whirr smoothly upwards from the sternum to the neck. A quick flick lifts her arm, so that it is braced by the shearer's elbow. The clippers nestle deep into the fleece above the soft skin of the armpits. I hold my breath, tar spray at the ready, but this ewe is rolled smoothly on to her back without incident. The shearer is adept and methodical. Sweat is dripping off his brow as he runs the cutters in long, single strokes from the rear flank to the head. The wool smells delicious. It is a rich, dense, ripe scent. Burying my nose in it, I think of how many hard frosts it has seen.

There is an art to throwing a fleece. As it is cast aside, I lift it and lay it clean side down, trying not to tear its soft, unmarked edges, while working quickly to clear it of dirt and muck. My hands dive into its weight, fingers picking away at the dags – matted, dung-encrusted locks of wool – as I untangle other debris from the main fleece. I remove the sweat fribs and other less desirable pieces of the fleece, with grass burrs, seeds, dried leaves and small twigs snared into the wool. A small, dusty pile will be used later to wrap around strawberry plants, to mulch my vegetable beds and stop up cold draughts in my cottage walls.

Once the main fleece is skirted, I fold its outer edges inwards, from both sides, towards its centre. Then the fleece is rolled, from the britch end to the neck, the neck wool is carefully parted and tucked into the fleece, and it is tied. After rolling the fleece, I dig a smooth stick into a pot of blue resin and mark the croft's signature on to the newly shorn ewe. A single dab positioned between the right shoulder and backbone enables the ewe to be identified at a glance, so that you don't have to catch her to check her ear tag and flock mark. There were times when it was used as a deterrent to the problem of stray sheep being appropriated into other flocks. I have heard tales of fistfights over sheep and one story of an entire flock disappearing off a hill, only to be found six miles down the road. These days the island is quiet and the sheep do not wander. Farming is no longer the mainstay of the island, nor does it dominate the community as it used to. The population is gradually increasing, its demographic is changing and the fights that so often used to take place over each blade of grass are becoming a thing of the past.

The fleeces are heavy and huge. The wool is usually simply packed into a large bag and carted away on a lorry for only a few pounds and pence from the Wool Board. There is an old saying that the Wool Board owns the wool on a sheep's back before it is shorn. This year, I have decided not to sell all my wool to the Wool Board. It barely covers the cost of the shearing. Instead I pack two-thirds of the clip separately and cover them. These are the best fleeces. I will comb through them again meticulously with my fingers and wash them in fresh rainwater. Then I will lie them flat outside to dry in the wind.

I will card the wool, pulling tufts and working it gently until it is finely combed. Once it is rolled into a ball, I will tease it into strands. Over the winter, I will meet with others to spin the wool. It is relaxing spinning yarn on to a wheel, the click of the treadle working rhythmically. From some of the fleeces I will make soft woollen throws, blankets and rugs. I am slowly learning these traditional crafts. Sometimes, I offer a basic exchange whereby artisans come to stay in the cottage and teach me. It is a lovely way to meet others and it opens a different gate to the crofting year, filled with softer voices, laughter, bright threads and stories.

As the gleaming, low early mornings lift, burning off the mist into a burnished brilliance that rises into a fragile trailing arc of sun, I pick tiny, fresh leaves from the hawthorn spires and sharp blackthorn, which are clustered with tight buds. Their barbs tear at my sleeves. It is amazing how much wear and tear the croft inflicts on work clothes. Sewing is a daily chore, but it is more than that. It is a meditative practice. I am not a good sewer but I find it relaxing. It is a metaphor for life: each type of stitch teaches you a different lesson with its flowing dive into the fabric. You learn, for example, that when using running stitch, it is often sensible to secure that loose row of thread by backstitching it. It keeps it from unravelling, helps each stitch to withstand the hard brunt of daily life. It anchors your effort so that each stitch counts.

These days, with a new generation reaching adulthood, an influx of international volunteers coming to work on the crofts and farms, and the emergence of a quiet yet burgeoning tourism, the island is changing. It wears its face differently. It matters less if you do not have kin of your own here. I live freely, without seeking others' permission, and on my own terms. I am making my own traditions and friendships that are steadfast, trustworthy and dependable.

When I think back to those early years on the croft, I wonder how we coped. That time was free in many ways, but it was emotionally arduous and physically gruelling. There was so much to learn, and so much that was invisible and difficult to navigate. The effort demanded by some of those harder years was punishing, but they also developed vital skills and brought the first inkling of the endurance required to thrive here. Those years alone have taught me all that is valuable in my life.

It helps to feel the seasons changing, to feel your hands chap and your cheeks roughen. I am still learning. In nature there are no hard edges. Perhaps this is why I seek out the wilds before I seek people. The natural world offers a peace like none other I know.

I do not worry now what each day will bring. I deal with times of hardship and plenty as they come. Worry is draining. It depletes and diminishes your vision and strength. I try to be open and adaptable. It allows each day to run smoothly when you live close to the soil. It enables you to work instinctively and proactively with nature. So long as you are attuned to your raw instincts, each day will unfold as it is meant to.

I am practising to be like earth. If I am cold, I light a fire. If I am hurt, I breathe and allow my tears to flow. If I am fearful, I step closer to the source of my fear. If I am alone, I go outside into the wilds for their solace and company.

Once the shearing is finished I kick off my boots and peel off my socks. The sun dapples my feet. I lie in the grass and watch the white clouds scudding over the hills.

Sometimes I dream that one day, when I become too old to work, I will offer this land to a young family with a child. I dream of sharing the beauty of this soil in a kinship of trust. My hands have been shoring up for the future. Planting seeds, acorns, birch feather and sycamore wings. I have been planting trees for the next generation: for wildlife to find shelter. I understand now that as long as you know where to go to find sanctuary, inspiration and protection, the land is a beautiful and forgiving place.

5

Air

I T IS MID-MORNING. The corrugated-iron roof of the old lambing barn is straining in a blast of northeasterly wind, unusual for the late summer. The yard dust lifts, whirling in gusts; the heavy air is laden, saturated with the thick scent of rain. But aside from a bullet-grey sheen, the skies remain clear. It is unsettling when you look to the skies to find the weather is at odds with itself. It makes your instinct more alert and on edge. I know a full-blown storm is imminent, scudding in from the horizon, not just from watching the gulls huddled against the feeders, or because the sheep are sheltering in the woods on the southwesterly aspect of the croft, or simply by watching the mercury sink low in the glass. I know it by all of this, but most of all I know it from the dull, leaden tang in my mouth, which stimulates saliva to spring to my tastebuds. I lift my face to scent and taste the air more keenly. That blunt-edged taste is a harbinger of either trouble or change.

These days my instinct is hard-wired to an internal library of nature's clues, so I listen and take heed of the small signals that my body absorbs. Sometimes I feel like litmus paper, soaking up atmospheric moisture and pressure. Today a wire thread of adrenaline is twitching, strung taut inside. I listen as the thin sheeting of the barn roof hums and shivers, trembling violently against its fixings, twisting and writhing, seeking to set itself free. Every few minutes it moans and shudders, before rippling in a belching spasm. It is terrifying to see that old, frayed, metal structure tearing itself apart. The perished, rusted metal is disintegrating, tiny flakes frittering away before my eyes as tiny, ragged shards splinter. It has been threatening to self-destruct for years. It is not a huge barn, maybe twenty foot high, yet with each gust the roof clatters, banging violently against the crumbling wall heads. And every few minutes an immense blast lifts the sheeting like two great wings. It has been like this for hours. I have despaired of trying to secure it.

My faithful hosepipe, whipping and coiling itself into sickening snakelike motions, has been a trusted friend and has given its all over the years. It has anchored the trusses, its ends laid out and tied to enormous rocks, an old rusting tractor axle and a thousand-kilogram solid-steel cattle crush, tensioning the entire roof down. I have salvaged all the debris from the croft to make this haphazard safety provision in the absence of funds to re-roof the barn. It is a strange affinity to have, but I am deeply attached to that section of hosepipe. It has saved me from disaster more times than I can remember. We have slogged it out together, battling extremes of gruelling weather over the last fourteen years.

As I watch with my heart in my mouth, trying to fathom what on earth to do, a momentous thought lands. There is nothing else I can do. And that is so absolute it is strangely calming and gives me strength.

There is always a point of no return when you suddenly step beyond your own fatigue, hesitation or sense of failure – to embrace your fear. And finally the roof shears over the walls, crumpling to the ground, and the barrelling wind tears into the hollow structure inside. I reach into my pocket, take out a sharp blade and, as that heavy tin sheeting clamours, I cut it free. I can't quite believe this is happening. All I feel is a euphoric relief. The weight of that roof has been pressing down on me all these years. There is a sense of freedom in letting it go. It is one less thing to waste my energy holding on to.

The roof is shuddering off the wall heads in convulsive gasps. I am frozen, unsure if more is to come. Its sharp, serrated edges, whirring like ragged disc blades through the air, carry the risk of inflicting serious damage or a hideous injury. Don't break up, I will it, as the separate panels start quivering. The roof will be impossible to control if it dismembers itself. Each sheet risks slicing or severing a limb in seconds. Thank goodness the livestock are safe, sheltering in the woods, well out of harm's way.

Hours later, I sweep up ripped metal and branches with a wire brush. The yard is eerily quiet in the radiant light soaking through a spattering rain. The wind-torn clouds are away, revealing the destruction and debris left behind. A tree is down, its trunk fissured in half and obstructing a gate. The barn, a desolate, drenched carcass of stone, looks more ancient and starkly beautiful. It is as if the years have been rolled back, hewing its bare structure to its origins. Inside, buckets splash with the sound of dripping water, and straw lies bedraggled and sodden in the yard. Fortunately, the hay is protected by a heavy tarpaulin cover. What now? I wonder, dismayed and appalled at the wreckage. As if in answer, a noise overhead startles me. A small bevy of swans is flying, their wings rhythmically strumming the sky like a lyre. The air through their wingtips oscillates and hums. It is a dreamlike moment. Visions of swans traditionally signify prosperity, luck and love, so I wonder if seeing a group in the air has the same portent. Take me with you, I think, as I watch them go. It is an extraordinary sight, seeing those heavy bodies so graceful and weightless.

I know not to worry. The wind is symbolic to me of the breath of change. It has stripped the barn of its past, and forced me, in the space of three hours, to envisage life on the croft differently. Sometimes the universe invites us to work according to its principle of destruction and alteration. To empty a space, discard an outworn routine or simply let go, so that a different future may fill that emptiness. The sight of the swans reminds me that if you can rise above the chaos, the mysterious flow of the wind offers a source of strength and renewal.

I slam on the brakes and lean heavily on the truck door with my shoulder. Leaving the key in the ignition and the engine running, I scour the verge, backtracking quickly but quietly. Did I really see it? I wonder, my eyes combing the steep bank. Suddenly, there it is, black wet feathers in a crumpled heap against the low stone dyke. As I crouch down, its ruffled head tilts and looks up at me. At first I think it is a baby rook, with the most beautiful milk-blue eyes. His wing is torn and his leg and foot damaged. He does not move as I gently fan out his wings. He is barely feathered, all downy fluff, neck hunched down into his shoulders. I try to stand him up but he falls over on to his side. It is then that I feel how cold and emaciated his body is. I fold my jumper into a cradle, gently scoop him into it and put him in the truck. I don't think twice. The bird is sick and he needs help. As I drive the six miles back to the croft, he stares up at me without taking his eyes off my face. I fall in love that day.

As soon as I get home, I fill a saucepan with water to hard-boil a fresh egg. When it is cool, I peel off the shell and feed small pieces, one by one, deep into the bird's gaping gullet. For some reason, the appreciative gargling sound he makes as he swallows melts my heart. His beak is long, contoured with a pointed tip, yet it is soft, delicate, hesitant. It is only then that I notice a greying ruff of feathers emerging at his crown, neck and back. A flicker of doubt creeps into my mind. I look at him closely, and in my heart I know he is not a rook, but a hooded crow.

On the island, hooded crows are notorious for maiming newborn lambs and are shot on sight. I wonder what I will do when he is well. Without a mother, he will be dependent on me and unable to fend for himself. And if he becomes tame, he will be insufficiently wary of humans and likely to be injured or killed. 'Don't worry,' I reassure him. 'Let's get you well before we work out the rest of it.' I keep hoping those greying feathers will somehow vanish. I stroke the bristly black ones at the brow of his beak. 'Rooks have those,' I tell myself hopefully. But when a farmer knocks on the door to borrow a syringe of penicillin for a sick lamb, he takes one look at the bird and asks suspiciously, 'Why the fuck is a hoodie in here?'

'It's a rook,' I say casually and then I wrap an old towel protectively around him, covering his emerging grey apron. My bird winks at me and leans into my arms. I take the medication from the fridge. When animals are sick, and the island veterinary box is low on supplies, it is good to be able to call on your neighbours. It is a bridging time when help becomes of far greater value than older hostilities.

The farmer steps closer. 'That's no rook,' he says. 'The only good crow is one with its neck wrung.'

'He is sick,' I sigh. 'I will find a way to rewild him, I promise.'

By that afternoon, my skin is crawling. My fingers itch and I scratch until I bleed. It feels as if something is eating the inside of my flesh. Looking up, I see my crow watching me from his small open pen, littered with straw and grass bedding, by the kitchen door. He is too ill to perch so I have piled up some sticks for him to crouch on instead.

I lift him up and inspect him more closely. When I part the downy fluff and newly emerging feathers, his skin is pockmarked and bare, covered in mites so small they are almost invisible. In the folds of a roll of skin in the soft hollow at the base of his shoulders, a dark fly buzzes, fat and soporific, feeding on an open wound in his flesh. I shudder, but I know I have to deal with this. I take the crow out to the roofless barn and clean him with a soft cloth. I find three more flies and no part of his body that is not covered in parasites. I have a medicine cabinet with antibiotic, painkiller and a mite drench, which I administer. 'I'm sorry,' I tell him, 'but you will have to stay here until the morning.'

I make a fresh pen, feed and settle him, and then I strip off outside in the yard and hose myself down with water from head to toe. Afterwards I run to the sea and jump into the waves. Later that night, I burn the clothes I have been wearing. Thankfully, I am no longer scratching. It is such a relief to be rid of that terrible infestation. Until the crow is well, and clear of these parasites, I wrap him in a towel and wear gloves. Each morning, I move his pen out on to fresh grass, under the trees. He sits and watches me, seemingly listening intently to every word I say. It takes five days to clear those bugs from his body. I do not bring him back into the house because I do not want him dissociated from his natural environment. 'You can't keep him,' I tell myself firmly, and yet I long to. He is a beautiful companion, intelligent and affectionate.

I carry him with me around the croft. It is weeks before he can walk or fly, managing only to hop awkwardly. So he is content to sit quietly in my arms. When I am digging outside, he sits on the ground and watches me. He loves to eat egg, black beetles and small pieces of melon, but most of all he loves black grapes. As he grows, his markings become more pronounced.

'We cannot help who we are,' I tell him.

I call him Feannag, which is Gaelic for crow, and shorten his name to Fea.

One day, Fea attempts a short flight in the garden. His wings will not carry him. He tries to land in a tree but falls to the ground. I lift him up, feed him and place him in the lower branches of the Scots pine by the wild berries. I have a plan in mind, and this morning I decide to put it to the test. I have read in a wildlife study that, contrary to popular opinion, crows do not attack youngsters in order to maim or kill them. They bombard them simply to encourage them to struggle to safety well above the ground. My research suggests that crows have an extraordinarily complex and sophisticated social structure. They mate for life and have been known to care for, foster and adopt other orphaned, sick or injured juveniles outside their own immediate family networks.

I am hoping that another crow will hear Fea calling when he is hungry, find him and feed him. I am taking a chance, but it is the only chance I have. I do not have long: after about an hour he will start to weaken. It is a bright fine day, windy and fresh. 'I can see you,' I tell him, as he watches me from the tree. At first he shuffles about, arranging the smaller twigs for comfort. Shortly before an hour has passed, he starts calling for food, his cries growing increasingly desperate. I force myself not to move, but it is torture to hear him calling and know that he can see I am not coming to help him. Suddenly, a rush of wings lands several branches above him. It is a huge adult hooded crow. I watch as she advances, ducking down to reach him. As she sidles up to him, she stretches out her beak. I am terrified she will harm him. Fea is calling and flapping his wings plaintively. Then, inexplicably, she shrugs away and flies off over the hill. I cannot bear to watch. His voice grows shriller and louder until eventually he stops calling and huddles down. Keep calling, I urge him silently. Use your voice, or how can anyone find you?

Half an hour later, he starts again, and rapidly the same enormous bird approaches him again. Only this time, as he tries to reach her, he slips through the branches. I force myself to keep still. I am terrified that he will hurt himself, but a lower spray breaks his fall. The adult bobs down to meet him, stepping closer until she is facing him. As he stretches his wings, opens his beak and starts to make that deep gargling sound, she tilts forwards and plunges her beak into his gullet. It is an extraordinary moment. I reach for my camera to capture it on film so I can review it more closely later.

After the adult flies off, Fea is settled and relaxed, his hunger assuaged. Over the next few hours, I watch as he is repeatedly fed in response to his calling. I realise that, judging by the increasing intervals, the currency of his food is higher than what I have been giving him. I am elated, because I know that he now stands a chance not just of surviving, but of integrating with his own kind. And I am thrilled that the risk I have taken has been worthwhile and to have witnessed an extraordinary act of compassion, one many would not believe is even possible.

A week later, Fea comes to find me in the garden. He is barely airborne but he manages short, clumsy test flights from the tree to the vegetable beds. I talk to him and he watches me intently. I know he must be fine, and I am grateful that although he has no need of me now, he chooses to sit comfortably close by me. For wildlife, as well as for humans, the main refuge from threat is within the protection of groups or family structures. Isolation is as much of an anathema to the corvus family as it is to us. This experience demonstrates that empathy for and acceptance of solitary, vulnerable individuals from outside blood kinships or familial groups is possible. It is an immensely heartening discovery.

I am standing at the window, watching the birds. The leaves have started to fall, and in the bright sunshine and wind, shadows and torn foliage whirl about the yard. Cleodie, my starling, is learning to feed, clinging on to the wire frame supporting my climbing rose and taking nuts, seeds and grapes from my bird feeders. I found Cleodie as a tiny nestling, only a matter of weeks old, on the ground. I realise that she is unused to the raucous struggle for food, not having experienced competition from siblings in the nest. It is a joy to see her now exploring the skies and trees. But now she is facing her first real test: learning to survive the colder months gusting in as the year dies back.

Suddenly, a sparrowhawk dives on to the feeders and, to my horror, Cleodie flings out her wings and screams for her life. Instinctively, I leap forwards to rap on the window. Before I get there, my moving shadow startles the predator, and it whirls about, its tawny wings elongating into a graceful take-off, swinging away over the roses and vegetable patch. I do not lose a minute. My legs are racing out of the kitchen door into the yard. Immediately, I notice a huge crow sitting on the shed. It is Feannag's foster mother. She caws abruptly twice, in quick succession. Whilst I instantly recognise this as an alarm call, I realise she is not responding to my presence, which is familiar in this setting, but to a different intruder. She shrugs into the air effortlessly and flies away after the hawk.

I gaze in amazement as she pursues it fearlessly, gaining height and plummeting down to attack it from behind. Slowly, they whirl away over the croft into the distance. I watch them locked in flight, each relentlessly seeking to gain territory and sway over the other. This mortal combat takes them circling high into the wind until they are tiny specks in the sky. When the crow returns to the croft, having successfully established her supremacy, it is a relief to know that, for now, the songbirds will be safe from the sparrowhawk and calm restored.

It is a reminder of the strange forces always at work, often unseen, within the landscape. In that circling flight, I was witnessing how predation and protection are facets of the same instinct. The crow, too, is a predator. In protecting her domain, she has her own self-interest at heart: in the springtime she will feed on the eggs of the songbirds she is defending now. Today the hawk has attacked the songbirds and the crow has vanquished it. Tomorrow, another duel may ensue with a different outcome. These forces are in constant flux in both the human and the wilder landscape. An island will forever be a closely guarded and shifting domain, of which I and the birds are each an intrinsic part.

6

Stars

ANOTHER SEASON HAS passed. It is late autumn and the ewes' fleeces are once more tousled and burred with dried leaves, heather and thistles that scratch and prickle my fingers as I untangle their knots. Cobnuts roll across the kitchen table, smooth shining brown balls of dense sweetness. I forage for pleasure now, and the days run as quietly as the leaves falling outside. They are growing shorter, and night falls swiftly after sunset, shuttering in the skies.

I am sitting on a low, rough-made stool by the flickering hearth. The dark skies outside suddenly feel breathtakingly close. In my lap, my hands cradle a box. As I open the lid, the dark wood inside gleams richly against the crimson crushed-velvet lining. I snap the safety catches to release the long bow nestling snug in its hollow. Its bone tip, threaded with a horsehair ribbon, glows pale as winter sunshine. As my fingers smooth its taut edge, it whispers with a soft, crackling sound that reminds me of early summer: of the grasses flowing wild and free over the croft, and the wind breathing through Fola's mane and tail.

It is a beautiful instrument. Perfectly moulded from rich, burnished wood, rounded at each end like a ripened fruit. My thumb plucks it gently, eliciting a vibrating, humming sound. Its voice is warm, lively, and distinctive, mellower than the sound of a fiddle. Hesitantly, I bring it closer and draw the bow across its body, so I can hear its sap ringing out of the wooden frame. As I tilt the bow, its voice quivers. I listen to its echo, as deep as the dark, porous night skies. To me, this viola is more precious than anything I own. It sings with its own clear beautiful note, transmuting the past into the present, lifting me up and transporting me with it.

The phone call came out of the blue. It was one of Cristall's daughters in New Zealand. I had been thinking of her, and then she rang as if she had heard that thought. Her voice startled me, it is so like her mother's. As bright as birdsong, rising and falling, just as I remember it, suddenly so alive and present it brought tears to my eyes. 'I have missed you,' I told her. 'I have missed you, too,' she said. For a while, we had lost touch with each other. Looking back, I think our grief was too raw for us to bear seeing it mirrored in one another. Sometimes you have to let go of the past in order to create a future. I was stunned as she explained that a sum of money had been bequeathed to me. 'She would have wanted you to have this,' Cristall's daughter told me. 'You were her other daughter. I know how much you meant to each other. It is right you should have it.'

As I put down the phone my hand was trembling. It was hard to know what to do with such an astonishingly generous gift. I wanted to be sure it was used wisely, and in a lasting way, not frittered away. I walked to the woods and sat in the midst of a circle of balsam trees, where I often go to think or dream. It helps to infuse ideas with clarity.

When the gift arrived, I first made donations to Cristall's favourite charities, then, for years, I did not touch it as I mulled over what to do with it. I knew in my heart I would like something that would interweave our past with my present, but it was difficult to think exactly what or how. I revisited all of our shared memories, of walking, sowing trees and leaves, cooking, painting, playing chess, emptying bottles of wine over long hours spent talking. One day, I was sitting with Isla outside, watching and listening to the birds. The birdsong reminded me of how much we loved music and how it seemed to allow us to feel the wilds more closely.

Music extracts all that is unharmonious from your thoughts and breaks down barriers. It touches the heart without the need for words. You feel it in your whole being. It offers escape, a visceral freedom of expression, and it helps you to work through experiences that are difficult to speak of. I learned to play the piano as a small child, yet here on the island, for years after Cristall died, I was unable to play. In time I came to appreciate that music keeps you company, too.

Suddenly, I knew what I was going to do with Cristall's gift.

It is daunting to hold an instrument that you have no idea how to play. I have chosen the viola precisely because it is a stranger to me. I want to start with a blank canvas, to approach the instrument without any preconceptions, prejudices or knowledge. My fingers feel awkward lifting the bow and yet the horsehair makes it familiar to the touch. The first time I draw it across the strings the sound it makes is like a tentative question. I do not know how to answer it, so I draw it again, and again, until the room vibrates with potential. My skin tingles listening to that sound. For the first few months, I only seem to be able to evoke openended questions from it. It is comical and frustrating not to be able to establish a dialogue. I keep trying to develop that conversation. Over time my patience rewards me. It is the start of a beautiful relationship.

I promise myself that I will learn to play by ear, rather than from a printed music score. It makes you listen more closely. 'No paper,' I tell the viola, shaking my head. 'I just want us to create together.'

There is an unresolved tension that sings from an instrument when you start to play it. It may sound strange, but although I am unskilled in handling it, the viola unlocks something inside me that has for too long been buried. When you have lived for so many years in solitude, each fresh human encounter can feel awkward and difficult at first. It is like being placed on a stage in the middle of an orchestra. You lift your bow, or open your mouth to sing, but as soon as you begin you realise that the orchestra is playing a different piece of music that you do not know. Like music, social interaction is a skill that improves with practice. Just as you have to learn each note in order to build them all up into a fluid piece of music, the small talk, signals and social constructs that form part of any brief exchange need to be rehearsed. You have to familiarise yourself with the dynamics of rhythm, cadence, pitch and tone. When you are out of practice this can be difficult. I am willing, longing to connect, and yet sometimes I strike a wrong note or I am out of step with my timing. I galvanise myself, even though it is tiring. I am just not used to talking. I never thought language would not come easily to me. It is a shock to realise that something I once took for granted I must now work at.

Playing my viola helps me to step on to that stage, to identify and navigate tricky points in the music. 'You can do it,' I tell myself. 'It is important to live without fear or regrets.' Yet sometimes it is easier said than done. Loneliness is hard to break down into its component parts, but each day, as I practise a combination of notes, I see how it is constructed of an emotive chord structure of distrust, hurt and lack of social support.

As I gain in confidence, I am able to play more fluently, and to produce a beautiful sound that sings of spiritual and creative growth and nurtures energy and the desire for company. Music is about making yourself vulnerable in a safe space. It is about facing your challenge and playing through it until the notes flow together. I understand now that it is not the number of social relationships you have that can make you feel full or empty, lonely or content, but how these connections play aloud in your heart, and whether the notes are true or false.

The joy of the viola is that, unlike the piano, it is light and portable. Each night, as I play in front of the fire, a thought flickers. I wonder if it is the key that might unlock the door to a wider musical community. I hold tight to that thought. I dream of being able to play with others.

Winter is a time of drawing inwards, yet I start to imagine a different way to spend the long dark colder months. The island is changing and so am I. In November, the cliffs are hewn sharper by salt spray and winds skirling off the sea. The heather bells brighten as the grass dies back and the browning hills darken. Hare dart furtively, and the bare shores glisten with whelks and limpets, clutching the rocks. Greylag quills litter the shingle and the skies advance north. The wind sings through the old ploughs, left standing, like an invisible loom still winding the threads of the land and its memories together, each day weaving a different past and present. In that metallic vibration, I hear the clink of heavy harnesses and the harsh calls chivvying the bowed heads of the old plough horses patiently working these fields. It is humbling to think of the simple joys and hardships of those bygone years.

My eyes naturally acclimatise to the darkness. The winter land rests quiet and still. Behind a craggy headland, a sharp blade of sunlight cleaves a path, glowing amber like a mythical beast. I watch as the dark line of the landscape deepens and hardens. An ancient ruin that once sheltered men, women and children in fiercer times torches bright against the skyline. I am glad those days of fear and struggle are gone. The landscape wears no airs and graces. It offers no false promises. I recognise in its stark simplicity a way of life I have grown to love beyond words.

I wonder if it is our everyday relationships with others that help to normalise our own quirks and idiosyncrasies. We ask for tolerance of traits that are different from others'. And yet, for all our social habits, we are as wary as the birds of difference or otherness. There were times I used to visualise the small clutch of people here as guillemots perched on a rock: watching the tides pass, squabbling and making our peace as the sun rises and sets each day. Now I understand that, like the birds, we are also following our own calling. There is always a time to take a solitary flight or to search for that wilder space beyond. But still each of us needs others to create a safe haven and home.

Music is teaching me to approach others with an active ear, to pick up their unique vibrations. It is as subtle as striking a tuning fork and feeling its resonance stirring inside, like interpreting welcome or warning in birdsong. It strips away superficialities, artificialities, and lays an intention bare. I am noticing how some folk emit true notes that resonate at a higher or middle frequency. They draw you closer with a warmth of tone that helps your own unique vibration to harmonise with theirs. I notice how my eyes lift, my voice brightens, my jaw relaxes and my limbs soften. Others' voices sound thinner, off-key or discordant, belying what their words or faces are signalling. Some are strident and overtly push you away. It changes the way I think, feel and respond to others. I am not only hearing the sounds, I am listening more deeply. And I notice how that draws kindred lives closer to mine.

And in the midst of that musical dialogue, I am learning the sound of my own wild call.

I remain shyer and more wary than I used to be. I rarely go out, and spend my days on the croft alone. Sometimes it makes me reflect on how profoundly and irrevocably our experiences can alter us. Sometimes it just makes me sad. I remember how, when I first came to the island, I was worried about this happening; that Rab and I might become different from the people we knew ourselves to be. Sometimes, when you have lost or forgotten a piece of music, you have to go back to the beginning and teach your fingers to play it again.

Trust is a golden, haunting note. Happiness is a strong, dominant chord, one of the most beautiful I know. It holds the possibility of resolving uncertainties, hurts and worries. It brings an uplifting end to darker, restless, minor chords. I am still improvising when it comes to forgiveness. I think that is in a key I am still learning. I am trying to let the past go. It is difficult, but over time it gets easier, and that encourages me. But some things take more time. I am hopeful that one day I will be able to be as confident and outgoing as I used to be. Sometimes you have to roll up your sleeves and just keep trying to improve at what you find the hardest.

As I light the lanterns, the moon is rising over the mountains. It glows pale, luminous on the freshwater loch below the croft and the silver sea beyond. A cluster of dark heads is gathered around the fire-light. Their silhouettes are etched clear against the flickering, golden flames. The gorse is crackling within a huge framework of sticks and branches. I am on the top of the hill, beside my favourite ash tree, where, not so long ago, I kept vigil as other flames purged me of the trappings of my past life.

Tonight I am circled with music and laughter, by harmonious voices, fiddles, a whistle and guitars. As I look at my tree, I am sure it is listening, gently rustling its leaves. Behind us, the ewes are cropping the short grass. At my feet, Maude's eyes are bright, reflecting the amber-lit flames. I think, everyone and everything I have is with me now in this moment, here. I smile as I tuck my viola beneath my chin and lift my bow. These friendships are still forming, and I am still inexperienced and young in my bowing, but I have journeyed a long way to find this bright constellation. I hope I will always be able to add the light of my own star to its shimmering pattern.

Sun and Moon

MY FINGERS FAN the knot of tiny roots. They are pale, translucent, covered in fine cilia. I breathe on them softly. As my fingertip nudges warm soil gently against the slender stem, I whisper, 'Live beautifully.' And then I mist the leaves of the silver birch tree with a fine spray of fresh rainwater, and place it in the sunshine. Its rising sap will be nourished by its being planted just before the mid-month. It is one of many that will one day stand in a great circle of silver and gold variegated birches beside the cottage on the croft. Its bright bark signifies hope for the future; its seasonal shifts represent trust in the natural movement of the cosmos and the great wheel of life.

I plant now according to the natural rhythms of the sun and the moon. The sunshine is hot on my bare skin as my hands weave soft ties in and out of a fishing net. It is thick, gnarled and coarse with wind and weather. It smells of the creels, salt and a cold, moving tide, even though these days it is washed with freshwater showers. The sweet peas are already thick with foliage, and the first flowers are opening as I thread old willow cane supports through the tangle of curling stems. At their base, I earth up the tiny plantings into the soil, pressing my fingers down around the roots that will bring nutrients to its growth and flowering.

I am learning how to live in closer alignment with bigger, unseen rhythms. As I tamp down the soil, I reflect on how all of life, its germination, growth, fruition and dying, is influenced by water and light, how all of it would be impossible without the sun and moon. Planting seeds in the right phase of the month makes all the difference to their growth. I feel so firmly anchored working like this. Swimming in the sea has immersed me daily in these rhythms over two and a half years as its ocean tides swell and ebb in harmony with these lunar phases.

A year has passed since I took possession of the gift of my viola. It is seven years since Cristall was killed on the road. As I look up, a swallow falls out of the sky, and then spins, twirling, lifting gracefully on its wingtip into the barn. The return of the swallows is magical. It feels like a promise. There is something wonderful about seeing those bare nests filled.

Springtime is always a hopeful time of year. The croft has never looked so beautiful. That day something that has been clouding my vision falls from my eyes. I have so much here to offer, I think. Fresh air, a beautiful home, a calm environment. Friendships that, whilst still young, are supportive, true and to be trusted. Above all, I know I have love to give. I cannot think of anything more I could need to make the dream I have held close to me all my days a reality. Years have passed and I have still not let go of that dream. The sense of longing has hemmed in my life and altered its structure and shape.

Years before I tried to have a child naturally, I made enquiries about adoption. Having suffered serious injuries previously, I was worried that, even if I was able to conceive, I might be unable to carry a baby to full term. Later, I decided I wanted first to see if I could conceive and carry myself, but in my heart I was still anxious. I invested years in this struggle for motherhood with nothing but a lot of heartache to show for it. Not long after we came to the island, I made an overseas adoption application. I chose China, whose one-child policy left female babies at risk of abandonment, infanticide or the orphanage. I had taken a close interest in a friend's successful overseas adoption and had watched her daughter grow from a toddler into a beautiful teenage girl. I learned first-hand of the risks, difficulties, challenges, successes and unknowns of this route. It upset me that it involved disruption of a mother's bond and culture. Yet, at the time, the orphanages were desperately under-resourced, lacking basic supplies, medication and care. The long-term prospects of children not adopted by local families or overseas applicants were unthinkable. I did my research at every level. The day I was approved to adopt and the long wait began, my dream of being a mother became a firm promise in my mind.

I wrote a diary for my child recording the beginnings of her journey to us. What was important was not the words themselves, but the feeling they awakened. Each night I would whisper, 'I want you to know, all this time of waiting, that you are not just a thought. You are real to me.' I planned one day to give this diary to her and read it with her, so that she would always know she was planned for and loved.

I did not mind that the process was slow because it made me confident that the stringent legislation in place to prevent the system being abused was being followed. I expected it to take at least eighteen months, and I was warned that the wait might be indefinite, but every year my application was reapproved and renewed. After five years, however, I grew anxious. I did not want to give up, for fear that I might find I was just months away from a placement. Having waited so long, I could not bear that thought. I consoled myself that eventually it would happen, by which time, if I was lucky, my daughter might already have a sibling born through my infertility treatment. I had always wished for more than one child. Only that was when my relationship began to implode and I lost every embryo. After Rab left, I hoped still to be able to adopt as a single parent, but sadly, my application was then rejected because of the change in my circumstances. It was a devastating blow. I had waited nine years for her when I had to let her go.

By then my little girl was tightly sewn into my heart. Suddenly I had to start unpicking those stitches. I struggled with this. It was too painful. Nearly four thousand threads – one for every day I waited for my child – now embedded deep in the tissue. When stitches have been in fabric for so long, their outline remains even after they have been removed. My heart still bears the white scars of that stitchwork, and what bound her to me, and tied me to her, is indelible.

I never imagined having a child would be this difficult. It seems to come to others so naturally. I have always forged close bonds with small children. 'There are so many ways you can be involved in other lives,' I tell myself. Yet the longing for a child of my own does not abate. 'You would make such a wonderful mother,' a friend says. 'Go with your heart.' And I know she is right. That is all you can do in life. It is important to live without regret, to keep trusting and stay open in the knowledge that nothing that is meant for you will ever pass you by. These days, I live by this creed.

I start exploring local adoption agencies.

'You live too far away,' one tells me. 'You are outside our one-hour catchment area.'

I ring another. 'You are not a first-choice candidate,' they inform me.

'That's OK,' I say. 'I don't mind being second best.'

'It's just that in most cases two parents will be preferred to raise a child.'

'I understand. But I have a lot of love to give and a beautiful home.'

We make an arrangement to talk further. I am hopeful. There may be only one of me, I think, but I have more than enough love and energy, and a strengthening support network around me. And it is true. Those hard, lonely years are gone. I discuss my decision with a close friend. She has three young children, whom I know and love. 'Here.' One of them thrusts a piece of paper at me. 'This is you.'

She has drawn me as a bird. I am feeding a young chick. 'This is your baby,' she says.

It is such a special gift that I frame it. Sometimes life is distilled to its essence when seen through the eyes of a child.

I decide to mark this time by creating something beautiful. I am making a quilt. One day, I hope I will wrap this soft fabric about my son or daughter. I have cut out the first square. It is a mother bird. I sew an appliqué on to a piece of lovely fabric, printed with swirls of leaves and berries, using a basting stitch.

'Will you make a square?' I ask my brother, sister, their children and a cluster of close friends. I have cut out the shape for each of them. I tell them, 'It is up to you to choose how you fill it.' Each of their pieces I will intersperse with others I am creating. When I throw out the quilt, I often look at its design and pattern. At its heart, I am leaving a space. I hope that one day that empty square will be filled and I will be able to sew down the edges permanently.

Every year, I plant a new tree on the croft. One day there will be a wood for us to walk through together, I think. One day, I will make a swing and hang it from the branches of these trees for the wind to blow. After I finish planting I walk to the hill. These days, I call it the Fire Hill. It is where I make all my wishes, for the sky to hear and the sun and moon to witness.

The wind is whispering through the leaves of my beautiful ash tree. I know this tree intimately. I come to sit with it each day and to reflect on all that is still to fill my life. I have its graceful shape and the rise of its sap tattooed on to my wrist, written into my body. It feels potent and healing to carry this symbol and bond on my skin. It will stay with me, be a part of me, for ever. I watch the wind brush the rippling skin of the water lapping the silver shores of the loch. The swallows are rising and falling in that fresh ruffle of glistening water and white sand. The sea shimmers all the way out to the horizon and beyond. I open my arms to the wind and cast my wish into its currents. I give my heart to the sun and moon. Beautiful things often come when we are least expecting it.

8

Wild

THE DEER ARE running, dark hooves rucking the earth, dislodging twigs and leaf litter, nicking loose shingle and grazing the stones as the tide turns around. In the moonlight, their shadows pour over the hillside an instant before I glimpse the beating life of them. They bound swiftly, tearing bracken, dense bodies hurtling out of the darkness before shuddering to a rippling standstill in the cold water. I inhale sharply, feeling the bristling presence of them, wet horns glinting, washed by the dark foam. A fine mist of breath sprays from flared nostrils as they stand proud, sinews pulsing at their throats with the blood of their running. Their taut flanks gleam darkly, glistening with sweat. I long to reach out and touch them. It is a tantalising moment that lifts me beyond the chill clasp of the sea.

In the water, I am indistinct, my hard lines and edges dissolved under the cold fire of the stars. Swimming at night feels like being reborn, some finer part of yourself wrapped in darkness and moon-light, cleansed by a cold, glittering amniotic sea. It instils a sense of wonder, offers a chance to tap into a wilder, braver and more beautiful world in which we are freed from all that holds us back or down. Swimming in moonlight is mesmerising. In the freezing water, you become so intensely locked into your physicality and yet your spirit is freed to journey expansively, beyond self-imposed limits or inhibitions. It is a beautiful sensation to feel my skin washed and salt-kissed. Like the birds, beasts lose their fear of you when you are in the water, and approach you differently; the part of me that is a predatory threat is neutralised. We face each other, and for these precious minutes, though I am alive and breathing in the waves, I am unseen. I gaze at the shad-ows of the deer etched starkly against the bright marbled shoreline. Their muscular necks flex as they raise their proud heads to scent the wind at the sea's edge, baring their long, white-boned front teeth.

I have never before seen the deer so close. The water is dark, shining and velvet-soft. As the sea laps and sighs over my skin, my human scent is undetectable, yet, with the breeze behind them, I can taste a trace of their fetid, musky odour. It is sweet, strong and acrid, like damp leaves fermenting into a rich fine dirt. I can hear their breath rasping, scorch-ing the air. It is a high, coarse, feral sound, seeking any hint of danger. I wonder if deer can smell human breath as well as our skin.

A single doe halts, ears flexing, lips puckered, eyes rigidly fixed, and for a moment watches my pale skin floating in the water. What does she see? I do not move, just let the waves lift and hold me, so that only my dark head and eyes are visible, resting on the lip of the tide. As our eyes meet for an instant, she flares her nostrils, mouth parted as if to snort an alarm. I drop my shoulders calmly, relaxing my gaze. It is not enough that it will convey observation rather than vigilance but that my intention neutralises, so that she will not sense my presence or interpret it as a threat. As I exhale slowly, lungs emptying, my buoyancy dips and I slip softly under the surface. Slowly, she lowers her head and crops the silver grass on the shore. As I bob quietly with the tide, I see that she is suckling a fawn.

For years, I have been fascinated and eluded by these shy, beautiful creatures. They draw me closer only to dart away to reconnect with their secret hinterland of soil, leaf, snapping twig and springing heather. I am in awe of their resilience. This year there has been a brutal, bloody cull that has decimated their numbers; a privately organised killing in the interests of protecting new plantings of trees on a marginal number of small crofts and farms. A herd of thirty has been reduced to a meagre four does. I am lucky to see these escapees. In the aftermath, they are wary.

Once, the island was covered in trees that shielded the deer within their rich thickets. I have taken a sharp blade and carved my own way through the forgotten or lost paths that lead back to a different world of myth, legend and folklore. Old texts eulogise the antlers and horns of the native deer as sturdily rounded, spiralled with growth and as magnificent as those of the elk. In ancient times, the deer were the sacred keepers of this island, revered for their shamanic strength. Their antlers lifted towards the sky, crowning the earth, they were a symbol of spiritual authority. As the trees were felled, burned for timber, fuel and manufacture, the deer lost their habitat. With it, the island arguably lost its older wisdom and ancient heart.

These days, when the deer swim back to the island, they find themselves outlawed. They run shy, fearful. In my heart, I welcome them. 'Come,' I whisper. 'The old ways are still here.'

In the years I have spent following their quiet tracks, gleaning clues and searching for glimpses of their hidden yet bold presence, I have come upon them at sunrise, picking furtively through the island's heartland, dipping in and out of the gloaming, foraging openly, fired by a fierce hunger. A rare sighting is over in minutes, as too often they spook and take flight, although they can be studied for longer if you seek them deliberately and quietly, and from a distance.

Sometimes I tease a bristling snag of pelt off the barbed fences and run my fingers along its rough tussocks. The hair is coarse, thick and stiff, ivory and peaty black like a wire brush.

It takes practice and perseverance to follow deer through the land-scape. A deer's hoof is divided into three parts – the compact horn, the sole horn and the cuneus – but the footprint it leaves is simply a cres-cent moon facing another crescent, in two graceful halves. Their tracks are larger than a sheep's cloven cleats, littered with dark, swollen pel-lets, larger and harder than those of other ruminants. It takes me a while to realise what is suddenly obvious. In daylight, my eyes are closed to their secretive forays, whereas after dark, the island comes alive with the soft rustling and thrashing of brush and fast-drawn flar-ing breath. On my night walks across the island, I pad quietly, ears pricked, eyes peeled for a glimpse of their dark shapes. Now that I have learned to acclimatise my eyes to the darkness, night vision has become a tonal score of shadows, resonating with a porous sound.

When you remove yourself from the noise of the modern world, you discover not simply a world within, but a deeper awareness of the instincts we have lost. Attuning to these requires time and silence. Being present with all of our senses allows us to imagine and inhabit the world differently. This intuition lies within all of us. Connecting with it allows us to tap into our wilder instincts and our deeper, un-inhibited selves.

After a while, it becomes second nature. Adapting our own body language takes practice, but it can be learned, through careful obser-vation, gaining an understanding of animal behaviour, and trial and error, to allow us to get close to a great many species. Working daily with animals is a beautiful way of letting a different perception soak into your eyes and saturate your awareness.

I hope that one day I will be able to approach the deer, to study their behaviour and to be instrumental in seeking ways for us all to cohabit and thrive successfully on this island. In the old lore, a deer crossing your path, whether in corporeal form or in a dream, is a sacred messenger. It is a visitation that was said to awaken compassion. The deer spirit represents the overcoming of obstacles, through peaceful means, facing the earth and all its elements and seasons. At each turn of the year, I celebrate the deer. I have become accustomed, by living close to the raw elements and the natural world, to honouring these old beliefs, rites and rituals. It helps me to broaden my vision and remain open to new ways to connect intuitively, physically and spiritually with all that is wild around and inside us.

I am on the boat back from Oban. The sea is alive and fresh out in the deeper tide. Above, the sky is dimming as the soft gloaming light falls on to the waves. I am on my way home from my first adoption meeting. There is a long way to go, but it is a start, and every journey must begin with a single brave step. I know that somewhere out there, another voice is waiting to find mine. I breathe in the glittering salt spray and reflect on how change is fresh, uplifting and invigorating.

The gulls are on the move again. They are blowing in off a south-easterly breeze. They come flying against the wind, rather than being lifted on to its back, which tells me that they are seeking a rich feeding ground or safe harbour. It reminds me of how I first came to the island, travelling in search of an anchor across an unknown passage of sea. I know I have come such a long way since those early, beautiful, desperate times, and I realise that I owe a debt of gratitude to every one of those bright, hard years. Everything has to break down in order to renew.

The gleeful cries of the gulls, spatters of feathers and bright chinks of sound tangling into a fishing boat's sun-filled nets, encapsulate for me how freely and universally wildlife is given to us all. Yet so often we walk the earth oblivious, never lifting our eyes to look through its open windows. Living wild teaches you to tread gently, to listen, not just with your eyes and ears, but with that finer instinct that lies even deeper than your heart. All it takes to untangle ourselves from everything that disconnects us or deracinates our lives from our beautiful earth is to find that animal instinct. Belonging is ultimately simple. Yet still we cage ourselves, subordinating our intuition to our rational mind as we wrestle with the everyday and existential anxieties that dominate almost every aspect of our lives. Setting aside some time to tap into our primal inner self, the part of us that resonates with our surroundings, is the first step to finding the freedom that eludes so many of us, towards reclaiming our own wilder spirit and voice.

Listening to the gulls, I imagine all the other islands to which that salt air may take them, out and away to where the sky meets the sea, and an infinite distance beyond. Whenever I hear them now, I never think of them as bereft, as once I did. There was a time when I longed to leave this island, but a meshing of circumstances held me down until that feeling passed. As the engine thrums, I turn to face the cliffs, the low-lying beaches and the tiny, pristine coves I now know intimately and love so well. The island's rippling grasses, hard rock face, hills and valleys are imprinted on my heart, its salt winds and fierce tides drenched into my flesh.

These days, wherever I am standing, I am rocked by the rhythmic voice of the land and the sighing of the sea, lapping and rolling, opening towards and away from me. 'I do not know what is coming, but I am ready,' I murmur. As the gulls skirl loudly, drifting over the shimmering water, to cleave to the contours and shelter of the island, I look to the empty skies, threaded by their joyful, raucous cries. I hold up my arms and call out to the wind. My voice merges with theirs, sending its own wild cry over the waves.

I cannot know what the future holds, or who it may bring to walk alongside me. Some days I wonder if I am destined always to be here alone, an island in a sea of solitude, or if one day a small hand will reach out to hold fast to mine. When I close my eyes, I imagine us sifting shells on the shore, or filling wet buckets with cockles for tea, or our arms lifting to wave and call out to the gulls. Sometimes I hear, in conversation with my own low voice, another, higher-pitched, singing out its own wondering questions as we discover together all the secrets our beautiful island holds.

'Every island is held by its sea,' I whisper softly to the wind. 'And one day soon, your beautiful tide will come and find me.'

Acknowledgements

In writing this book, I drew much support and encouragement from friends: first inspiration from Antoinette Wysocki; an early conversation with my dear friend Tree Sheriff; the incredible support of Eleanor Mills, and her early advocacy of my work. Their love and support came at a time when it really mattered, and without it this book might not have been written at all.

Special thanks to my agent, Sarah Williams at the Sophie Hicks Agency, for her diligence, care, and remarkable way of ensuring that I kept going back to the raw story, journeying closer to some truths that were difficult to face, let alone to tell. And to the incredible support, guidance and expertise of my publisher Susanna Wadeson, editor Helena Gonda, copy-editor Caroline North, publicist Tabitha Pelly and the entire team at Transworld. This is our book – I am so lucky to have found such a family to work with and such a beautiful home for it.

Thank you, dear Rab – for those tough, beautiful island years, and for your generosity, reconnection and friendship, inspired by our reading this book together.

My gratitude also to the community, for the good times and those of difficulty and struggle. Your unique influence has been instrumental in helping to shape who I am and to find my voice. To call this island my home. And to know how Belonging comes differently to each of us.

My love and gratitude to Jane Garnett and the women of the My Heart is in the Highlands retreat, to whom I gave my first reading. And to Achara Tait and family, and Georgina Martin, for your

ACKNOWLEDGEMENTS

friendship and keeping your radar tracking west; and Sarah Belfield, for uplifting me.

And to my other close constellations of love, inspiration and support. Special thanks to Damian and Tassya, and my family, to Elena, for your beautiful heart and wisdom, and above all to David and Ginnie, Liz and family – simply for being there.

Most of all, I drew much from the nature around me: the fierce sea, the raw elements, the strong mountains, the wildlife and the changing seasons. Beautiful moments – standing alone, drawing strength and courage from this source, watching the dawn rise and the tides always rushing in with such a welcome – helped me to find my place again in the world.

Above all, this book is dedicated to Cristall, who was my inspiration. And to Maude, my beloved dog, friend and faithful companion, who was always at my side.

I am an island
Reading group questions

What does this book have to say about solitude, and resilience?

Do you think the idea of moving to a remote island would hold a similar appeal for you? Why/not?

What does the book's structure and language contribute to the overall narrative?

How is the difference between loneliness and isolation navigated and how might you have coped?

Did reading this book deepen your understanding of how trauma is written within the body? How might you have coped?

Did you empathize with Tamsin and why?

A lot of the events in this book are sad, but is there cause for hope? To what extent did you find it an inspirational read?

How did the setting impact your reading experience?

Did you connect with the landscape as a presence and character within the book?

How did you find the writing style merged genres? Did this help you to experience the narrative more closely?